THE ROSE COOKBOOK

featuring Pink Ribbon recipes

The Rose
a non-profit organization for Breast Cancer Screening
Houston, Texas

THE ROSE COOKBOOK _____

by **THE ROSE**

Additional copies of **THE ROSE** Cookbook may be obtained at the cost of $14.95 plus $2.00 postage and handling, each book.

Send to:
THE ROSE
12700 No. Featherwood, Suite 260
Houston, TX 77034

ISBN: 0-9647648-0-6
Copyright © 1996

THE ROSE
Houston, Texas
First Printing   June, 1996

Introduction

THE ROSE *Cookbook featuring Pink Ribbon Recipes* represents the efforts of many volunteers and countless hours of work. Proceeds from the sale of this book will be used in the fight against breast cancer to help reduce the cost in terms of both lives and dollars.

Funds will be used to provide breast cancer screening and diagnostic procedures to medically underserved "working poor" women. These women have little or no financial resources, no insurance and, ironically, because they work, are not eligible for public assistance. It takes every dollar, dime, nickel, and penny they earn just to put food on the table, clothing on their backs and provide a roof over their heads for themselves and their dependent children or aged parents. Procrastination, even in the face of a lump or other condition signaling the need for concern, is the norm for these women. Consequently, if they do have breast cancer, when they finally seek help their chances for survival are often greatly diminished. **THE ROSE** is the "only game in town" for these needy women.

We hope you will join us in our fight against breast cancer. Your purchase of **THE ROSE** Cookbook could help save a woman's life.

For every 10 cookbooks sold,
One needy woman can be screened!

Dedication

This first edition of **THE ROSE** Cookbook is being dedicated to the more than 180,000 women who will be diagnosed with breast cancer in 1996.

Every recipe that is in this book is a recipe from someone who has personally faced the effects of breast cancer or has experienced it through a mother, sister, aunt, grandmother, or friend.

This cookbook was made possible by the Diann Meriwether Memorial Fund. Diann's support of **THE ROSE** was unwavering throughout her life and this cookbook is one more gift from a very special lady — a gift that will help women in their battle with breast cancer. Special thanks to her family for allowing us to remember her in this special way.

Cookbook Committee

Chairman and Editor-in-Chief: Suzanne Vax-Laverdiere
Cookbook Consultant: Dianne Ibenthal
THE ROSE Staff Advisors: Dorothy Weston
Louise Mitchell
Amy Rigsby

Committee Members:

Janet Bodiou	Zorida Gillebaard
Davy Konikowski	Georgie McIrvin
Nancy Maranto	Keith Mayberry
Donna S. Myers	Gretchen Nakayama
Gail Pepitt	Helen Perry
Gail Phillips	Babette Schlesinger
Charles F. Vatterott, III	Alan Weston

Linda Yarger

Typists:

Jan LeBlanc   Kelly Ubernosky

Cover Design:

Hill/A Marketing Design Group, Inc.
Chris Hill
Andrea Pastrano

Smith Photography
Ralph Smith

Linda Hofheinz

Acknowledgements

Georgie McIrvin deserves special recognition for her work with the "Pink Ribbon Inns". She contacted bed and breakfast inns across the State of Texas and got a number of them to contribute a portion of their room rate, a night's lodging, or a special one-time donation in support of **THE ROSE**.

Our support groups, the Rose Buds and the Rose Garden, have played an important and ongoing role in the development of the cookbook. Many of our "Pink Ribbon" recipes come from the members of these two groups.

Table of Contents

Appetizers and Dips 8

Breads 24

Salads 36

Soups and Sandwiches 54

Casseroles 68

Main Dishes 84

    Main Dishes 84
    Meats 91
    Poultry 95
    Seafood 107
    Pasta 112

Vegetables 122

Desserts 150

    Desserts 150
    Cakes 174
    Cookies 196
    Pies 210

Extraordinary Extras 218

Special Guides 230

Texas Pink Ribbon Bed and Breakfast Inns 240

Organization

"Every woman who pays, helps another who can't!"

THE ROSE is a qualified 501(c)(3) "grassroots" charitable organization, Texas-based, locally founded and operated. The services we provide through our three community-based, FDA approved, and American College of Radiologists accredited centers include: full mammographic screening, diagnostic workups, ultrasounds, ultrasound guided core breast biopsies, and fine needle aspirations.

Since 1987, when **THE ROSE** opened its first center, we have provided more than 51,000 total procedures including over 5,000 "sponsored" (provided without charge). In 1995 alone, we served over 8,500 women through 10,144 procedures, sponsored 860 women with 1,002 procedures, and diagnosed 56 cancers.

THE ROSE is about concern and care for women — from Dr. Dixie Melillo, who together with Dorothy Weston, founded **THE ROSE** in 1986...to the competent, caring staff who go the extra mile to ensure that every patient receives the highest standard in quality care...to the dedication of our radiologist...to the committed members of the Board of Directors, Cancer Fighters of Houston, "Friends of **THE ROSE**" chapters and the many foundations, corporations, and organizations who support our efforts.

Editor's Note:

This cookbook is a collection of recipes encompassing two centuries. Many recipes have ingredients that were "the norm" in their time. All recipes can be "tinkered" with to suit palate and lifestyle.

We have tried to honor the original recipe author whenever possible. However, a few recipes came to us without any name. They, too, are preserved here for all to enjoy.

Appetizers & Dips

Nopales con Queso
(Cactus with Cheese)

2 (10 ounce) cans "nopalitos" or 1 bag fresh nopales (cactus pieces)
1 to 2 tablespoons butter
1 white onion, finely chopped
1 can green chilies or 2 to 3 jalapeños, seeded and chopped
1 package lowfat cream cheese
Salt
Ground pepper

If using canned nopales or chilies, rinse and drain. For fresh nopales, boil in lightly salted water for 2 to 3 minutes, then rinse and drain. In a pan or the microwave, melt butter and sauté the onion in it. Add the 'nopales' and chilies. Cook until the onion is transparent. For microwave, cook for 1 minute at a time, stir, then cook for another minute. Season to taste. Scatter the cream cheese over the dish. When it starts to melt, serve at once.

Note: This is wonderful as a lunch with rice and a salad. My kids love it with warm tortillas, white rice and fresh fruit. They also like to scoop it up with Doritos. It looks strange, but is wonderful! Fresh nopales are available in winter and early spring.

Nancy Hannan

Shrimp Ring

1 (10½ ounce) can condensed tomato soup
8 ounces cream cheese
2 packages unflavored gelatin powder
2 soup cans of small shelled shrimp, washed and drained
2 tablespoons water
2 tablespoons lemon juice
1 cup chopped celery
1 cup chopped green onions
Salt, white pepper, and Tabasco to taste
Cooking oil spray

Blend softened cream cheese and tomato soup in blender. Put mixture in a pot and heat on low until mixture is warm. Remove from heat. Mix gelatin in water and lemon juice (mixture will be very thick). Add gelatin and stir well. Let mixture cool a little, then add all other ingredients. Add salt, pepper, and Tabasco. Spray a ring mold lightly with cooking oil spray before pouring into a ring mold. Refrigerate overnight. Unmold on a bed of Boston lettuce and garnish with parsley. Serve with buttery crackers. Serves 20 as an appetizer.

Note: This is a very popular appetizer at New Orleans get-togethers, whether formal or potluck or at work. Fits a Tupperware mold - but there's never any left!

Frances L. Smith, M.D.

APPETIZERS AND DIPS

Shrimp Marinade

3 cups cooked shelled shrimp
½ cup vinegar
½ cup salad oil
2 tablespoons chopped chives
2 tablespoons chopped fresh parsley

2 tablespoons chopped dill pickle
1 teaspoon salt
few drops garlic juice to taste
Tabasco sauce to taste

Put all ingredients in a jar. Store in the refrigerator 24 hours - shake frequently. Will keep two weeks.

Shirlee Nicholson

Tortilla Roll-Ups

1 pint sour cream
24 ounces cream cheese, softened
½ teaspoon garlic salt or powder
1 package dry taco seasoning

4 ounces ham, shredded (optional)
Juice of one lime
2 to 3 jalapeños, chopped
10 green onions, tops only
1 package large flour tortillas (burrito size)

Mix together all ingredients except flour tortillas. Spread this mixture in a thin layer on each flour tortilla. Tortillas are easier to work with if heated in microwave for ½ minute. Roll up tightly and wrap each tortilla individually in foil or plastic wrap. Put in refrigerator at least three hours, better if overnight. Take out of refrigerator about 30 to 40 minutes before serving. Cut into ½ inch to ¾ inch slices with serrated knife and lay on side to look like jellyroll slices. If desired, put a dab of picante sauce on top of each. Delicious! Better on the second or third day.

Janice Schwausch

Lemon cups filled with tartar sauce make an eye-appealing border for seafood.

APPETIZERS AND DIPS

Quick and Easy Mexican Appetizer

1 (8 ounce) package cream cheese, softened (non-fat or regular)
1 can chili without beans (approximately 19 ounce size)
1 bunch green onions, finely chopped
½ pound cheddar cheese, shredded

Spread softened cream cheese in bottom of a 9 or 10 inch pie plate. Pour chili over cream cheese and sprinkle chopped green onions over chili. Top with grated cheese and place in 350 degree oven till heated thoroughly and cheese is melted, approximately 15 to 20 minutes. Spoon onto tortilla chips and serve immediately to avoid soggy chips, or let guests make their own.

Note: My guests always clean the plate when I serve this and more than one has remarked that they are going to make a dish for supper one night. Besides tasting great, there is no mess to clean up afterward!

Nancy Maranto

Black Bean Salsa

1 (15 ounce) can black beans, rinsed and drained
1 can shoepeg corn, drained
2 medium tomatoes, diced
1 red bell pepper, diced
1 green bell pepper, diced
½ cup finely chopped red onion
1 or 2 thinly sliced jalapeño peppers, seeds and all
⅓ cup fresh lime juice
⅓ cup extra virgin olive oil
⅓ cup chopped cilantro
1 teaspoon salt
½ teaspoon cumin
pinch of cayenne pepper

Combine all ingredients in a large bowl, mix well, cover and refrigerate 24 hours. Bring to room temperature before serving. Serve with baked tortilla chips.

Ellen Limitone

APPETIZERS AND DIPS

Stuffed Mushrooms

30 large mushrooms
1 stick butter, melted
salt and pepper
½ tablespoon flour
½ cup heavy cream
¼ cup grated Swiss cheese
2 tablespoons minced shallots
Italian bread crumbs
3 tablespoons minced fresh parsley

Wipe off mushrooms. Stem. Dip caps in 2 or 3 tablespoons of melted butter. Salt and pepper caps. Chop stems and sauté with shallots and 2 tablespoons butter. Add flour and stir one minute. Stir in cream and simmer to thicken. Stir in parsley and crumbs until it is a stuffing consistency. Adjust seasoning if desired with garlic salt, red pepper, etc. Fill caps with stuffing and put cheese on top. Drizzle butter on top. Bake at 375 degrees in top third of oven for about 15 minutes. Serve warm.

Note: This great appetizer or party food was shared by Liz Bugh, a neighbor, many years ago. It is one of the most requested things I make. The recipe can easily be doubled.

Jeanne Whitehead

Pizza Fondue

1 onion, chopped
½ pound ground beef
2 tablespoons margarine
2 (10½ ounce) cans Chef-Boy-Ardee pizza sauce
1 tablespoon cornstarch
1½ teaspoons fennel seeds
1½ teaspoons oregano
¼ teaspoon garlic powder
10 ounces grated cheddar cheese
1 cup grated mozzarella cheese

Brown beef and onion in margarine. Drain beef. Mix cornstarch and seasonings with pizza sauce in separate bowl. Add to skillet with meat and onions. When mixture thickens and begins to bubble, add cheeses in thirds, stirring well after each addition. When cheeses are melted and blended, put in fondue pot and serve with pretzels and bread sticks.

Kathy Guillame

APPETIZERS AND DIPS

Cheese Ball

1 pound Velveeta cheese
½ cup jalapeños
1 clove garlic or garlic powder to taste

2 ounces cream cheese
1 tablespoon Worcestershire sauce
Chili powder

Mix all ingredients except chili powder and heat in double boiler stirring until well blended. Refrigerate overnight. Make balls and roll in chili powder.

Jean Whitten

Cheese Ball

2 (8 ounce) packages cream cheese, softened
1 (10 ounce) package cheddar cheese, shredded
1 (8 ounce) can crushed pineapple, drained

2 tablespoons chopped green onion or chives
2 teaspoons Worcestershire sauce
⅔ cup chopped pecans

Mix all ingredients well and divide into two balls and roll in two-thirds cup chopped pecans. Chill.

Kathy Lopez

Chipped Beef and Olive Cheese Ball

1 teaspoon minced onion
1 tablespoon dry sherry, white wine, or vermouth
1 (8 ounce) package cream cheese, softened

2 tablespoons mayonnaise
1 (3 ounce) package chipped beef
¼ cup chopped olives

Soften minced onion in dry sherry. Blend cream cheese with the mayonnaise, stir in onion and dry sherry mixture. Add chipped beef and olives. Form into a ball and chill. Serve with crackers.

Ginny O'Connor

APPETIZERS AND DIPS

Cheese Roll

2 pounds Velveeta cheese
1 (8 ounce) package cream cheese
1 teaspoon garlic powder
1 cup chopped nuts

Soften cheese to room temperature. Mix all ingredients together with hands. Roll in a ball and roll out in 3 or 4 rolls. Sprinkle wax paper with paprika and chili powder and roll each log on the wax paper. Can be frozen in tinfoil.

Gaylene Adams

Angel of Death Cheese

1 head of garlic, separated into cloves
8 ounces ricotta cheese
4 ounces Gorgonzola cheese
1 cup whipping cream
¾ teaspoon salt
⅓ cup pecans, finely chopped
Cheesecloth

Peel garlic cloves and boil in small saucepan for 15 minutes. Drain well and mince in garlic press until 2 tablespoons puree obtained. Discard remainder. Beat ricotta well and add crumbled Gorgonzola. Mix until smooth. Gradually add cream and stir well. Add salt and garlic puree. Stir well. Line large strainer with a 12 x 18 inch piece of cheesecloth and set over a bowl. Spoon cheese mixture over cheesecloth and press cheese into a loose ball. Tie ends of cheesecloth together. Refrigerate 24 hours or up to 4 days. When ready to serve, unmold onto platter and press nuts on top. Let stand at room temperature for 1 hour before serving with crackers.

Ellen Limitone

Candles burn longer and slower if stored in the refrigerator before using.

APPETIZERS AND DIPS

Oyster Roll

1 (8 ounce) package cream
 cheese, softened
1 can smoked oysters
1 tablespoon chopped onion

1 tablespoon mayonnaise
Dash of garlic salt
Dash of Worcestershire sauce

Combine all ingredients except oysters. On waxed paper, pat out flat into ¼ inch rectangles. Cover and place in refrigerator to harden, approximately 20 minutes. Remove from refrigerator and place chopped oysters on top of each rectangle. Beginning at long end, roll up and chill again. Serve with a variety of crackers. May be made one day ahead. Keep covered.

Gaylene Adams

Cheese and Sausage Biscuits

1 pound pork sausage
4 cups biscuit baking mix

1 can cheddar cheese soup
½ can water

Combine all ingredients, using fingers to mix. Shape into one inch balls or drop onto ungreased baking sheet as biscuits. Bake at 350 degrees for 15 minutes.

Kathy Lopez

Sausage Balls

3 cups biscuit baking mix
1 pound Jimmy Dean or Owen
 sausage

16 ounces grated cheddar
 cheese

Combine all ingredients until mixed well. You will probably have to use your hands. Form into small balls and place on cookie sheet. Bake at 375 degrees for 15 to 20 minutes or until golden brown.

Diann Meriwether

APPETIZERS AND DIPS

Meat Popovers

1 pound ground beef
1 onion, finely chopped
1 teaspoon fresh ginger, finely chopped
4 cloves garlic, finely chopped
2 teaspoons cumin powder
2 teaspoons coriander powder
1 teaspoon black or rock salt (optional)
1 whole green pepper (optional)
2 tablespoons vegetable oil

Heat oil in skillet, sauté onions, garlic, ginger, whole green pepper for one minute. Add the cumin powder and coriander powder; sauté for one more minute. Add ground beef, rock salt and salt to taste. Stir well, cover and simmer on low to medium heat till done; drain.

For the crust, ready-made flour tortillas are ideal. If you have to make the tortillas, use the following recipe:

1 cup white flour
½ teaspoon baking powder
1 tablespoon shortening
salt to taste
water for mixing

Mix all ingredients except water. Add water a little at a time and knead into a soft dough that is not too sticky. Take small balls of dough (8 to 10) and roll them into a tortilla as thin as you can. Bake the tortillas on a hot griddle just a few seconds on either side. Cut tortillas in half. Keep a paste of flour and water handy for sealing the popovers. Take one-half of a tortilla, double it at the center of the rounded edge so that the edges overlap slightly. Put some flour paste over the edges and press so they stick together. You now have the pocket that you fill about ¾ full of meat filling. Fold the open edge over; let it overlap the cone. Seal again with flour paste. After all the cones have been made, deep fry them in vegetable cooking oil until crisp and brown. These can be frozen and reheated in the 400 degree oven. Yum-yum.

Elizabeth Henson

Cold Salmon Mold

1 (1 pound) can salmon
1 (8 ounce) package cream cheese
1 tablespoon lemon juice
1 tablespoon hot horseradish
½ teaspoon salt
½ teaspoon liquid smoke
½ cup chopped pecans
3 tablespoons minced parsley
1 tablespoon grated onion

Drain and flake salmon, remove skin and bones. Combine salmon, cream cheese, lemon juice, horseradish, salt, liquid smoke, grated onion and mix thoroughly. Chill well (overnight seems to blend flavors best). Combine chopped pecans and parsley. Shape salmon into ball and garnish with nuts and parsley.

Ethel Ankner

APPETIZERS AND DIPS

Stella's Spicy Pecans

2 cups pecans
Olive oil

1 teaspoon lemon pepper
⅛ teaspoon cayenne

Rub with a small amount of olive oil. Sprinkle with 1 teaspoon lemon pepper and ⅛ teaspoon cayenne pepper and mix well. Microwave on high for 2 minutes. Stir and microwave 45 more seconds. Stir well. Adjust seasonings if needed. Serve as a snack or sprinkle over foods to add zest.

Helen L. Kainer

Almond Chicken Dip

1 (8 ounce) package of cream cheese
1 teaspoon Worcestershire sauce
⅛ teaspoon garlic powder

1 (4 ounce) can mushroom pieces, including liquid
1 (5 ounce) can boned chicken
½ cup sliced almonds

Soften cream cheese. Blend Worcestershire sauce and garlic powder. Add mushrooms with liquid, chicken and almonds. Mix well and serve warm or cold with crackers. Makes 3 cups. Best the second day.

Diann Meriwether

Anchovy-Olive Dip

1 cup sour cream
½ cup finely chopped stuffed green olives

1½ teaspoons anchovy paste
½ teaspoon grated onion

Combine, mix well and chill.

Carolyn Thompson

Artichoke Dip

1 (14 ounce) can artichoke hearts in water, drained and cut up
1 cup mayonnaise
¾ teaspoon garlic powder
1 cup Parmesan cheese
4 ounces grated mozzarella cheese

Mix all ingredients together and bake at 300 degrees for 30 to 40 minutes.

Gail Culberson

Avocado Dip

6 large avocados
12 ounces picante sauce
1 (16 ounce) carton sour cream
Monterey Jack cheese
1 (8 ounce) carton sour cream cheese

Mash avocados well and mix with picante sauce. Spread in a 9 x 13 inch glass baking dish. Spoon sour cream over all. Sprinkle grated Monterey Jack cheese on top. Serve with chips.

Diann Meriwether

Skip Dip

1½ pounds lean ground meat, browned
3 ounce garlic cheese roll
3 ounce jalapeño cheese roll
1 can cream of mushroom soup
1 (9 ounce) jar hot picante sauce

Cut the 2 cheese rolls in small pieces, add to meat and melt. Stir in mushroom soup and picante sauce. Mix well while heating. Serve with a variety of chips. Add chopped peppers if you want it hotter.

Gaylene Adams

Cheese Dip

1 (8 ounce) package cream cheese, softened
1 stick oleo, soft
1 small jar pimentos, drained
1 small onion, chopped
1 teaspoon paprika
Dash of garlic salt
3 to 4 tablespoons salad dressing
1 heaping teaspoon mustard

Mix all ingredients well. Serves 12.

Shirley Bobo

Curry Dip and Marinated Broccoli

1 large bunch broccoli florets
¾ cup olive oil
¼ cup wine vinegar
2 tablespoons dill weed
1 teaspoon sugar
2 to 3 garlic cloves, chopped

Mix broccoli and all the above ingredients. Store in a plastic bag in refrigerator over night. Drain before serving.

2 cups fat free or regular mayonnaise
1 tablespoon catsup
¼ teaspoon Worcestershire sauce
3 teaspoons curry powder

Mix ingredients well and serve with marinated broccoli florets.

Elaine Doubrava

Raw Vegetable Dip

¼ teaspoon turmeric
1½ teaspoons curry powder
½ teaspoon garlic powder
2 teaspoons sugar
½ teaspoon salt
2 teaspoons lemon juice
¼ cup crushed parsley flakes
2 cups mayonnaise - fat free
½ cup sour cream - fat free
Raw vegetables: cauliflower, broccoli, celery, cucumbers, cherry tomatoes, zucchini, etc.

Mix all ingredients for sauce and refrigerate long enough to blend flavors. Serve with favorite raw vegetables, cut into bite-sized pieces.

Lucille (Max) Ankner

APPETIZERS AND DIPS

Chipped Beef Dip

1 (2½ ounce) jar of chipped beef
1 package low fat or no fat cream cheese
½ cup low fat or no fat sour cream
2 tablespoons milk
1 tablespoon minced onion
¼ teaspoon garlic salt
¼ cup chopped green or red bell pepper
½ cup chopped pecans

Shred chipped beef in a food processor or blender. With cream cheese at room temperature, place all ingredients except pecans in bowl and add chipped beef. Mix well and put in glass pie plate. Sprinkle chopped pecans on top and bake at 350 degrees for 20 minutes. Serve with Wheat Thins.

Joan Moon

Phil's Cheese Dip

2 pounds of Velveeta cheese
2 pounds of ground chuck or ground round
1 medium bottle of Pace picante sauce
1 medium chopped onion
1 chopped jalapeño pepper

Cook ground meat, onion and jalapeño pepper. Drain well and cook till dry. Place in crock pot and add cheese which has been cut into chunks and picante sauce. Cook till cheese is completely melted. Stir often. Great for parties and will serve about 25 people.

Eva McIntyre

Broccoli Dip

1 chopped onion, sautéed in ¼ cup butter
1 cup sliced mushrooms, sautéed in ¼ cup butter
2 packages frozen chopped broccoli, cooked and drained
2 cans cream of mushroom soup
2 rolls Kraft garlic cheese
1 cup slivered almonds
Accent
Tabasco
Salt to taste

Sauté onions and mushrooms and set aside. Combine broccoli, soup, and cheese and stir until smooth. Add onions, mushrooms and slivered almonds. Season lightly wwith Accent, Tabasco, and salt.

Serve hot with round melba thins. Makes 4 quarts. Freezes nicely.

Lucille (Max) Ankner

APPETIZERS AND DIPS

Mexican Style Chips-N-Dip

1 can low-fat refried beans
1 (8 ounce) package low-fat cream cheese
1 (12 ounce) jar salsa
1 package shredded low-fat cheese
1 bag nacho chips

Preheat oven to 350 degrees. Use a 9 x 13 inch glass pan. Spread refried beans in pan. Spread softened cream cheese on top of refried beans. Pour salsa over cream cheese. Sprinkle cheese on top of salsa. Heat in oven until cheese is melted and serve hot. Quick, easy, and inexpensive. Great when watching sports, movies or for unexpected guests.

Kelly Jo Myers-Madoian

Cousin Iola's Chili Dip

2 pounds ground chuck
1 tablespoon cooking oil
⅛ teaspoon pepper, or to taste
2 teaspoons cumin, or more
1 pound Velveeta cheese
2 cans condensed tomato soup
1 envelope dry onion soup mix
2 teaspoons oregano, or more
⅛ teaspoon garlic salt
1 clove garlic, pressed

Sauté beef in hot oil. Add remaining ingredients except cheese. Simmer five minutes. Add cheese and stir until melted. If too thick, add water. Makes two quarts. Serve in chafing dish with tostados.

Helen L. Kainer

Spinach Dip

3 packages frozen chopped spinach
6 large cloves garlic, finely minced
8 ounces fat-free cream cheese
1 cup freshly grated Parmesan cheese, well packed
1 can water chestnuts, drained and slivered
1 can artichoke hearts, drained and chopped
1½ teaspoons Adobo or other garlic seasoning
4 to 6 dashes Tabasco sauce
⅓ to ½ cup reduced fat Hellmann's mayonnaise

Cook spinach with minced garlic in small amount of water, just until thawed. Drain well in colander. Add all other ingredients and season to taste with Tabasco sauce. Stir well and refrigerate. To serve, heat in microwave until hot and surround with toast made from slices of fat-free French bread drizzled with low-fat margarine and sprinkled with freshly grated Parmesan cheese.

Frances L. Smith, M.D.

Spinach Dip

1 (10 ounce) package chopped spinach, thawed and drained
1 cup mayonnaise
1 cup sour cream
1 envelope Knorr's vegetable soup mix
1 can water chestnuts, drained and chopped
1 small onion, chopped

Combine the above. Chill for at least 4 hours. Serve with fresh vegetables or crackers.

Kathy Lopez

APPETIZERS AND DIPS

Fruit Dip

32 ounces Dannon nonfat yogurt
10 ounces Polander or Smucker's Simply Fruit, black cherry

1 to 2 teaspoons vanilla
Few drops of almond flavoring

Place the yogurt in a clean cheesecloth and using a funnel, drain overnight in the refrigerator. Discard the liquid. Mix in the fruit and flavorings. I use this as a dip for fruit such as apples or pears and also as a topping for toast and bagels.

Henrietta Hall

Relish Dip

2 firm tomatoes, seeded and chopped
3 to 4 green onions, sliced
2 (4.5 ounce) cans chopped chilies

1 (4 ounce) jar pimento olives, sliced
1 tablespoon red wine vinegar
1 tablespoon cooking oil

Mix all ingredients and refrigerate overnight for flavors to blend. Serve as a relish with hamburgers or as a dip with corn chips. Yields 1 quart.

Merline Fogtman

BREADS

BREADS

Oatmeal Muffins

1 cup regular oats, uncooked
1 cup low-fat buttermilk
1 large egg
1 banana, mashed (¼ cooking oil can be substituted if desired)
¼ cup honey
1 cup whole wheat flour
1½ teaspoons baking powder
½ teaspoon baking soda
½ teaspoon salt
¼ cup sesame or flax seeds

Combine oats and butter milk in a bowl and let stand for 30 minutes. Stir in egg, banana, and honey. Combine flour and remaining ingredients in a large bowl. Make a well in center and add oatmeal mixture, stirring until just moistened. Spoon mixture into greased muffin pans, filling ¾ full. Yields 12 to 15 muffins.

Nancy Maranto

Pineapple Muffins

1 cup pineapple
1 cup flour
2½ teaspoons baking powder
¾ teaspoon salt
¼ teaspoon cinnamon
¾ cup Ralston Bran 100% Wheat cereal
⅓ cup salad oil
⅓ cup brown sugar
1 egg, beaten

Combine all ingredients and mix well. Drop by spoonfuls in well greased muffin tins and bake at 400 degrees for 20 to 25 minutes. Yields 12 big or 24 small muffins.

Anne Meyn

Orange Yogurt Muffins

1¾ cups flour
⅓ cup sugar
¼ teaspoon salt
½ teaspoon baking soda
⅔ cup margarine
1 egg, beaten
¼ cup corn oil
1 (8 ounce) carton orange flavored yogurt
optional: dates, raisins, blueberries, shredded coconut or nuts, if desired

Combine flour, sugar, salt and soda. Cut in margarine with pastry blender until mixture is the size of small peas. Add beaten egg, corn oil and yogurt. Stir just until all ingredients are moistened, or batter will get too stiff. Grease a muffin tin and spoon batter into cups, filling each ⅔ full. Bake in 375 degree oven for 20 minutes or until well browned. Makes 1 dozen muffins.

Note: For stronger orange flavor, a teaspoon of orange extract may be added.

Elaine DeSouza

BREADS

Banana Carrot Bran Muffins

1 cup skim milk
1¾ cups bran
¾ cup whole wheat flour
1 tablespoon baking powder
½ cup egg substitute

¾ cup grated carrots
1 banana (mashed)
2 tablespoons oil
½ cup brown sugar
¼ cup nuts (optional)

Mix together skim milk and bran and whole wheat flour. Mix egg substitute, carrots and mashed banana. Add remaining ingredients. Mix then stir into bran mixture; mix just until moistened. Pour into muffin tins either oiled or use muffin papers. Bake at 350 degrees for 18 to 20 minutes. Makes 12 muffins.

Note: These are made also for people with special diets.

Virginia Sattler

Pumpkin Bread

1 teaspoon baking powder
3½ cups flour
2 teaspoons baking soda
1½ teaspoons salt
1 teaspoon cinnamon-allspice
1 teaspoon nutmeg

1 cup salad oil
4 eggs
⅔ cup water
2 cups pumpkin
3 cups sugar
1 cup chopped nuts

Sift dry ingredients in bowl. Make a well and add remaining ingredients. Mix until smooth. Put into 3 loaf pans (greased and floured). Bake at 350 degrees. Cool slightly in pan. Place pans on rack to finish cooling. Wrap in foil or plastic. Store in refrigerator. Will freeze beautifully. Make at least 2 days before serving.

Jean Whiten

Raisin Scones

2 cups Bisquick mix
¼ cup sugar
⅓ cup milk

1 egg, beaten
½ cup raisins

Mix Bisquick, sugar, and raisins together. Mix milk and egg together, then combine with Bisquick. Stir only until moistened. Grease a 6 x 10 inch pan. Drop batter onto pan, making 6 mounds. Bake at 375 degrees for 25 minutes. Sprinkle lightly with granulated sugar while cooling.

Elaine DeSouza

Cinnamon-Raisin Scones-Sticks

2½ cups reduced fat baking mix (Bisquick is one brand)
½ cup raisins

½ cup skim milk
¼ cup plain non-fat yogurt
½ teaspoon ground cinnamon

Heat oven to 450 degrees. In a large bowl, combine baking mix, raisins, milk, yogurt and cinnamon. Mix to form a soft dough. Turn dough out onto surface dusted with baking mix and roll dough into baking mix to coat. Knead dough 5 times. Roll into a 10 x 6 inch rectangle. Cut crosswise into 10 1-inch strips. Place about 1 inch apart on ungreased cookie sheet. Bake 10-12 minutes or until golden brown. Makes 10.

Sharon Kiel Gutormson

Zucchini Bread

3 eggs
2 cups sugar
1 cup oil
2 cups grated zucchini
1 teaspoon salt
1 cup chopped nuts

3 cups flour
1 teaspoon baking soda
½ teaspoon baking powder
1½ teaspoons cinnamon
2 teaspoons vanilla

Beat eggs. Add sugar. Add oil and vanilla slowly. Add all dry ingredients. Fold in zucchini and nuts. Bake in 2 loaf pans lined with waxed paper at 350 degrees for 1 hour or until a toothpick comes out clean.

Gailyn Malone

BREADS

Zucchini Nut Bread

2 eggs, well beaten (egg substitute may be used)
⅓ cup canola oil
1 cup honey
1 teaspoon vanilla extract
2 cups unpeeled zucchini, grated
2 cups whole wheat flour
1 teaspoon baking soda
½ teaspoon baking powder
1 teaspoon sea salt or regular salt
1 teaspoon cinnamon
1 teaspoon allspice
¼ teaspoon cloves
¾ cup walnuts, chopped

In a large bowl, beat eggs. Mix in oil, honey, and vanilla. Stir in zucchini. In a separate bowl, combine flour, baking soda, baking powder, salt and spices. Stir the dry ingredients into the zucchini. Fold in nuts. Turn batter into a well-greased and floured loaf pan. You may use a non-stick spray on the pans. Bake in preheated oven at 350 degrees for 55 minutes or until toothpick inserted in the center comes out clean. Cool before removing bread from pan, and cool completely before serving. Makes 1 regular loaf or 4 small loaves. Freezes well.

Yvonne Constantino

Zucchini Bread

1½ cups grated zucchini
1 cup vegetable oil
2 cups sugar
3 eggs
1 tablespoon vanilla
3 cups flour
1 tablespoon cinnamon
¼ teaspoon baking soda
1 teaspoon salt

Pat zucchini dry with paper towels. Beat eggs light and foamy. Add next 4 ingredients. Mix lightly, but well. Sift dry ingredients. Add to wet mixture. Stir until well blended. Add nuts. Pour into 2 well greased and floured 9 x 5 x 3 inch pans. Bake at 350 degrees for 45 to 60 minutes.

Wanda Szot

BREADS

Banana Nut Bread

½ cup margarine
1 cup sugar
2 eggs
¾ cup mashed ripe bananas

1¼ cups sifted flour
¾ teaspoon baking soda
½ teaspoon salt
1 cup chopped pecans

Cream margarine and sugar, add eggs and mix well. Stir in bananas, sift in flour, salt, and baking soda. Add nuts last, beat well for at least 2 minutes. Pour into greased loaf pan and bake at 350 degrees for 40 minutes. Do not overbake. Test with toothpick. Will keep for weeks if wrapped in plastic wrap and refrigerated.

"Pete" Davie

Whole Grain Wheat Bread

1½ cups whole grains of wheat or whole wheat flour
2 cups milk
2 envelopes active dry yeast
4 cups all-purpose flour (approximately)

½ cup butter or margarine, softened
2 eggs
¼ cup sugar
2 teaspoons salt
Melted butter or margarine, as needed

If using whole grains of wheat, grind in blender 40 seconds to 2 minutes depending on the texture of bread you desire. Pour ground wheat or whole wheat flour into a large mixing bowl. Heat milk to scalding; cool to lukewarm. Add yeast to milk, put in blender and let stand 5 minutes.

Meanwhile, add 3¾ cups all-purpose flour to whole wheat flour and mix. To blender mixture add butter, eggs, sugar, and salt. Blend 20 seconds. Pour over flour and mix with wooden spoon until all dry ingredients are moistened. Turn out onto floured board, knead until smooth and elastic, adding small amounts of all-purpose flour as necessary. Return to bowl, brush with melted butter. Cover and let rise in warm place until double — about 1½ hours. Knead dough down and divide in half. On lightly floured surface, roll half of dough to 10 x 12 inches. Fold in thirds, then tuck in ends. Place in buttered 9 x 5 x 3 inch pan. Brush with butter. Cover; let rise until doubled — 45 to 60 minutes. Bake at 375 degrees (glass) 400 degrees (metal) for 40 to 45 minutes. Turn out onto rack. Let cool completely before slicing.

Ethel Ankner

Fresh bread can be cut into thin slices if the knife is heated on the stove every 4 or 5 slices.

BREADS

Beer Bread

3 cups self-rising flour
2 tablespoons sugar

1 can room temperature beer

Mix all ingredients. Pour into buttered loaf pan. Let rise 30 minutes in a warm place. An oven heated to 225 degrees and then turned off makes an excellent place to let bread rise. Allow bread to rise for 30 minutes. Preheat oven to 350 degrees and bake bread for 60 to 70 minutes. A non-stick bread pan works best. Invert and remove bread immediately upon removal from oven. When partially cooled, this bread slices best with an electric knife. This bread is fantastic toasted or not and it is so easy to make and delicious.

Gailyn Malone

Dilly Bread

2 teaspoons sugar
1 tablespoon instant onion
1 tablespoon butter, melted
2 teaspoons dill seed
1 teaspoon salt
¼ teaspoon baking soda
1 package dry yeast
¼ cup warm water

1 cup cottage cheese at room temperature, or non-fat yogurt or buttermilk can be used
1 egg lightly beaten, or 2 egg whites
2¼ to 2½ cups whole wheat or unbleached flour

Combine sugar, onion, butter, dill seed, salt and baking soda. Mix yeast and water and add to dry ingredients. Stir together and add the cottage cheese and egg. Add sufficient flour to make a stiff dough. Beat well, cover with a damp towel and set in warm place to rise until doubled in size, about 85 to 90 minutes. Turn into a well-greased casserole dish approximately 8 inches in diameter. Brush top with butter and sprinkle with salt if desired. Bake at 350 degrees for 40 to 50 minutes. Turn out on rack to cool. It goes well with roasted or smoked meats but is equally great with an assortment of cheeses and salads.

Note: I have been making this bread for over 23 years and always have to restrain myself and anyone else around from eating it all immediately.

Nancy Hannan

BREADS

Garlic Bread Sticks

1 package hot dog buns
1 stick margarine, melted

Garlic powder

Cut buns lengthwise. Each bun makes 4 bread sticks. Dab margarine on 1 side of each bun and place close together on a cookie sheet. Sprinkle with lots of garlic powder and bake at 200 to 225 degrees for 1 hour.

Gaylene Adams

Manuela's Greek Bread

1 stick margarine
½ cup mayonnaise
1 bunch chopped green onions
1 small can chopped black olives, optional
1 cup shredded mozzarella cheese
garlic powder to taste
Salad seasoning
1 loaf French bread

Cut loaf of bread in half. Mix together first 6 ingredients and spread mixture on French bread. Sprinkle salad seasoning over top. Bake in oven at 350 degrees until cheese melts and bread is crisp around edges.

Linda Gibson

English Muffin Bread

(For a bread machine)

This is a really good, easy way to get that English muffin taste and texture. Great bread to have set on the timer for a hot breakfast bread. In order to have the proper texture, there will be a sunken top to this bread. Select correct amount of ingredients for your machine.

	Small	Medium	Large
water	⅔ cup-1 tbs.	1 cup-1½ tbs.	1¼ cups
sugar	1 tsp.	1¼ tsp.	2 tsp.
salt	½ tsp.	⅔ tsp.	1 tsp.
baking soda	dash	⅛ tsp.	¼ tsp.
bread flour	1½ cups	2 cups	3 cups
nonfat dry milk	1½ tbs.	2 tbs.	3 tbs.
yeast	1 tsp.	1½ tsp.	2 tsp.

Lucille (Max) Ankner

Cornbread

1¼ cups flour
¾ cup cornmeal
4 tablespoons sugar
5 teaspoons baking powder
1 egg
1 cup milk
2 tablespoons butter or margarine, melted
½ teaspoon salt

Sift together flour, cornmeal, sugar, and baking powder. Add 1 egg, slightly beaten, milk, margarine, and salt. Mix well. Bake in square pan at 375 degrees for 20 minutes, or for bread sticks, bake at 450 degrees.

Janice Schwausch

Southern Cornbread

1 cup cornmeal
1 cup unbleached flour
4 teaspoons baking powder
1 teaspoon salt
1 cup milk or buttermilk
1 egg
4 tablespoons cooking oil

Mix together cornmeal, flour, baking powder and salt. Combine milk, egg, oil and stir into dry ingredients. Bake at 425 degrees in iron skillet for 20 to 25 minutes.

Janice LeBlanc

Brown Sugar Shortbread

1⅓ cups raw (or brown) sugar
1 cup butter
1 teaspoon pure vanilla
2 cups flour
¼ teaspoon salt
¼ teaspoon baking powder
Ground nutmeg

Cream sugar and butter together by hand. Add vanilla. Add all dry ingredients except nutmeg and work in with hands. When well mixed, press into greased 8-inch square pan and sprinkle nutmeg on top. Bake in 375 degree oven for 30 minutes.

Ethel Ankner

BREADS

Mexican Cornbread

1 cup yellow cornmeal
½ teaspoon baking soda
¾ tablespoon salt
1 cup milk
2 eggs, beaten
1 stick margarine, melted

1 cup grated sharp cheddar cheese
1 medium chopped onion
½ cup chopped jalapeño peppers
1 cup frozen whole kernel corn

Combine in large bowl cornmeal, baking soda, salt, milk, eggs, and margarine. Mix well. Pour ½ mixture in a well greased 10 x 10 inch baking dish or iron skillet. Add to remaining mixture in bowl grated cheese, chopped onion, jalapeño peppers, and corn. Mix well and spread over mixture in baking dish. Bake at 350 degrees in preheated oven for 1 hour until golden brown on top.

Sharlene Farrar

Mexican Cornbread

¾ pound ground meat
1 cup yellow cornmeal
½ cup flour
1 tablespoon sugar
1½ teaspoons baking powder
½ cup milk
2 eggs, slightly beaten

1 (8 ounce) can cream style corn
¼ cup oil
½ cup minced onions
2 jalapeño peppers, chopped fine
1 cup grated cheese

Brown meat and drain well. In a large bowl mix together cornmeal, flour, sugar, baking powder. Add eggs and ½ cup milk and mix well by hand. Add cream corn, oil, minced onion, jalapeño peppers and mix well. Spread one-half of cornmeal mixture in baking dish. Add hamburger meat and half of cheese. Top with rest of mixture and more cheese. Bake at 375 degrees for 30 to 45 minutes until golden brown.

Anna Belle Baugus

Broccoli Cornbread

1 stick margarine
2 boxes Jiffy cornbread mix
12 ounces cottage cheese
4 eggs, beaten

1 (10 ounce) package frozen chopped broccoli
1 cup chopped onion

Mix all ingredients together well. Bake in a greased pan for 45 to 55 minutes at 350 degrees.

Betty Baker

Corny Cornbread

2 eggs
1 (17 ounce) can whole kernel corn, drained
1 (16 ounce) can creamed corn

1 (8 ounce) box cornbread mix
1 (8 ounce) carton sour cream
1 stick margarine, melted

Preheat oven to 350 degrees. Beat eggs in a large bowl; add corn, creamed corn, cornbread mix, sour cream, and margarine; mix well. Pour into a greased 9 x 13 inch baking dish. Bake at 350 degrees for 45 minutes. Makes 8 to 12 side dish servings.

Note: To lighten up, use low fat sour cream and margarine and egg substitute.

Janice LeBlanc

Housework is something you do that nobody notices unless you don't do it.

BREADS

Injun Fry Bread

3 cups flour
4 teaspoons baking powder
3 teaspoon salt
2 tablespoons sugar

1¼ cups lukewarm water
1 tablespoon vinegar
(optional)

Mix all dry ingredients together, add the liquid all at once and blend to a biscuit dough stage. The less the mixture is handled, the lighter it will be. Separate into 4 sections. Let stand for 5 minutes. Roll out to ⅛ inch thick. Fry in hot oil until golden brown.

Helen L. Kainer

Sour Dough Buttermilk Biscuits

6 to 8 cups flour
1 package dry yeast
1 cup warm water
¼ cup sugar
¼ teaspoon baking soda

4 teaspoons baking powder
2 teaspoons salt
¾ cup oil
2 cups buttermilk

Dissolve yeast in warm water. Mix together all dry ingredients and add yeast mixture, oil, and buttermilk and blend until it makes a stiff dough. Store in a covered, greased bowl in refrigerator. You may need to punch it down every so often. This will store for 2 weeks. To bake, pinch off and shape. Place in greased pan and let rise. Bake at 450 degrees till nicely browned. These are delicious and another of my favorite recipes from my mom.

Susan Munson

Bread flour (hard wheat flour) that is unbleached makes the best yeast dough. All purpose flour can be used but will not produce the same results.

SALADS

SALADS

Melon Salad

1 small cantaloupe, cut into bite size pieces or balls
¼ cup wine or ginger ale
½ teaspoon dried crushed red pepper flakes
Pinch of salt

Combine all ingredients, cover and refrigerate at least 2 hours, stirring occasionally. Yields 4 servings.

Nancy Maranto

Glazed Fruit Salad

2 (20 ounce) cans pineapple chunks
1 (11 ounce) can mandarin orange slices, drained
3 large bananas, sliced
1 cup maraschino cherries, drained
1 cup pecans, finely chopped
1 (3¾ ounce) package vanilla instant pudding

Reserve liquid from pineapple. Mix pineapple, oranges, cherries and bananas. Gently add pecans. In large mixing bowl, mix pudding with 1 cup pineapple juice on high speed for 1 minute. Pour over salad, mixing gently. Chill before serving.

Anna Belle Baugus

Heavenly Salad

1 (3 ounce) package lime
  gelatin
1 cup whipped cream

1 cup nuts
1 cup Velveeta cheese
1 (#2) can chunk pineapple

Mix gelatin according to package directions. Refrigerate, but don't let it jell too thick. Combine pineapple, cheese and nuts, then add Jell-O and whip well. Add Cool Whip and pour in well greased mold. Refrigerate till completely set.

Jean Whitten

Cranberry Crown Salad

1 pound cranberries
2 apples
½ pound marshmallows,
  cut in fourths

1 cup sugar
1 cup whipped cream
6 to 8 pineapple slices

Grind cranberries and apples. Add sugar and marshmallows. Let stand overnight in refrigerator. Before serving, add whipped cream. Place a large mound of salad on a lettuce leaf. Cut pineapple in half. Put half over top and use the other half to form crown. If you want, you add a can of drained pineapple and/or 8 ounces of nuts in cranberry mixture before adding the whipped cream.

Note: This was one of my mother's favorite cranberry salad recipes when she worked for a restaurant in Fort Wayne, Indiana. This recipe is about 50 years old. She served this around Thanksgiving and Christmas and everyone liked it.

Virginia Sattler

Cranberry Salad

1 pound ground cranberries
1½ cups sugar
1 large can crushed pineapple, drained
1 cup chopped pecans
1½ cups miniature marshmallows
1 large container Cool Whip

Combine cranberries and sugar and let stand in refrigerator overnight. When ready to serve, add all remaining ingredients.

Maxwell Miller Suarez

Dump Salad

1 (15 ounce) can pineapple chunks, drained
1 pound cottage cheese
2 cups Cool Whip
1 package orange Jell-O

Mix dry Jell-O with other ingredients. Pour into a bowl and it's ready to serve.

JoAnne Moore

Napa Cabbage Salad

1 head Napa or Savoy cabbage, chopped
5-8 green onions with tops, thinly sliced
¾ cup thinly sliced almonds
2 packages Ramen noodles, crumbled
½ cup raw sunflower seeds

Dressing:
1 cup sugar
1 cup vegetable oil
½ cup vinegar
3 tablespoons soy sauce
½ teaspoon salt

Preheat oven to 350 degrees. Spread almonds, Ramen noodles and sunflower seeds evenly on a cookie sheet. Put in oven and roast until they all are a deep, golden brown. Check frequently and shake or stir to evenly roast them. This may take 8 to 15 minutes, depending on the oven.

Clean and chop the cabbage and onions and combine in a large salad bowl. Just before serving, add the roasted nuts, etc., and toss with dressing.

Note: The noodles get soggy if left in the salad for very long. If making this ahead, keep the noodles and nuts in a separate container, combine with cabbage and dressing just before serving.

Sharon Kiel Gutormson

SALADS

Apricot Salad

1 small package apricot Jell-O
1 (8 ounce) can crushed pineapple
1 cup buttermilk
8 ounces Cool Whip

Combine Jell-O and pineapple with juice in saucepan and simmer for 5 minutes. Whip with a whisk and add buttermilk and Cool Whip. Refrigerate before serving.

Jane Alexander

Fruit Salad

1 cantaloupe, halved and seeded
½ honeydew melon, seeded
¼ cup superfine or granulated sugar
¼ cup fresh lime juice
2 tablespoons fresh lemon juice
1 tablespoon orange flavored liqueur, optional
1½ teaspoons grated lime peel
1 cup fresh strawberries, sliced
1 cup black or red seedless grapes

Use a melon baller to scoop out cantaloupe and honeydew balls. Set aside. Reserve the shells for serving. In a large glass (non-metal) bowl, combine the sugar, lime juice, lemon juice, orange liqueur, and lime peel. Stir until sugar is dissolved. Add the melon balls, strawberries and grapes. Toss gently to coat. Cover the bowl with plastic wrap and refrigerate for at least 1 hour to blend flavors. Serve in bowls or melon shells.

Anna Bell

SALADS

Waldorf Salad

2 medium apples, chopped, about 2 cups
¾ cup chopped celery
¼ cup pecans or walnuts, chopped
1 (6 ounce) carton piña colada yogurt

Mix all ingredients completely, folding in yogurt. Refrigerate before serving.

Note: This is my husband Frank's recipe.

Joan Moon

Seven Layer Salad

1 head lettuce, chopped
1 small head cauliflower, chopped
1 (10 ounce) package frozen English peas, uncooked
1 package Good Seasons Italian salad dressing, dry
1 pound bacon, cooked and crumbled
1 cup mayonnaise
2 cups grated sharp cheddar cheese

Layer ingredients in above order in large bowl or 9 x 13 inch dish. Cover with plastic wrap and refrigerate overnight. Toss just before serving. If you halve the recipe, still use the whole package of peas. Serves 12.

Diann Meriwether

Avocado-Cranberry Salad

Arrange avocado halves or quarters on lettuce. Top with mixture of cubed, canned cranberry sauce and diced celery. Serve with French dressing.

Carolyn Thompson

SALADS

Broccoli Salad

1 large head of broccoli
½ cup raisins
½ cup salted peanuts
½ cup chopped celery, optional
2 to 3 slices bacon, cooked and crumbled
½ cup mayonnaise
½ cup sugar
¼ cup vinegar

Clean and chop broccoli into bite size pieces. In large bowl, combine broccoli, raisins, peanuts, celery and bacon. Set aside. In small bowl, combine mayonnaise, sugar and vinegar, stirring until sugar dissolves. Pour over salad and toss well. Refrigerate until ready to serve.

Dorothy Schuchardt

Broccoli Salad

5 cups broccoli, chopped
½ cup chopped onion
½ cup golden raisins
1 cup low fat mayonnaise
¼ cup plus 1 tablespoon sugar
3½ tablespoons vinegar

Combine broccoli, onion and raisins and set aside. Mix mayonnaise, sugar and vinegar until sugar is dissolved. Pour over salad and refrigerate until ready to serve. Good if topped with spicy pecans (see below).

Note: I use the vinegar off sweet pickles in place of plain vinegar.

Helen L. Kainer

Stella's Spicy Pecans

2 cups pecans
Olive oil
1 teaspoon lemon pepper
⅛ teaspoon cayenne pepper

Rub with a small amount of olive oil. Sprinkle with 1 teaspoon lemon pepper and ⅛ teaspoon cayenne pepper and mix well. Microwave on high for 2 minutes. Stir and microwave 45 more seconds. Stir well. Adjust seasonings if needed. Serve as a snack or sprinkle over foods to add zest.

Helen L. Kainer

SALADS

Pineapple Coleslaw

2 cups shredded cabbage
1 grated carrot
⅛ teaspoon salt
1½ teaspoons vinegar
¼ cup drained pineapple, crushed or tidbits
3 tablespoons cream or mayonnaise

Combine all ingredients. Toss together to blend. May be served immediately or chilled in a covered dish until serving time.

Diann Meriwether

Black Bean Salad

1 (16 ounce) can black beans, rinsed and drained
2 to 3 ripe tomatoes, chopped
1 green bell pepper, chopped
1 to 3 jalapeño or serrano chilies, seeded and chopped
½ bunch cilantro or parsley, chopped
1 bunch green onions, chopped
Juice of ½ lemon and 1 lime
¼ cup olive or safflower oil
Sea salt and pepper to taste

In a salad bowl, mix the beans, bell pepper, tomatoes, chilies, cilantro, and green onions. In a small bowl whisk the juices and oil together. Whisk in the salt and pepper, pour over the salad and serve. Yields 4 to 6 servings.

Note: To prepare jalapeños, serranos, or other hot chilies, I usually hold the chili by the stem and cut it almost lengthwise. Then, being careful not to touch the inner surfaces with my fingers, I use the tip of the knife to scrape out the veins and seeds. Seeds make food hot, but have no flavor. I then quarter the pieces lengthwise and chop or mince. If you do get a chili burn on your fingers, putting table salt, cooking oil, or bleach on them may help. The best way to prevent it is to wear rubber gloves while preparing chilies. If the chilies are too hot on your tongue, try holding some bread on your tongue. The temptation is to bathe the effected area with cold water. However, the capsaicin, the active substance in chilies, is soluble in oil, not water. Fresh chilies are good sources of vitamins A and C. This recipe is quick and easy and is good as a summer lunch. Serve with French bread, Italian bread, or corn tortillas.

Nancy Hannan

SALADS

Garden Rice Salad with Lemon Herb Dressing

1½ cups cooked brown rice
1¼ chopped tomatoes
¾ cup slightly cooked peas
¼ cup chopped green onions
¼ cup sliced black olives
1 tablespoon pine nuts

2 tablespoons fresh lemon juice
1 teaspoon olive oil
¼ teaspoon black pepper
½ teaspoon dried oregano
½ teaspoon dried sweet basil
Pinch of garlic powder

Combine rice, tomatoes, peas, onions, olives and pine nuts and set aside. Mix remaining ingredients in small bowl to make up dressing. Pour dressing evenly over vegetables. Toss and refrigerate until ready to serve.

Gail Greenberg Kirk

Carrot Salad

4 medium carrots
1 small can crushed pineapple, drained
½ cup raisins

½ cup pecans
½ cup milk or cream
2 tablespoons mayonnaise
Dash of salt

Grate carrots and mix with pineapple, raisins, pecans and salt. Mix mayonnaise with milk or cream and pour over salad. Refrigerate until ready to serve.

Dorothy Schuchardt

Carrot Raisin Salad

¾ cup grated carrots
¼ cup shredded coconut
2 tablespoons raisins

1 tablespoon lemon juice
2 tablespoons mayonnaise

Combine all ingredients and chill. Serve on a bed of lettuce.

Diann Meriwether

Winter Fruit Salad

¼ cup red wine vinegar
1 tablespoon plus 1 teaspoon brown sugar
1 tablespoon vegetable oil
2 teaspoons low sodium soy sauce
1 teaspoon curry powder
1 clove garlic, minced
5 cups loosely packed torn romaine lettuce
5 cups loosely packed torn red leaf lettuce
2¾ cups coarsely chopped, unpeeled Red Delicious apples
3 large oranges, sectioned and chopped, or 2 cups orange pieces
2 tablespoons chopped toasted almonds

Combine vinegar and next 5 ingredients; stir with a wire whisk until well blended. Set aside. Combine lettuces, apples, and oranges in a large bowl; toss gently. Add vinegar mixture, tossing gently to coat. Sprinkle with almonds. Serves 8.

Annette Carr

Sinner's Repent Big Time Salad

1 pound fresh broccoli
1 medium zucchini, cut into strips
2 carrots, cut into strips
2 shallots, minced
2 cloves garlic, crushed
2 tablespoons fresh cilantro, minced
¾ teaspoon crushed red pepper
¼ cup water
¼ cup lemon juice
2 tablespoons cooking oil
2 green onions, chopped

Wash, cut, and peel broccoli. Cut the stalks into ¼ inch slices. Combine tops, stalks, zucchini, and carrots in large bowl and set aside. Combine shallots, garlic, cilantro, and pepper; stir well. Add shallot mixture, water, lemon juice and oil to broccoli mixture, tossing gently. Top with green onions. Serves 8.

Always use fresh garlic instead of powder for better flavoring. Press it instead of chopping for better digestion.

Sunshine Spinach Salad

1 cup nonfat honey mustard dressing
2 tablespoons orange juice
3 oranges, sectioned
½ teaspoon grated orange peel, optional
8 ounces fresh spinach leaves, torn in pieces
1 small red onion, thinly sliced
6 slices turkey bacon, cooked and crumbled

Mix together honey mustard dressing and orange juice, whisking thoroughly until blended. Add orange peel. In a large serving bowl, mix spinach, orange sections, bacon and onion slices. Add dressing and toss lightly. Makes 6 servings.

Gretchen Nakayama

Spinach Rice Salad

1 cup raw rice
½ cup bottled Italian salad dressing
1 tablespoon soy sauce
½ teaspoon sugar
2 cups fresh spinach, cut in thin strips
½ cup sliced celery
½ cup sliced green onions
⅓ cup cooked and crumbled bacon

Cook rice according to package directions and transfer to a large bowl. Cool slightly. Combine dressing, soy sauce and sugar. Stir into warm rice; cover and chill. Fold in remaining ingredients just before serving. Makes 6 to 8 generous servings. This is a great summer potluck dish.

Barbara Nelson

Diana's Delight

2 (3 ounce) boxes apricot jello
1 cup buttermilk
1 large can crushed pineapple
1 (8 ounce) container Cool Whip

Do not drain pineapple. Mix pineapple and jello together and cook together until hot. Set aside and cool. Add buttermilk and Cool Whip. Stir and refrigerate.

Diana Plasse

SALADS

Macaroni Salad

4 ounces small shell macaroni, uncooked
2 hard-boiled eggs, chopped
½ cup shredded Chinese cabbage
⅓ cup chopped green or red bell pepper
¼ cup chopped celery
¼ cup fat-free mayonnaise
1 tablespoon chopped sweet pickles
1 tablespoon Ranch dressing
Salt and pepper to taste

Cook macaroni according to package directions. Drain and rinse with cold water, drain and cool. Combine macaroni with remaining ingredients, tossing lightly. Cover and chill 1 to 2 hours. Yields 4 servings.

Nancy Maranto

Yogurt-Cucumber Salad

1 cucumber, peeled and sliced
1 pint plain yogurt
1 tablespoon dried mint
Dash of salt, optional
1 or 2 cloves garlic, crushed

Cut peeled cucumber into quarter slices. Cut up several leaves of mint in small pieces, or use about 1 tablespoon of dried mint. Add salt to taste, if desired, and 1 or 2 mashed garlic cloves. Mix ingredients together in medium size bowl. Chill in refrigerator until served. Serve in small bowls.

Note: The above is a general recipe. Ingredients and amounts can be varied according to taste. This basic recipe is great served as an accompaniment dish with cabbage rolls or wonderful by itself.

Norma Maria

Boiled eggs will peel better when cracked and put in cold water after boiling.

Pasta Salad

24 ounces spaghetti, cooked, rinsed, and drained
2 to 3 celery stalks, chopped
1 red bell pepper, chopped
1 small can black olives, sliced and drained
16 ounces hard salami or ham
16 ounces Italian dressing, fat free
Cavender's Greek seasoning

In a large bowl, mix together cooled spaghetti, celery, red pepper, and black olives. Chop the salami or ham and add to pasta. Add several shakes of Greek seasoning and part of the Italian dressing. Toss well and continue to add Greek seasoning and Italian dressing to desired taste. Yields 10 to 15 servings.

Note: Easy and filling. You may change the chopped vegetables and meat. I've made it using celery, red pepper, fresh mushrooms, black olives, and cooked, chopped chicken. I have also added shredded cheese on top.

Joy Caka

Mexican Chef Salad

1 chopped onion
3 to 4 chopped tomatoes
½ to 1 head lettuce, chopped
4 ounces grated cheese
½ to 1 bag Fritos or Doritos, slightly crushed
1 pound ground meat, browned and drained
1 can ranch style beans, drained and washed
¼ teaspoon salt, if needed
Catalina dressing, optional

Mix all ingredients together and serve.

Dorothy Schuchardt

Pasta salads are at their best when served at room temperature, or very soon after being assembled.

SALADS

Potato Salad for a Crowd

8 pounds of potatoes
¾ cup finely chopped onion
1 tablespoon plus 1 teaspoon salt
½ teaspoon pepper
1 cup Italian salad dressing
2 cups Light Miracle Whip
2 cups chopped celery
12 hard boiled eggs, chopped
Bacon, crumbled, optional

Cook unpeeled potatoes covered in boiling salted water 30 to 40 minutes or until tender. Drain and cool slightly. Peel and cut into cubes. Toss with onion, salt, pepper and Italian dressing. Cover and chill thoroughly, at least 8 hours. About 2 hours before serving, add the Light Miracle Whip, celery and eggs. Toss until well coated. Chill until ready to serve. Keep the salad cold during the serving period. Makes 24 servings.

Note: It's important to keep the salad cold during preparation. Serve in bowls nested in a large pan filled with ice and refrigerate any leftover salad at once. I use this recipe for family reunions and always get rave reviews.

Ruth Gates

Lazy Ladies Salad

4 ounces cooked chicken, cut in strips
2 oranges, peeled and sectioned
¼ cup thinly sliced red onion
4 cups spinach, rinsed and torn
2 tablespoons corn oil
2 tablespoons orange juice
2 tablespoons white wine vinegar
½ teaspoon dry mustard
¼ teaspoon ground ginger
⅛ teaspoon pepper
⅛ teaspoon salt

Combine in serving bowl chicken, oranges, onion and spinach and toss. Mix remaining ingredients for orange salad dressing. Shake well and chill. Shake again before serving. Makes 4 servings.

A few drops of vinegar in boiling water in which an egg is to be boiled will prevent the egg from breaking.

Chicken Salad in Orange Halves

4 whole cooked and diced chicken breasts
½ cup chopped green apple
½ cup chopped pecans
½ cup seedless grapes
¼ cup finely chopped celery
¾ cup mayonnaise
1 tablespoon orange juice
¼ cup sour cream
1 tablespoon wine vinegar, optional
1 tablespoon soy sauce, optional
2 teaspoons minced onion, optional
½ teaspoon curry powder, optional

Combine mayonnaise, sour cream, orange juice, and spices and mix well. Add remaining ingredients and mix. Cut 3 large oranges in half, remove fruit from shell and fill with chicken salad. Wrap each orange half individually.

Note: The optional spices can be omitted for the less adventurous.

Judy Durand

Low-Fat Chicken and Grape Salad

1 pound skinless, boneless chicken breasts, cooked and diced
½ cup low fat sour cream
½ cup non-fat yogurt
½ cup light mayonnaise
1½ cups seedless grapes, red, green or a mixture
1 cup diced celery
¼ cup chopped pecans
2 tablespoons poppyseeds
Salt and coarse black pepper to taste

Poach chicken in enough water to cover. Cool, dice and set aside. In bowl, combine sour cream, yogurt, and mayonnaise. Add chicken, grapes, celery, pecans, and poppyseeds. Season with salt and pepper. Serves 4.

Eileen Scott

SALADS

Jambalaya Rice Salad

⅓ cup red wine vinegar
3 tablespoons Dijon mustard
1 teaspoon salt
2 teaspoons pepper
1 cup olive oil
1 egg
1 to 2 tablespoons olive oil
1 medium onion, finely chopped
½ teaspoon crushed red pepper flakes
1 teaspoon thyme
2 bay leaves
1 teaspoon salt
2 cups chicken broth
1 cup long grain white rice
3 celery ribs, cut in ½ inch pieces
1 small green bell pepper, cut in 1 inch pieces
1 small red bell pepper, cut in 1 inch pieces
4 thinly sliced scallions
1½ cups diced, cooked chicken
1½ cups diced, cooked ham
1 large head of lettuce
2 ripe tomatoes cut in 6 wedges each
18 large cooked shrimp

For the dressing, in a food processor or blender, combine the egg, vinegar, Dijon mustard, ½ teaspoon salt and pepper. Process for 1 minute, then add the 1 cup olive oil in a steady stream. Continue to process until all oil is added and blended. Refrigerate. To prepare the rice, sauté the onion in 1 to 2 tablespoons olive oil until tender. Add the pepper flakes, thyme and bay leaves and cook, stirring for 2 to 3 minutes. Stir in chicken broth, 1 teaspoon salt and 1 cup rice. Heat to boiling. Reduce the heat to low, cover the pot and cook for 20 minutes or until rice is tender and liquid is absorbed. Let stand for 5 minutes. Scrape into a large bowl, remove the bay leaves and let cool. Add the chopped celery, bell peppers, chicken, and ham. Toss to mix. To serve, place lettuce leaves torn into pieces on six plates. Mound about 1½ cups of the rice salad on each plate. Garnish with 2 tomato wedges and 3 shrimp each. Drizzle salad dressing over each plate. Serve with additional fresh pepper and remaining salad dressing. Yields 6 servings.

Note: This recipe can be made a day ahead. It can be a complete meal accompanied by French bread and iced tea. A very southern dish and quite colorful. I have used egg substitute and sautéed the onion and spices in chicken broth.

Nancy Hannan

Exposure to direct sunlight softens tomatoes instead of ripening them. Leave the tomato stem up in any spot where they will be out of direct sunlight.

SALADS

Southwestern Chicken and Vegetable Salad

4 boneless, skinless chicken breasts, cooked and cut in strips
⅓ cup olive oil
¼ cup lime juice
2 tablespoons chopped fresh cilantro
1 tablespoon capers
½ teaspoon salt
½ teaspoon chili powder
½ teaspoon cumin
2 tablespoons pine nuts
1 pound fresh green beans
½ teaspoon salt
2 medium tomatoes, cut in wedges
Fresh basil or cilantro leaves, optional

Combine olive oil and next 6 ingredients in a bowl or jar and mix thoroughly. Adjust lime juice to taste. Pour dressing over chicken, add pine nuts and toss gently. Place in plastic ziplock bag and chill 1 to 2 hours. Wash green beans and remove ends. Pour 1 inch of water in a skillet, add ½ teaspoon salt and bring to a boil. Add green beans and cover. Reduce heat and cook 8 to 10 minutes or until crisp-tender. Drain and plunge beans into ice water to stop the cooking process. Arrange beans and tomatoes on plates and top with chicken and pine nuts. Drizzle with any remaining dressing. Garnish, if desired. Yields 4 servings.

Nancy Maranto

Oriental Salad

12 ounces cooked seafood such as tuna, crab or lobster (chicken can be used)
10 ounces frozen peas
1 cup celery, chopped
1 medium onion, minced
¾ cup mayonnaise
1 tablespoon lemon juice
¼ teaspoon curry powder
1½ teaspoons soy sauce
¼ teaspoon garlic salt
½ cup slivered almonds
2 tablespoons margarine
3 ounces chow mein noodles

Drain seafood well. Mix peas, celery, and onion and chill. Combine with mayonnaise, lemon juice, curry powder, soy sauce, and garlic salt and chill overnight. Sauté almonds in 2 tablespoons margarine. When ready to serve, add noodles and nuts to salad.

Gaylene Adams

SALADS

Zero Salad Dressing

1 cup tomato juice
1 tablespoon finely chopped onion
1 tablespoon finely chopped bell pepper
2 teaspoons lemon juice

Combine all ingredients and shake well. Keep in the refrigerator. Delicious to use as a dressing on salads, meats, or chips. Contains "zero" calories.

Shirlee Nicholson

Green Goddess Dressing

1 small clove garlic, pressed
3 tablespoons anchovies (boneless, skinless)
3 tablespoons chopped green onions, tops and all
⅓ cup parsley (no heavy stems)
1 tablespoon lemon juice
3 tablespoons tarragon wine vinegar
1 cup mayonnaise, low fat
½ cup sour cream, low fat
Salt and pepper

Blend first six ingredients in blender until well mixed. Combine mayonnaise with sour cream. Add the blender ingredients and mix well. Add salt and pepper to taste. Easy on the salt; the anchovies are salty. Makes one pint.

Sharon Kiel Gutormson

French Dressing

1 can Campbell's tomato soup
½ cup vinegar
1 teaspoon salt
1 teaspoon red pepper
1 teaspoon paprika, optional
1½ cups oil
1 tablespoon onion juice
1 tablespoon prepared mustard
½ teaspoon black pepper
1 clove garlic, minced
¼ cup sugar

Combine all ingredients and pour over your favorite green salad.

Note: This is a 1930 recipe from the Ritz in New York City.

Shirlee Nicholson

Honey Dressing

¼ cup water
2 tablespoons honey
1 envelope garlic salad dressing mix
⅔ cup salad oil

Mix vinegar and honey in cruet or jar with tight-fitting cover. Add salad dressing mix. Cover and shake well. Add salad oil; cover and shake again. Makes 1 cup. Serve over orange and grapefruit salad.

Sharon Kiel Gutormson

SOUPS & SANDWICHES

SOUPS AND SANDWICHES

Cabbage Soup

1 pound of ground meat
1 onion
1 cabbage, cored and cut in pieces
1 can Ro-Tel tomatoes
1 can stewed tomatoes
Seasoning to taste
½ can water

Brown meat in a large pot or Dutch oven. Add remaining ingredients and simmer until cabbage is done. Use 2 cans of Ro-Tel tomatoes if you like it hot. It can be frozen; great with French bread; best with cornbread.

Ruth Ferguson

Cheese and Cabbage Soup

1 envelope Butter Buds dissolved in 1 cup water
7 cups water
24 ounces potatoes, cubed, not peeled
8 chicken bouillon cubes or 1 envelope chicken broth
1 onion, chopped
1 cup celery, chopped
1 cup carrots, sliced
1 medium head cabbage, cored and cut in large pieces
1 pound Velveeta cheese, cubed

Combine all ingredients except cheese in large pot or Dutch oven and simmer for 1½ hours. Stir in Velveeta cheese and simmer gently until melted, stirring occasionally.

Dolores Kennedy

SOUPS AND SANDWICHES

Potato Soup

3 to 4 cups peeled and sliced red potatoes
3 cups sliced yellow onions
1½ to 2 quarts water
1 teaspoon salt, or less

6 chicken bouillon cubes
Pepper to taste
3 to 4 tablespoons butter
½ pint cream

Boil potatoes and onion in salted water. Add bouillon cubes. Reduce heat and simmer 45 minutes. Drain and cream in blender. Return to pot. Add pepper, butter, and cream. Heat and serve. Consider toppings like grated cheese, bacon bits, or fresh chopped chives.

Bobbi Walters

Potato Soup

3 cups diced potatoes
½ cup diced celery
½ cup diced onion
1½ cups water
3 chicken bouillon cubes

1½ teaspoons salt
2 cups milk
1 cup sour cream
4 tablespoons flour
1 tablespoon chopped chives

In pan, combine potatoes, chives, celery, onion, bouillon cubes, salt, and water and cook for 20 minutes. Add 1 cup milk and heat without boiling. In a bowl, mix 1 cup milk, sour cream, and flour. Slowly add to soup stirring constantly and heat to serving temperature.

Sue Simmers

Turkey and Sweet Potato Soup

2 tablespoons margarine or butter
1½ cups chopped onion
1½ cups thinly sliced parsnips
1½ cups thinly sliced carrots
1 cup thinly sliced celery
2 tablespoons all-purpose flour
5 cups turkey or chicken broth
1 pound raw, boneless, skinless turkey or chicken meat, cut in bite-size pieces
2 cups cubed, peeled yams or sweet potatoes
½ cup uncooked long-grain brown rice
1 teaspoon poultry seasoning
⅛ teaspoon ground nutmeg
1 (10 ounce) package frozen green peas or 1⅔ cups fresh peas
1 (10 ounce) package frozen corn or 1⅔ cups fresh corn kernels
Salt and pepper
Chopped fresh parsley

Melt margarine in large pot or Dutch oven over moderate heat. Add onion, parsnips, carrots and celery. Cook 3 to 5 minutes, stirring occasionally, until onion is translucent and vegetables are golden. Sprinkle flour over vegetables and stir to blend. Stir in broth, turkey, yams, rice, poultry seasoning and nutmeg. Cover and bring to a boil. Reduce heat to moderately low and simmer 35 minutes or until rice and vegetables are tender. Add corn and peas and bring to a boil. Simmer 10 minutes longer until vegetables are tender. Season with salt and pepper. Sprinkle with parsley before serving. Yields 2½ quarts.

Annette Carr

Oatmeal will add texture and body to a long cooking soup. Add a handful at the beginning.

Taco Soup

1 pound lean ground meat
1 large onion, chopped
3 (16 ounce) cans ranch style beans, rinsed and drained
1 (16 ounce) can whole kernel corn, undrained
1 (16 ounce) can chopped tomatoes, undrained
1 (15 ounce) can tomato sauce
1½ cups water
1 (4½ ounce) can chopped green chilies
1 (1¼ ounce) package taco seasoning mix
1 (1 ounce) package ranch style salad dressing mix

Cook meat and onion in a large Dutch oven over medium-high heat until meat is browned. Drain excess grease. Stir in beans and next 7 ingredients. Bring to a boil, reduce heat and simmer uncovered for 15 minutes. Serve with choice of toppings such as tortilla chips, grated cheese, shredded lettuce, chopped fresh tomatoes, chopped avocado, and sour cream. Yields 3½ quarts.

Note: I have used venison meat or a mix of beef and turkey.

Merline Fogtman

Taco Soup

1½ to 2 pounds lean ground beef or turkey
1 large onion, chopped
1 package taco mix
1 package Hidden Valley Ranch Dressing Original (not dip mix)
1 can kidney beans with juice
1 can pinto beans with juice
1 can whole kernel corn with juice
1 can Ro-Tel tomatoes, chopped
1 can stewed tomatoes with juice
1 (8 ounce) can tomato sauce

In large pot or Dutch oven, brown meat and onion. Add remaining ingredients and simmer for 10 to 15 minutes. This is a really quick meal, makes a big pot of soup, and is delicious with cornbread. Add additional water if desired.

Helen S. Dartez

SOUPS AND SANDWICHES

Pancho Villa Stew

2 pounds pork loin, cut in 1 inch cubes
¼ cup flour
2 tablespoons vegetable oil
2 (4 ounce) chorizo sausages, cut in ½ inch slices
3 (14½ ounce) cans chicken broth
1 (14½ ounce) can whole tomatoes, drained
3 (4 ounce) cans diced green chilies
1 large purple onion, sliced into rings
3 cloves garlic, pressed
2 teaspoons ground cumin
2 teaspoons cocoa powder
1 teaspoon dried oregano
¼ teaspoon salt
1 (2 inch) stick cinnamon
2 (15 ounce) cans black beans, rinsed and drained
1 (15½ ounce) can white hominy, rinsed and drained
1 (10 ounce) package frozen whole kernel corn
½ cup beer or tequila
Flour tortillas

Dredge pork in flour and set aside. Heat oil in large Dutch oven over medium heat. Add pork and brown, stirring often. Add sausage and cook 2 minutes, stirring often. Add broth and next 9 ingredients. Bring to a boil, reduce heat and simmer 1 hour. Add beans and next 3 ingredients; simmer 30 minutes. Remove cinnamon stick and serve with hot buttered tortillas. Yields 3 quarts.

Note: Don't let the long list of ingredients scare you. This dish is well worth the effort. You can choose to serve over rice.

Merline Fogtman

Mexican Chicken Soup

1 cooked chicken, deboned and cut in small pieces
1 large can tomatoes, chopped
2 large onions, chopped
1 clove garlic
2 cups cooked pinto beans
1 (3 ounce) can chilies
Salt and pepper to taste

Combine all ingredients and simmer for 2 hours.

Elizabeth Henson

Gazpacho

1 (28 ounce) can tomatoes
½ cup diced green bell pepper
1 medium cucumber, diced
½ cup celery, diced
¼ onion, diced
1 teaspoon chopped chives
2 teaspoons chopped parsley
1 clove garlic, minced
2 tablespoons olive oil
1 cup beef or chicken bouillon
2 to 3 cups tomato juice
3 tablespoons red wine vinegar
1 teaspoon Worcestershire sauce
Salt and pepper to taste

Place tomatoes in a large bowl and chop in small pieces. Add remaining ingredients and chill in refrigerator for at least ½ day. This is low fat, low in calories and really the best Gazpacho I've ever had.

Eileen Scott

Old Fashioned Vegetable Soup

2 or 3 soup bones with meat
2 tablespoons oil
8 cups water
⅓ cup barley
1 onion, chopped
1 cup sliced carrots
2 cups potatoes, chopped
1 cup celery, chopped
2 (1 pound) cans tomatoes
1 cup whole kernel corn
2 cups green peas
3 sprigs parsley, chopped
1 tablespoon salt
¼ teaspoon rosemary
¼ teaspoon marjoram
¼ teaspoon thyme
½ bay leaf, crushed
3 peppercorns

Cut meat off bones into small pieces and brown in hot oil in large skillet or Dutch oven. Add water and bones and simmer, covered, for 1½ to 2 hours. Remove bones and skim fat from top. Add barley and simmer for 45 minutes. Add onion, carrots, potatoes, celery, tomatoes, corn, peas, parsley, salt, rosemary, marjoram and thyme. Tie bay leaf and peppercorns in cheesecloth bag and add to soup mixture. Simmer for 25 to 35 minutes or until the vegetables are tender. Remove bag before serving. Yields 10 to 12 servings.

Diann Meriwether

Farm Market Soup Stew

2 tablespoons extra-virgin olive oil
½ pound slab bacon, rind removed, cut in ½ inch cubes
6 medium carrots, halved lengthwise and cut into ½ inch pieces
3 medium onions, diced
4 cloves garlic, minced
2 leeks, 3 inches of green left on top, well washed and diced
1 small cabbage, cored and cut in 1 inch pieces
1 russet potato, peeled and diced
½ cup dried green split peas
8 cups defatted chicken broth
1 cup chopped flat leaf parsley
2 teaspoons dried thyme
1 teaspoon dried tarragon
Salt and pepper to taste
4 medium zucchini, cut in ½ inch pieces
¾ pound Swiss chard or spinach, cut crosswise into 1 inch pieces
6 plum tomatoes, seeded and diced

Heat oil in a large, heavy pot over medium-low heat. Add bacon and cook, stirring for 10 to 12 minutes. Add carrots, onions, garlic, and leeks. Cook over low heat for 15 minutes to wilt the vegetables, stirring occasionally. Fold in cabbage, potatoes, split peas into pot and cook 10 minutes. Add broth, ½ cup parsley, thyme, tarragon, salt and pepper. Bring to a boil, reduce heat and simmer for 30 minutes. Add zucchini and cook 15 minutes, stirring occasionally. Add Swiss chard and cook 8 to 10 minutes. Stir in tomatoes and remaining parsley. Cook 5 minutes longer. Serve piping hot. Yields 8 to 10 servings.

Annette Carr

To absorb grease from the top of soup, drop a leaf of lettuce into the pot. Remove and discard when it has served its purpose.

Minestrone

2 tablespoons olive or vegetable oil
1½ cups coarsely chopped onion
1 cup thinly sliced carrots
1 cup thinly sliced celery
1 cup chopped green bell pepper
2 teaspoons minced garlic
4 cups cubed zucchini
1 (35 ounce) can Italian plum tomatoes, undrained
2 (13 ounce) cans chicken broth or 3½ cups water
2 teaspoons dried basil or ¼ cup chopped fresh basil
½ teaspoon dried oregano
3 cups thinly sliced cabbage
1 (20 ounce) can chickpeas, drained
1 (20 ounce) can red kidney beans, drained
8 ounces green beans, cut in 1 inch pieces
½ cup uncooked elbow macaroni
Salt and pepper
Chopped fresh parsley
Fresh grated Parmesan cheese

In an 8 quart pot, heat oil over moderate heat. Add onion, carrots, celery, green pepper, and garlic and cook 3 to 5 minutes, stirring occasionally, until onion is translucent. Stir in zucchini, tomatoes, broth, basil and oregano. Cover pot and reduce heat to moderately low and simmer about 40 minutes, stirring occasionally. Add cabbage, chickpeas, kidney beans, green beans, and macaroni and simmer 15 minutes longer, stirring once or twice until cabbage and macaroni are tender. Season with salt and pepper. The soup will be thick, almost a stew. If you like a thinner soup, add more broth or water. Sprinkle generously with parsley before serving. Serve with grated Parmesan. Makes 15 cups.

Annette Carr

Over salted soup may be corrected by slicing a raw potato into the soup and boiling for a short time. Remove the potato before serving.

Creole Gumbo

1 pound bacon, cut up
1 ham steak, cut up
2 large onions, chopped
2 bell peppers, chopped
1 pound okra, sliced
4 cans tomatoes
4 cans water
1 can Ro-Tel tomatoes
1 can tomato paste
1 tablespoon salt
1 teaspoon cayenne pepper
3 bay leaves
4 or 5 cloves garlic, whole
1 teaspoon celery salt
1 tablespoon Worcestershire sauce
1 lemon
3 to 4 pounds raw shrimp, cleaned and deveined

In large pot or Dutch oven sauté bacon and ham till bacon is done. Remove meat and set aside. Sauté in remaining grease onions, peppers, and okra. Add all remaining ingredients except shrimp. Cut the lemon in half and squeeze juice into pot, then add the lemon. Simmer slowly for about 3 hours. Remove the lemon and bay leaves. Add shrimp and cook until shrimp are pink and tender (not too long). Serve over rice.

Note: 12 boiled crabs can be used instead of shrimp or a combination of both.

Shirlee Nicholson

Cold Strawberry Soup

2 pints strawberries, cleaned and washed
1 pint light white wine
1 ounce orange liqueur
2 ounces brown sugar
2 ounces sour cream

Cut half of the strawberries into large squares. Blend the other half of the strawberries together with the white wine and orange liqueur for about ½ minute in the blender. Chill well, and pour into champagne glasses. Garnish with cut strawberries, sprinkle on a little brown sugar and top with teaspoon sour cream. Serves 6.

Ethel Ankner

Sippy Consommé

1 (10½ ounce) can condensed consommé
½ soup can apple juice
1 teaspoon lemon juice
Dash nutmeg

Combine soup, apple juice, and lemon juice. Heat; stir now and then. Garnish with nutmeg. Makes 2 to 3 servings. (7 ounce mug or bowl, 53 calories).

Sharon Kiel Gutormson

Crawfish Gumbo

1 cup cooking oil
1 cup flour
1 cup chopped celery
1 cup chopped onion
1 gallon water
1 (6 ounce) can tomato paste
2 tablespoons margarine or butter
1 (10 ounce) can Ro-Tel tomatoes
3 pounds crawfish tails
1 pound crab meat
½ cup chopped green onions, tops only
½ cup chopped bell pepper
½ cup parsley
Garlic to taste
Salt and pepper to taste
Gumbo filé

Heat oil in a large heavy pot. Add flour to oil and make a dark roux, stirring constantly. Add celery and onions. Sauté 30 minutes. Add water. In a separate pan, brown tomato paste in margarine. Cook until it loses its bright red color. Add ½ of the tomato paste to the can of Ro-Tel tomatoes. Add this mixture to the large pot and simmer 1 hour. Add crawfish, crab meat, green onions, bell pepper, and parsley. Adjust seasonings to taste and simmer 20 to 30 minutes. This is a thin gumbo. If you want it thickened, add a little cornstarch dissolved in water. Serve on rice and let each person add filé to his own taste. Yields 12 servings.

Diann Meriwether

Fresh Spinach Soup

2 pounds fresh spinach leaves
6 tablespoons butter
Salt and freshly ground pepper
1¼ cups heavy cream
1¼ cups chicken stock

Wash the spinach leaves, changing water several times; drain thoroughly. Put spinach in a thick-bottomed saucepan with butter, and simmer gently, stirring continuously, until spinach is soft and tender.

Whisk in electric blender or put through a wire sieve. Season to taste with salt and freshly ground black pepper. Combine with cream and chicken stock, and heat through. Serve immediately. Serves 4.

Lucille (Max) Ankner

Wild Duck Gumbo

1 green bell pepper, chopped
3 stalks celery, chopped
3 onions, chopped
3 cloves garlic, minced
3 tablespoons cooking oil
1 pound smoked sausage, cut in ½ inch pieces
3 tablespoons flour
2 tablespoons cooking oil
4 quarts hot water
4 large ducks, cut in serving pieces
1½ teaspoons black pepper
1½ teaspoons salt
⅛ teaspoon red pepper
Water
Green onion tops, chopped
Gumbo filé
Cooked white rice

Cook vegetables in 3 tablespoons oil until soft. Cook sausage pieces and add to the vegetables and set aside. Make a roux of the 3 tablespoons flour and 2 tablespoons oil. Be patient; just keep stirring and it will slowly turn to dark brown. Add the roux to the vegetable mixture. Add hot water. Season the duck pieces with the salt, black pepper, and red pepper. Fry the duck in hot oil until dark brown, adding each piece of duck to the vegetable mixture as it turns brown. Pour a little water into duck pan and stir until all the drippings are dissolved and pour into the vegetable mixture. Cook the gumbo slowly until the duck is tender, about 2 to 3 hours. Remove from heat to cool. Debone the duck. This can be done by pouring the gumbo through a large strainer and putting everything except the bones back into the pot. The gumbo may be frozen and reheated. Just before serving, chop green onions to sprinkle on top of each bowl of gumbo which is served over cooked white rice. Add ⅛ teaspoon gumbo filé to each bowl, if desired.

Diann Meriwether

Crab Sandwiches

2 English muffins
1 (7 ounce) package frozen crabmeat, thawed and drained
4 slices tomato
Salt and pepper
⅓ cup finely chopped celery
1 teaspoon lemon juice
Mayonnaise - fat free
4 slices cheddar cheese

Split English muffins and broil until lightly browned; top each with a fourth of the crabmeat. Place a slice of tomato on each and sprinkle with salt and pepper.

Combine celery, lemon juice, and enough mayonnaise to make a spreading consistency; spread over tomato slices. Top with cheese slices and broil until cheese melts. Makes 2 to 4 servings.

Lucille (Max) Ankner

SOUPS AND SANDWICHES

Veggie Pita Pockets

1 package of pita pockets, whole wheat
1 (4 ounce) can mushroom pieces
½ large onion, thinly sliced
2 cups broccoli stems and pieces
1 cup shredded chicken pieces
¼ cup water
⅛ cup white wine vinegar
1 clove garlic
4 ounces shredded cheese
Mrs. Dash herb seasoning to taste
Salsa

Add water, wine vinegar and garlic in a large skillet. Add broccoli, onion, and chicken and simmer until tender and liquid cooks down. Add seasonings and mushrooms and heat but do not overcook. Preheat oven to 350 degrees. Cut pita pockets in half and fill with veggie mixture. Sprinkle cheese on top of the mixture. Place pockets upright side-by-side in a glass baking dish. Bake for 8 to 12 minutes or until cheese melts. Add a little salsa on top and serve.

Note: Great for lunches and for those times when you don't know what to serve. My mother (who has worn a pink ribbon every day since I was diagnosed) made these for me during treatment. They were tasty and healthy and made with tender loving care. She is proud to tell people about BSE and Breast Cancer Awareness, just as I am proud of her - she is terrific!

Kelly Joe Myers-Madoian

Vegetarian Pita Sandwiches

¾ pound firm tofu
1 medium cucumber, shredded
1 medium yellow squash, shredded
1 medium tomato, chopped
2 green onions, chopped
3 eggs, hard-boiled, chopped
3 tablespoons slivered, toasted almonds
2 tablespoons reduced calorie creamy Italian dressing
5 ounces fresh spinach
6 (6 inch) whole wheat pita bread rounds, cut in half
½ cup alfalfa sprouts

Wrap tofu in several layers of paper towels; press lightly to remove excess moisture. Remove paper and crumble the tofu. Combine tofu and next seven ingredients; stir well. Remove stems from spinach. Wash leaves, drain well. Line each pita pocket with spinach leaves. Spoon ⅓ cup mixture into each pocket. Top with alfalfa sprouts. Makes 6 servings.

SOUPS AND SANDWICHES

Stroganoff Sandwiches

1 pound ground beef
1 pint sour cream
3 tomatoes
1 package stroganoff mix

8 ounces sharp cheddar cheese
2 bell peppers
2 large loaves French bread

Split bread loaves, butter and lightly toast in oven. Brown meat, add stroganoff mix and sour cream. Chop tomatoes and peppers. Grate cheese. Top bread with meat mixture, then tomatoes, peppers and cheese last. Heat in a 350 degree oven for about 20 minutes until cheese is melted.

Deby Koudelik

Cancun Tuna Sandwiches

1 can water packed tuna
2 tablespoons low fat salsa (Guiltless Gourmet)

1 tablespoon low fat mayonnaise

Drain tuna and mix all ingredients well. Serve on crackers or as a pita pocket sandwich. Sprinkle with low fat Monterey Jack cheese. Light and refreshing.

Pam Hosford

Grilled Chicken Sandwich

1 cup finely diced cooked chicken or turkey
1 teaspoon lemon juice
½ cup chopped celery

¼ cup fat free mayonnaise
⅛ teaspoon salt
6 slices bread
3 tablespoons margarine

Sprinkle chicken with lemon juice. Mix in celery, mayonnaise, and salt. Makes into 3 sandwiches. Fry in margarine, turning once, until golden brown on both sides.

Lucille (Max) Ankner

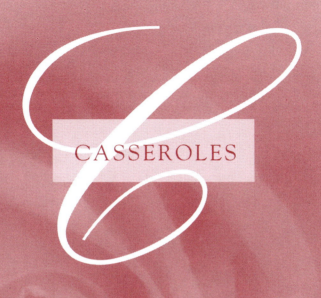
CASSEROLES

CASEROLES

Pizza Spaghetti Casserole

1 (3½ ounce) package sliced pepperoni
½ stick margarine
2 (8 ounce) cans tomato sauce
1 pound ground meat
1 package sliced mozzarella cheese
1 to 2 cups grated mozzarella cheese

1 (7 ounce) box spaghetti
1 (4 ounce) can sliced mushrooms, drained
1 medium onion, chopped
Parmesan cheese
½ teaspoon basil
½ teaspoon oregano

Boil pepperoni 5 minutes, drain on paper towel. Cook and drain spaghetti. Add margarine and generous amount of Parmesan cheese. Brown onion and ground meat and drain. Add tomato sauce and seasonings, simmer, covered for 20 minutes. Add mushrooms and stir well. Layer in a 9 x 13 inch baking dish the spaghetti, grated mozzarella cheese, pepperoni, meat sauce, and sliced mozzarella cheese. Bake uncovered at 350 degrees for 20 minutes.

Billie Menn

Mom's Macaroni Casserole

1 (8 ounce) package macaroni, cooked
1 pound lean ground meat, cooked and drained
2 (8 ounce) cans tomato sauce
1 can condensed tomato soup

1 can corn, drained
2 tablespoons brown sugar
Dash of oregano
Salt and pepper to taste
½ to 1 pound mozzarella, grated

Mix all together and bake at 350 degrees until bubbly.

Susan Munson

Most times, hot water will revive your wilted plants.

Easy Egg Casserole

6 eggs, beaten
2 cups milk
1 teaspoon salt
1 teaspoon dry mustard
1 box cheddar cheese croutons (Kroger's)
8 ounces cheddar cheese, grated
8 to 16 ounces bacon, cooked and crumbled

Blend all ingredients and pour into a lightly greased 13 x 9 inch baking dish. Bake in a 350 degree oven for 20 minutes. Can be put together the day before and refrigerated overnight. Serves 10. Great served with a fruit cup and cinnamon rolls for a great brunch menu.

Darlyne Fratt

Breakfast Casserole

6 eggs
2 cups milk
1 teaspoon salt
6 slices bread, torn into small pieces
1 teaspoon dry mustard
8 ounces or 1½ cups grated cheese
1 pound sausage
4 ounces mushrooms, optional

Brown sausage, drain and cool. Beat eggs and add milk, salt, mustard and beat again. Add bread and mix lightly. Add cheese, sausage, mushrooms and mix well. Pour into a 9 x 13 inch baking dish and refrigerate overnight. Bake at 350 degrees for 45 minutes or until brown around the edges.

Gaylene Adams

CASSEROLES

Make Ahead Breakfast Casserole

1 pound sausage
2 slices of bread cut into cubes
4 ounces shredded sharp cheddar cheese
6 eggs
2 cups milk
½ teaspoon salt
½ teaspoon dry mustard

Crumble sausage in a skillet and cook over medium heat until browned. Drain well. Spread bread cubes in a buttered 12 x 8 x 2 inch glass baking dish. Top with sausage and cheese. Combine eggs, milk and seasonings and beat well. Pour over sausage and cheese. Cover and refrigerate overnight. Bake at 350 degrees for 30 to 40 minutes or until set. Serves 6 to 8 people.

Belva Evans

Brunch Casserole

16 slices white bread
½ pound Kraft Old English cheese, or sharp cheddar
1 pint milk
6 eggs
1 teaspoon salt
½ teaspoon Worcestershire sauce
½ cup melted margarine
1 can cream of mushroom soup
Sautéed mushrooms
Optional: ham, chicken, bacon, Canadian bacon

Cut crusts off bread. Cut bread into 1 inch cubes. Spray glass baking dish with Pam and place bread cubes in it. Use blender to grate cheese in milk. Beat eggs well. Add milk, cheese, salt, and Worcestershire sauce. Pour mixture over bread cubes. Pour melted margarine over top. Cover with plastic wrap and refrigerate at least 4 hours or overnight. Place meat on top of casserole, if desired. Bake at 325 degrees for 15 minutes. Turn oven down to 300 degrees and bake for 45 minutes. Sauté mushroom pieces. Add mushroom soup and heat. This makes a sauce to pour over individual servings. Serves 8.

Note: This is my family's traditional Christmas morning brunch and so easy, because you prepare it the night before and bake while sharing gifts. We have juice, coffee, and coffee cake with it.

Ginny O'Connor

Sesame-Cheese Casserole Bread

3 tablespoons sesame seeds
1 egg
1½ cups milk
3¾ cups Bisquick baking mix
1 cup cheddar cheese, shredded (4 ounces)
1 tablespoon parsley, chopped
¼ teaspoon pepper

Heat oven to 350 degrees. Grease a 2-quart baking dish. Sprinkle sesame seeds evenly on bottom and sides. Beat egg in mixing bowl on low speed. Beat in remaining ingredients on medium speed for 30 seconds. Pour into casserole dish. Bake until toothpick comes out clean, about 40 to 45 minutes. Invert and remove casserole immediately.

Eva McIntyre

Sloppy Joe Casserole

1 (8 ounce) package shell macaroni
1 package French's sloppy joe mix
½ pound ground turkey meat, cooked and drained
1 (6 ounce) can tomato paste
1 (8 ounce) can tomato sauce
1 cup water
1 (16 ounce) carton low fat cottage cheese
1 cup grated low fat or fat free cheddar cheese

Cook macaroni and drain. Brown meat and add Sloppy Joe Mix, tomato paste, tomato sauce, and 1 cup water. In a greased 2½ quart baking dish layer half the macaroni, half the cottage cheese, and half the meat mixture; repeat. Top with grated cheddar cheese and bake at 350 degrees for 40 to 50 minutes or until bubbling. Serves 8.

Sue Clark

CASSEROLES

Mexican Casserole

2 pounds ground meat, browned
1 can cream of chicken soup
1 can cream of mushroom soup
1 (10 ounce) can mild enchilada sauce
1 (3 to 4 ounce) can chopped green chilies
1 large can milk
1 can ranch style beans
10 ounces nacho or taco flavored Doritos, crushed
Grated cheese

Mix all ingredients except cheese. Place in large baking dish and sprinkle with cheese. Bake at 350 degrees for 30 minutes.

Note: The wonderful thing about this recipe is that you can easily double or triple it for large groups. Just use a large oven-proof pot and increase the baking time until it is bubbly.

Gailyn Malone

Mexican Casserole

1 pound ground meat
1 can cream of mushroom soup
1 can cream of chicken soup
1 can Ro-Tel tomatoes with chilies
Shredded cheddar cheese
Flour tortillas

Brown meat and drain. Add soups and Ro-Tel tomatoes. Let simmer a few minutes. Break tortillas into bite size pieces. Layer tortillas, sauce and grated cheese in 9 x 13 inch greased baking dish. Bake at 350 degrees for 20 to 30 minutes. Serve with salad and French bread.

Note: Our daughter-in-law made this for us the first time she had us over for dinner in 1982. It has remained one of our favorite meals.

Joan Louth

Tigerina

2 pounds ground meat
1 large chopped onion
Garlic powder to taste
Salt and pepper to taste
1 teaspoon chili powder
1 large can tomatoes, drained

1 can shoepeg corn, drained
¾ pound shredded cheese
½ cup sliced black olives
1 package flat noodles,
  ½ inch wide

Sauté onions, ground meat, garlic, salt and pepper. Add chili powder and tomatoes. Cook noodles according to package directions. Spray a 9 x 13 inch baking dish with cooking spray. Cover bottom of dish with small amount of meat mixture. Layer the noodles, shoepeg corn, meat mixture, cheese, and black olives. It usually works out to be 2 layers. Bake at 350 degrees for 30 minutes.

Gaylene Adams

All-In-One Casserole

1½ to 2 pounds ground meat
1 large onion, chopped
1 (16 ounce) can tomatoes, chopped with liquid
1 can diced Ro-Tel tomatoes and green chilies

1 can ranch style beans, undrained
3 cans minestrone soup
1¼ cups water

Sauté and drain ground meat. Combine all ingredients in crock pot and simmer on low 2 to 3 hours or longer. Freezes well. Serve with Broccoli Cornbread.

Betty Baker

CASSEROLES

Pork Chops and Rice Casserole

4 pork chops, thin cut
1 tablespoon garlic salt
1 cup uncooked rice
1 tablespoon cooking oil
1 teaspoon salt

1 can cream of mushroom
  soup
½ cup water
1 tablespoon chopped
  pimientos

Sprinkle pork chops with garlic salt and brown in skillet until done. Cook rice with 1 tablespoon cooking oil and 1 teaspoon salt. Add to rice 1 can cream of mushroom soup, ½ cup water, and pimientos and mix well. Place pork chops in 9 x 13 inch baking dish and pour rice mixture over top. Cover with foil and bake in a 350 degree oven for 30 to 40 minutes until pork chops are tender.

Albina H. Elliott

Italian Beef Casserole

1 pound ground meat
8 ounces mushrooms, drained
1 tablespoon cooking oil
2 packages frozen broccoli,
  cooked and drained
1 cup sour cream

1 can condensed cream of
  celery soup
6 ounces grated mozzarella
  cheese
1 teaspoon garlic salt
½ teaspoon pepper
1 small onion, chopped

Brown meat and mushrooms in oil. Add broccoli, soup, sour cream and seasoning. Pour into 2 quart baking dish. Top with grated cheese. Bake uncovered in a preheated oven at 350 degrees for 35 to 45 minutes.

Diann Meriwether

St. Paul's Rice Casserole

1 cup chopped green onions
1 cup chopped celery
1 cup chopped bell peppers
1 pound of Jimmy Dean breakfast sausage
2 envelopes chicken noodle soup mix
1 cup rice
6 cups water, boiling
2 cups grated cheese

In a large pan, cook soup mix and rice in boiling water approximately 20 minutes until done. In large skillet, cook vegetables with sausage approximately 20 minutes. Drain any grease. Combine with soup mixture. Bake in a greased 9 x 13 inch baking dish at 350 degrees for 35 minutes. Top with cheese.

Billie Menn

Green Rice Casserole

2 cups uncooked rice
2 cups grated cheddar cheese
1 package frozen chopped spinach
½ cup margarine, melted
1 teaspoons salt or to taste
2 eggs, slightly beaten
2 cups milk
1 small onion, chopped fine

Cook rice and spinach separately. When done, combine rice, cheese and spinach. Add margarine, salt and onion and mix well. Combine eggs and milk and add to mixture. Pour into a 9 x 13 inch greased baking dish. Bake at 350 degrees for 45 minutes.

Janice LeBlanc

Sterling becomes more beautiful with use as it develops a "patina".

Hominy Casserole

1 onion, chopped
2 to 3 stalks of celery, chopped
1 bell pepper, chopped
1 large can hominy, drained
1 can cream of mushroom condensed soup
1 small jar Cheese Whiz

Mix together and bake in casserole dish at 350 degrees for 35 to 40 minutes.

Diann Meriwether

Hamburger Casserole

1¼ pounds ground meat
½ cup chopped onion
½ cup chopped bell pepper
1 (8 ounce) can tomato sauce with mushrooms
1 (#2) can French style green beans
½ teaspoon salt to taste
½ teaspoon garlic salt
⅓ teaspoon cumin powder
1 can of crescent dinner rolls
1 egg, slightly beaten
1 cup grated Monterey Jack cheese
10 ounces grated cheddar cheese

Sauté onions and bell pepper, add ground meat and brown. Drain any grease. Add tomato sauce, green beans, salt, garlic salt, and cumin powder and simmer. Line the bottom of a large pie pan with the crescent dinner roll dough to make a crust. Combine the egg and cheese and spread over the bottom of the pie pan. Add meat mixture and top with grated cheddar cheese. Bake at 350 degrees for 20 minutes. Add more cheese if desired.

Elizabeth Henson

Company Casserole

8 ounces medium noodles
1 pound ground beef
2 (8 ounce) cans tomato sauce
8 ounce package cream cheese
1 cup cottage cheese
¾ cup sour cream
½ cup chopped green onion
2 tablespoons chopped green pepper
2 tablespoons melted butter

Cook noodles, rinse, and drain. Brown and crumble meat. Stir in tomato sauce. Combine softened cream cheese, cottage cheese, sour cream, onion and green pepper, and beat.

In a greased casserole, layer the noodles, meat-tomato sauce, and sour cream-cheese combination, beginning and ending with noodles. Pour melted butter over the mixture. Bake at 350 degrees for one hour. Serves 8.

Note: This may be frozen before baking.

Ethel Ankner

Jalapinto Rice Casserole

½ cup chopped onion
2 to 3 garlic cloves, chopped
1 tablespoon olive oil
1 pound ground turkey
Salt and pepper as desired
2 (15 ounce) cans Trappey's Jalapinto pinto beans
2 bags Success brown rice, cooked
1 (14 ounce) can stewed tomatoes, "Cajun Style", chopped and drained
1 can Ro-Tel diced tomatoes and green chilies
1 cup no-fat cheddar cheese, shredded

Sauté onion and garlic in olive oil until tender. Add ground turkey, salt and pepper, and brown. Stir in beans, rice, tomatoes, and mix well. Pour into 9 x 13 inch greased baking dish. Sprinkle cheese over top and bake at 350 degrees for 20 minutes until cheese is melted. Serves 6 to 8 people.

Note: This a heart healthy recipe. I made changes to lower fat content and cholesterol. This recipe is also a little spicy. If you want a less spicy dish, use plain pinto beans and substitute another can of stewed tomatoes for the Ro-Tel tomatoes.

Elaine Doubrava

Green Rice Casserole

1 stick margarine
1 cup celery, chopped
1 bunch green onions, chopped
1 can cream of chicken soup
1 can cream of celery soup
1 cup water
1½ cups uncooked rice
1 small can sliced water chestnuts, drained
1 teaspoon salt

Sauté green onions and celery in margarine. Add the remainder of all ingredients and mix well. Bake in a greased, covered casserole dish for 1 hour at 350 degrees.

Note: This special dish was usually prepared by my "Granny" on special occasions. When I make it, I always think of her. It's so delicious and easy to make.

Georgina Mahoney

CASSEROLES

Broccoli Cheese Rice Casserole

2 boxes Uncle Ben's long grain and wild rice
2 packages frozen chopped broccoli
1 (14 ounce) can chicken broth, low salt variety
2 (8 ounce) cans of chopped mushrooms, drained
2 (8 ounce) cans of whole water chestnuts, drained
2 cups grated nonfat cheddar or 16 ounces Kraft Free cheese slices
1 cup low fat croutons, crushed
1 to 1½ teaspoons Mrs. Dash salt free extra spicy seasoning
Butter Buds butter substitute

Prepare the rice as directed on the package using the Butter Buds as flavoring. Cook the broccoli according to package directions, then add to the rice. Add mushrooms, water chestnuts, chicken broth, grated cheese, and Mrs. Dash. Bake in a large casserole dish that has been sprayed with nonfat cooking spray. Top with croutons and bake covered at 350 degrees for 30 to 35 minutes. Remove cover the last 10 minutes. Serves 12 to 14.

Sue Clark

Green Chili Rice

4 cups cooked rice
1½ to 2 cups sour cream
¾ to 1 pound Monterey Jack cheese, thinly sliced
1 can chopped green chilies
Cheddar cheese, grated, enough to cover top
1 teaspoon salt to taste

Mix rice, sour cream, green chilies and salt. Spray a 9 x 13 inch baking dish with cooking oil spray. Spread a thin layer of rice mixture in dish, add a layer of Monterey Jack cheese, another layer of rice, then cheese. Top with cheddar cheese and bake at 350 degrees for 30 minutes.

Leslie LeVack

Arroz Central Cafe Rice Casserole

1 cup long grain rice, rinsed well
½ onion, chopped
1 (4 ounce) can chopped green chilies, drained
1 clove garlic, minced
1 tablespoon butter, melted
1 tablespoon olive oil
2 cups chicken stock

Sauté rice, onion, chilies and garlic in butter and oil. Add stock and place in 1½ quart baking dish. Cover and bake at 350 degrees for 30 minutes. Makes 4 to 6 servings.

Merline Fogtman

Chicken and Rice Casserole

1 cup rice
2 tablespoons margarine
1 can onion soup
1 can beef bouillon soup
6 chicken breasts, skinned

Soak rice for 30 minutes. Combine all ingredients in a shallow baking dish; lay chicken, rib side down, on top of mixture. Cover with foil and bake at 350 degrees for 1 hour. Serves 8 people.

Eva McIntyre

Bean Casserole

1 pound hamburger (extra lean), turkey or chicken, ground
½ pound bacon or turkey bacon, cut up
1 cup chopped onion
1 cup ketchup
½ cup brown sugar
1 tablespoon dry mustard
1 can baked beans
1 can kidney beans
1 can lima beans

Sauté the hamburger, bacon and onion until meat is lightly browned. Add other ingredients. Bake at 350 degrees for one hour. (This freezes well).

Lucille (Max) Ankner

One-half spoonful is measured lengthwise of the spoon.

Chicken Tetrazzini Casserole

4 ounces margarine (½ stick)
1 medium bell pepper, chopped
5 tablespoons flour
½ pound cheese
1 can cream of mushroom soup
1 (3 ounce) can sliced mushrooms
1 chicken, cut up
1 tablespoon garlic salt
2 tablespoons soy sauce
4 ounces pimentos
4 ounces thin spaghetti

Boil chicken with celery, onion and salt. Cool and debone to equal 4 cups of chicken. Sauté bell pepper in margarine. Remove peppers, add flour and milk to make cream sauce. Grate cheese and add half of it to the sauce. Add soup, mushrooms with juice, diced chicken, and other ingredients. Boil the spaghetti in chicken stock. Grease a 9 x 13 inch baking dish. Put in spaghetti. Pour the mixture over and top with remaining cheese and bake at 350 degrees for 30 to 40 minutes.

Diann Meriwether

Chicken Casserole

4 cups chicken, cooked and boned
4 tablespoons diced onions
2 cups diced celery
1½ cups mayonnaise
2 cans cream of chicken soup
1 cup sliced almonds
2 cups cornflake crumbs

Mix well. Put in a greased 9 x 13 inch baking dish and bake at 325 degrees for 30 minutes.

Barbara Gibbs

Almond Chicken Casserole

2 cups cooked diced chicken, boiled in broth, save the broth
1 package Uncle Ben's long grain and wild rice
1 chopped onion
1 can French style green beans, drained
1½ cups mayonnaise
2 ounces pimentos
1 can water chestnuts, drained and chopped
2 cans cream of celery soup
1 cup sliced almonds
2½ cups chicken broth
Parmesan cheese for top

Cook rice and onion in 2½ cups broth. Mix all ingredients, use ½ cup of almonds. Pour mixture into a 9 x 13 inch greased baking dish, scatter remaining ½ cup almonds on top, sprinkle generously with Parmesan cheese, then paprika. Bake uncovered at 350 degrees for 40 minutes.

Pauline Harp

Biscuit-Topped Casserole

1 to 2 pounds ground beef or turkey, browned
1 can or 2 cups frozen mixed vegetables
1 to 2 cups diced potatoes
1 package onion soup mix
Biscuit mix or canned biscuits

Cook vegetables and potatoes until almost done and add onion soup mix. Combine with browned meat. Pour into a greased 8 inch square baking dish. Use larger dish if needed. Prepare biscuit mix according to package directions and top casserole. Bake at 400 degrees until done. Canned biscuits can be used.

Helen L. Kainer

CASSEROLES

Tuna-Noodle Casserole

6 ounces medium noodles
12 ounces tuna, drained
½ cup mayonnaise
1 cup celery, chopped
⅓ cup onion, chopped
¼ cup bell pepper, chopped
1 (10 ounce) can cream of
  celery soup
½ cup milk
4 ounces sharp cheddar
  cheese, grated
½ cup slivered almonds,
  toasted
salt to taste

Cook noodles in water, drain. Sauté celery, onion and bell pepper. Blend cream of celery soup with ½ cup milk and heat. Add cheese and stir till cheese melts. Combine noodles, sautéed vegetables, tuna, mayonnaise and salt. Combine with soup-cheese mixture and pour into a greased 9 x 13 inch baking dish. Top with toasted almonds and bake at 425 degrees for 20 minutes.

Note: This is a frequent supper meal at our house. It can also be frozen and popped into the oven for those nights when there's not much time for cooking.

Mary Jane Morgan

Tagglarene Casserole

4 tablespoons cooking oil
1 onion, chopped fine
2 cloves garlic, pressed
1 green pepper, seeded and
  chopped
1 pound ground beef or
  turkey
1 (4 ounce) package noodles
2 cans tomato sauce
Water
1 small can cream-style corn
1 small can pitted black
  olives
1 can mushrooms, drained
Dash cayenne pepper
Salt and pepper to taste
Grated sharp cheese

Sauté onion, garlic and green pepper in oil until golden. Add ground meat and cook until pink does not show. Add tomato sauce, noodles and enough water to cover noodles. Cook until noodles are tender. Add corn, olives, mushrooms, cayenne, salt and pepper to taste. Place in 2-quart casserole and cover with cheese. Bake in 325 degree oven for 35 minutes.

Sharon Kiel Gutormson

The three kitchen items that spread the most bacteria are the can opener, the meat grinder, and the cutting board. Keep them clean.

MAIN DISHES

MAIN DISHES

Chili Con Carne

1 pound lean ground beef
1 can chili beans or kidney
   beans
2 cans tomato soup
½ teaspoon salt
1 teaspoon chili powder
2 tablespoons sugar
2 medium onions, chopped

Brown meat, add onions and lightly sauté. Add remainder of ingredients and simmer about 30 minutes.

Note: This was my father's (Maxwell S. Bowman) recipe. The more times it is reheated, the better it tastes. My father would eat his chili con carne served over mashed potatoes. Sounds strange, but it's good, try it.

Ginny O'Connor

Turkey Chili (Spicy)

1 pound ground turkey
1 package chili mix
1 (14 ounce) can Mexican
   stewed tomatoes
   (Del Monte)
1 (10 ounce) can Ro-Tel diced
   tomatoes and green chilies
1 (15 ounce) can kidney or
   pinto beans
½ onion, chopped
2 cloves garlic, chopped
Salt and pepper to taste

Brown ground turkey. Add onion and garlic and sauté. Add chili mix, tomatoes, and beans. Simmer over medium heat for approximately 20 minutes. Add water if it gets too thick. Serves 4.

Elaine Doubrava

Can Can

1 can cream of chicken soup
1 can cream of celery soup
1 soup can instant rice (dry)
1 soup can water
2 soup cans boned chicken (or
   cooked chicken breasts)
Optional: celery, pimentos,
   green chilies for color and
   taste
1 can onion rings

Mix first five ingredients (add optionals if desired) and pour into 1½ quart casserole dish, cover, and bake at 325 degrees until brown. Top with onion rings.

Anna Belle Baugus

Southwestern Quiche

1 (9 inch) pie shell
1 teaspoon chili powder
10 ounces grated colby and Monterey Jack cheese
3 eggs, lightly beaten
1½ cups milk
1 teaspoon salt
¼ teaspoon white pepper
1 (4 ounce) can diced green chilies
1 (2¼ ounce) can sliced black olives

Sprinkle pie crust with chili powder. Spread cheese on bottom of pie shell. Mix remaining ingredients together and pour over pastry. Bake at 350 degrees for 45 minutes or until knife inserted in center comes out clean.

Ellen Timitone

Quiche Lorraine

1 unbaked pie shell
½ cup chopped chives
8 ounces Swiss cheese, diced
1 can crab meat, drained
½ cup mayonnaise
2 tablespoons flour
½ cup milk
2 eggs, well beaten

Mix all ingredients together and pour into unbaked pie shell. Bake at 350 degrees for 30 to 35 minutes or until golden brown on top. Let stand 2 to 3 minutes before serving. Instead of crab, you may substitute lobster, salmon, tuna or vegetables, like spinach.

Yvonne Constantino

Hamburger Pie

1 pound lean hamburger meat
1 can green beans
2 cups mashed potatoes
Salt
Pepper
Garlic powder
Cheese or butter

Brown meat and drain. Season green beans to taste. Using a square Pyrex 2 quart baking dish, layer hamburger, green beans and potatoes. Top with cheese or butter. Cook for 10 minutes at 400 degrees.

The men love this one!

Pat Thompson

MAIN DISHES

Sausage Ring

2 pounds sausage
½ cup crackers, crushed
2 eggs
½ cup skim milk
¼ cup chopped onion
1 cup apples, peeled and chopped

Mix all ingredients well and pat into a ring-shaped mold (approximately 12 inches wide x 3 inches tall) and place on a cookie sheet. Bake one hour at 350 degrees. Serves 8 people. Can be served with scrambled eggs in the center or with "Easy Baked Eggs with Cheese Sauce". Can be baked ahead and also freezes well.

Nancy Maranto

Easy Baked Eggs with Cheese Sauce

4 eggs, boiled
3 tablespoons butter
3 tablespoons flour
1 cup skim milk
½ to 1 cup grated sharp cheddar cheese (low fat can be used)

Halve the boiled eggs and place in a buttered glass baking dish. Melt butter over medium heat in saucepan and stir in flour. Remove from heat and slowly add milk, stirring to prevent lumps. Return to heat and cook until thickened, stirring constantly. Add cheese and stir until melted. Spoon cheese mixture over eggs and bake in 325 degree oven until hot and bubbly, approximately 20 minutes.

Nancy Maranto

Quick and Easy Pastie Pie

2 cups leftover roast, turkey or chicken, chopped
2 potatoes, medium-sized, peeled and diced
3 carrots, peeled and sliced into small pieces
⅔ cup frozen peas
1 small onion, diced
1 teaspoon marjoram, optional
1 teaspoon Cavender's seasoning
Salt and pepper to taste
2 cans crescent rolls

Peel the carrots and potatoes and par cook them in water. While they are cooking, cut up the leftover meat and dice the onion. Heat up the meat, peas and onion in the microwave for two minutes (put a little water for moisture). Spray a cookie sheet with non-stick spray. Open one of the cans of crescent rolls and lay the dough out flat on the cookie sheet. Drain the potatoes, carrots and the meat mixture and combine in a bowl. Add seasonings. Place the meat mixture on the dough. Open the remaining can of rolls and place on top of the meat. Seal the sides. Bake at 375 degrees until golden brown. Serves 4 to 6.

Note: My husband who hates leftovers and my children love this dish!

Louise Mitchell

Tijuana Torte

1½ pounds ground beef
1 medium onion, chopped
1 pound can stewed tomatoes
1 (8 ounce) can tomato sauce
1 (4 ounce) can green chilies, diced
1 package taco seasoning
flour tortillas
1 to 1½ cups sour cream

Brown beef and onion in pans; add other ingredients (except cheese). Simmer 10 minutes to 15 minutes. Spread ⅓ of mixture in 9 x 13 inch baking pan. Place a layer of tortillas on top; add more mixture, then cheese. Add layer of sour cream, then repeat layer of tortillas, beef mixture and cheese. Bake at 350 degrees for 25 minutes, until cheese is bubbly. Serves: 4 to 6.

Leslie LeVack

Black Bean Pizza

1 tablespoon olive oil
1 to 2 tablespoons minced jalapeño peppers
1 teaspoon chili powder
1 minced garlic clove
1 prepared pie crust
1 medium tomato, chopped
1 can black beans, drained and rinsed
1 cup green pepper strips
½ cup green onion, thinly sliced

Preheat oven to 425 degrees. In a small bowl, combine oil, jalapeños, chili powder, and garlic. Spray pizza pan with vegetable cooking spray. Pat dough in pan and brush with oil mixture. Bake 6 to 8 minutes. Top crust with chopped tomatoes, beans, pepper and onions. Bake an additional 14 to 18 minutes or until crust is brown. If you wish, you may top off with grated cheese and add tomato paste to the chopped tomatoes.

Ruth Kirk Soloff

Saltimbocca a la Romana

"Jump in the mouth"

8 (2 ounce) thin slices of veal fillet
8 slices Prosciutto di Parma
8 sprigs fresh sage or 4 dried bay leaves
2 ounces olive oil
6 tablespoons Marsala or white wine
¼ cup lemon juice

Beat each fillet of veal until very thin. Rub each with lemon juice and pepper. Top with sage leaves or bay leaves, crushed. Roll up and secure with toothpicks. Fry in hot olive oil until golden brown on all sides. Sprinkle with lemon juice. Add wine to pan, lower the heat, cover and cook about 15 to 20 minutes. Serve with multi-colored pasta. Yields 4 servings.

Anci Waugh

MAIN DISHES

Curly Noodle Dinner

1 pound ground beef or turkey
1 (14 ounce) can stewed tomatoes
1 (8 ounce) can whole kernel corn with liquid
1 package Oriental noodles, beef or pork flavored

Brown meat well in 10 inch skillet and drain off any fat. Stir in stewed tomatoes with liquid and corn with liquid. Stir in the seasoning packet from the noodles and bring to a boil. Reduce heat, cover and simmer about 10 minutes or until noodles are tender. This recipe refers to the package of Oriental noodle soup and not the cup of soup noodles. For variation, add ½ teaspoon chili powder.

Note: This is a favorite with my teenage grandson, Wayne. When he and his friends come in hungry, I fix a big pot of it and add picante sauce. Sometimes I add chopped bell pepper for color. Served with hot cornbread and chocolate cake for dessert, it really fills them up. And we all know how hard it is to fill up teenage boys!

Janice LeBlanc

Rolled Cabbage Leaves

1 head tender, green cabbage
1 pound diced lamb (shoulder or breast)
1 cup rice soaked for 10 minutes
½ teaspoon cinnamon
1 tablespoon salt
Pepper to taste
¼ teaspoon allspice
1 (29 ounce) can tomatoes, minced
¼ cup lemon juice
3 tablespoons margarine, melted

Trim core of center of cabbage. Boil cabbage head in water for about 5 minutes. Drain and separate leaves. Cut off coarse vein at end, enough to roll easily.

Mix uncooked lamb and rice, add spices and melted margarine. Roll about 1 tablespoon in half of large leaf or use whole large leaf and roll with about 2 tablespoons mixture. Line bottom of a 5 quart pot with 2 or 3 leaves, then lay cabbage rolls evenly in pot. Add 2 cups water or enough to cover the rolls and cook covered 20 to 30 minutes on low heat. Add minced tomatoes and cook 5 more minutes. Add lemon juice and simmer an additional 5 minutes. Serves 4 to 5 people as a one dish meal with pita bread and Mediterranean tossed salad. Delicious with shish kabobs.

Variations: Add whole cloves of garlic over rolls during first cooking stage. Add can of tomatoes to meat and rice mixture for a more moist texture. Ground meat or turkey can be substituted for lamb.

Norma Maria

MAIN DISHES

Baked Stuffed Cabbage

1 (3 pound) cabbage
1 cup rice, cooked
1 large onion, chopped
¼ pound margarine
1½ pounds ground beef or pork
1 egg
1½ teaspoons salt
Pepper to taste
2 tablespoons margarine
2 tablespoons flour
1 large can tomatoes

Place cabbage in boiling water and let stand a few minutes. Separate leaves from stem and trim off hard parts. Sauté onions in margarine and add rice. Mix together meat, egg, salt and pepper. Roll the meat in cabbage leaf. Place in pot which has the bottom covered with leaves. Place the fold on bottom. Brown the flour in butter and add tomatoes. Pour over cabbage rolls and cook or bake slowly for 2 hours.

Wanda Szot

Arroz Con Pollo

2 chicken breasts, skinless, cut into small cubes
1 cup rice
½ can Ro-Tel diced tomatoes and chilies
Garlic powder to taste
½ teaspoon cumin powder
1 cube chicken broth
½ fresh bell pepper
½ fresh medium onion
salt and pepper to taste
1 tablespoon cooking oil

Heat cooking oil in skillet and brown rice then remove from skillet. Brown chicken pieces, then simmer with bell pepper and onion. Add rice, Ro-Tel tomatoes, spices, and 2 cups water. Bring to boil and simmer for 30 minutes until done.

Chicken Pot Pie

1 package Ready pie crust
2 cans white chicken
1 (10 ounce) package frozen vegetables (peas and carrots)
½ cup onion, chopped
1 (10¾ ounce) can cream of potato soup
⅓ cup milk
½ teaspoon poultry seasoning

Line 9 inch pie plate with one crust. Combine all ingredients in bowl and add salt and pepper. Top with second crust, crimp edges and cut slits in top. Bake at 350 degrees for 40 to 45 minutes.

Helen L. Kainer

MAIN DISHES

Chicken Pot Pie

4 chicken breasts, skinned
2 quarters water
Salt and pepper
2 cans mixed vegetables
2 large potatoes, cut in small pieces
½ cup margarine
½ cup flour
1 cup milk
2 boxes 9-inch pie crusts (in refrigerated section)

Combine chicken, water, salt, and pepper. Bring to a boil, reduce heat and simmer one hour or until chicken is tender. Remove chicken, cool, debone and cut in bite size pieces. Add vegetables and potatoes to broth and simmer 8 to 10 minutes. Add chicken, 2 to 3 cups water, margarine, and continue to simmer. Mix ½ cup flour and 1 cup milk and pour into broth mixture. Stir until thickened. Turn off heat. Grease 9 x 13 inch baking dish. Roll out one pie crust and cut to fit bottom of baking dish. Pour chicken and vegetables in dish. Roll out other pie crust and fit on top. Make a few slits. Bake at 400 degrees for 20 to 25 minutes until top crust is lightly browned.

Note: This recipe is quick and easy to prepare. Serve with a salad and you have a complete meal.

Joy Caka

Dressing-Topped Chicken Pot Pie

1 package stuffing mix
1½ cups vegetable juice from the canned vegetables
2 teaspoons liquid Butter Buds
2 cups cooked chicken (canned chicken can be used)
2 cans low-salt mixed vegetables, drain and save liquid
1 (10 ounce) can cream of chicken soup
1 cup celery, chopped
1 small green pepper, chopped
1 small onion, chopped

Spray a microwave casserole pan with vegetable spray. Put one can of mixed vegetables in the bottom, ½ of the chicken on top. Add the other can of vegetables and the remainder of the chicken. Pour the chicken soup on top. Cook the celery, pepper, and onion in the vegetable juice until tender. Add more water if needed. Add stuffing mix and Butter Buds in the pan and mix well. Spoon the stuffing on top of the vegetable and chicken mixture so it is completely covered. Microwave 8 to 10 minutes. Serves 8 to 10.

Mabel E. Lucas

Fajitas

1 pound meat (beef, chicken, or shrimp)
3 tablespoons oil
2 tablespoons cornstarch
2 tablespoons oil
2 tablespoons lemon juice
½ teaspoon ground oregano
½ teaspoon ground pepper
⅛ teaspoon Liquid Smoke flavoring
1 cup sliced bell pepper
1 cup sliced onion
1 cup thin tomato wedges
½ cup salsa

In medium bowl, combine all of the spices, 2 tablespoons oil, cornstarch, and lemon juice. Add meat and stir to coat. Refrigerate 2 to 8 hours. In a 10-inch skillet, heat 3 tablespoons cooking oil until very hot. Sauté meat until just cooked; remove to plate. In drippings, sauté pepper and onion wedges until tender crisp. Return meat to skillet and toss with pepper and onion wedges. Top with tomato wedges and salsa and simmer 1 minute. Serve with flour tortillas, refried beans and rice. Garnish with grated cheese, sour cream, and guacamole. Serves 4.

Merline Fogtman

Pork Roast with Miso

5 pound pork roast
1 piece fresh ginger 2 to 3 inches long, mashed
2 cloves garlic, crushed
½ teaspoon ajinomoto
¾ cup miso
½ cup sugar
¾ cup soy sauce

Mix miso, soy sauce and sugar in a large pot then add ginger and garlic. Mix well. Place pork in the pot and simmer over medium heat for 2½ to 3 hours until fully cooked.

Note: The ajinomoto and miso can be found at health food or Oriental grocery stores.

Leiola Onishi

You will not smell of garlic if parsley equal to the amount of garlic is added to your recipe.

Pork Chops With Oregano

4 center cut pork chops,
  1 inch thick and trimmed
  of fat
1 tablespoon olive oil
Salt and pepper to taste
1 tablespoon dried oregano
¼ cup fresh lemon juice
½ cup sherry

Spray large baking dish with cooking spray. Drizzle olive oil on top of each chop and spread with fingers. Add salt and pepper. Sprinkle each chop heavily with oregano and place in baking dish. Add lemon juice and sherry. Bake at 350 degrees for 45 minutes to one hour until done. Serve with baked sweet potatoes, green vegetable, and salad.

Ellen Limitone

Million Dollar Meatballs

2 eggs or 2 egg substitutes
½ cup bread crumbs
½ cup grated Parmesan
  cheese
1 pound ground beef or ½
  pound each of beef and
  ground turkey
3 tablespoons cooking oil
  or ¼ cup defatted chicken
  broth
2 tablespoons lemon juice
1 (¾ ounce) envelope brown
  gravy mix
Salt and pepper to taste
2 teaspoons beef soup base
2 cups water

Combine eggs, crumbs, and cheese in mixing bowl. Add ground meat, salt and pepper and mix well. Shape into meatballs. Brown in cooking oil in large skillet. Drain off oil. Stir in 2 cups water, lemon juice, beef soup base and contents of gravy mix. Simmer 15 to 20 minutes or until meatballs are cooked. Serve with noodles. Makes 4 to 6 servings.

Joy Caka

Belgian Pot Roast

3½ pounds boneless chuck
  roast
2 tablespoons shortening
1 (15 ounce) can beef gravy
¼ teaspoon rosemary leaves,
  crushed
¼ teaspoon pepper
4 medium pears, cut in half
  (about 1½ pounds)
1 (10 ounce) package frozen
  (or fresh) Brussels sprouts

In large heavy pan, brown meat in shortening; pour off fat. Add gravy and seasonings. Cover; cook over low heat for 2 hours and 30 minutes. Add pears; cook 15 minutes. Add Brussels sprouts; cook 15 minutes more or until done. Stir occasionally. Thicken gravy if desired. Serves 6. Makes about 2 cups of gravy.

Ethel Ankner

MEATS

E-Z Steak

1 round steak, trimmed of fat and cut in pieces
1 onion sliced in rings
8 ounces fresh mushrooms, sliced
1 bell pepper, cleaned and cut in rings, optional
1 package au jus mix prepared according to package directions
Salt and pepper to taste

Spray a non-stick skillet with cooking spray and brown meat. Add onion, bell pepper, and mushrooms. Simmer covered until vegetables are tender crisp. Pour au jus gravy over all, cover and cook until done.

Note: 1 can of beef stock mixed with ¼ cup cornstarch can be substituted for the au jus gravy mix.

Elizabeth Payne

Steak Kabobs

2 tablespoons soy sauce, reduced sodium
2 tablespoons honey
1 tablespoon grated fresh ginger, or 1 teaspoon ground ginger
1 clove garlic, crushed
1 teaspoon grated lemon peel
¼ teaspoon crushed red pepper flakes
12 ounces boneless sirloin steak, cut in 1 inch pieces
8 cherry tomatoes
4 large mushrooms, halved
1 bell pepper, cut into square pieces

In a shallow glass dish, combine soy sauce, honey, ginger, garlic, lemon peel, and red pepper flakes. Mix well. Add beef and coat well. Cover with plastic wrap and refrigerate for at least 2 hours, stirring occasionally. Preheat broiler. Remove beef from marinade. Using 4 10-inch metal skewers, alternately skewer beef, tomatoes, mushrooms, and bell pepper and place on broil pan. Broil 2 inches from heat, turning 2 or 3 times until meat is done and vegetables are brown; about 10 minutes for medium.

Anna Bell

Sunday Pork Tenderloin

2 pork tenderloins
¾ cup dry vermouth or apple juice
⅔ cup applesauce
¼ cup finely chopped peanuts
¼ teaspoon salt
¼ teaspoon fennel seed
¼ teaspoon garlic powder
Pepper to taste

Marinate pork in vermouth for 1 to 3 hours. Cut a tunnel down middle of pork and fill with applesauce, peanuts, and spices. Hold together with toothpicks. Sprinkle with black pepper. Bake in 9 x 13 inch pan for 30 to 40 minutes at 375 degrees.

Lucille (Max) Ankner

MEATS

Stuffed Meat Loaf

1½ pounds lean ground beef
1 egg
4 tablespoons seasoned bread crumbs
4 to 5 green onions, minced
1 teaspoon salt
½ teaspoon basil leaves
½ teaspoon black pepper
½ cup shredded cheddar cheese
1½ cups broccoli, zucchini, or macaroni
1 tablespoon melted butter
1 tablespoon ketchup

In a bowl, combine the beef, egg, 2 tablespoons of the bread crumbs, ¾ of the onion, ¾ teaspoon salt, the basil and the pepper. Mix well and set aside. If using fresh broccoli or zucchini, bring a pot of water to boil. Drop the broccoli or zucchini in for 3 to 4 minutes and drain well. If using macaroni, cook according to directions. If using frozen broccoli or zucchini, thaw and drain well. Mix with the cheese, remaining bread crumbs, green onion, and salt. Press half of the meat mixture into a loaf pan, forming an indent along the center, and leaving a 1-inch layer on the sides. Fill the indent with the vegetable or macaroni mixture. Top with remaining meat mixture and seal well around the edges. Mix the melted butter and ketchup and brush on top of loaf and bake at 350 degrees for 1 hour.

Note: Can be frozen or served cold.

JoAnne Moore

No-Work Meat Loaf

1½ pounds ground meat
1 cup packaged herb-seasoned stuffing mix
1 (8 ounce) can seasoned tomato sauce
1 egg
1½ teaspoons salt
¼ teaspoon pepper

Mix ingredients well. Shape into a loaf and place in a shallow baking dish or jellyroll pan. Bake at 350 degrees about 1 hour.

Carolyn Thompson

Broiled Flank Steak

3 pounds flank steak
1½ garlic cloves, pressed
1 tablespoon soy sauce
2 tablespoons red wine
1 teaspoon sugar

Mix above ingredients and marinate steak at room temperature for 2 hours or more. Broil 7 minutes on first side and 5 minutes on reverse side. Slice thinly against the grain. Serves 8.

Sharon Kiel Gutormson

Chicken Alfredo

4 cooked chicken breasts, boneless, skinless and cut into small pieces
1 (8 ounce) can mushrooms, sliced and drained
1 cup evaporated skim milk
¼ cup liquid Butter Buds
¼ cup flour
4 teaspoons chicken broth
¼ cup Parmesan cheese
¼ teaspoon minced garlic
¼ teaspoon black pepper
¼ teaspoon salt
10 to 12 ounces cooked fettuccine

In a saucepan over low heat, blend flour, liquid Butter Buds, skim milk, and chicken broth. Add minced garlic, salt, and pepper. Continue to cook over low heat, stirring constantly until the sauce thickens. Stir in Parmesan cheese. Combine sauce with chicken and mushrooms. Fold into cooked pasta and serve immediately. If sauce is too thick, add a little more milk and chicken broth. Serves 6.

Sue Clark

Citrus Salsa Chicken

4 boneless, skinless chicken breasts
Pepper to taste
1 tablespoon grated orange peel or zest
½ cup orange juice
3 tablespoons honey
1 tablespoon low sodium soy sauce
1 teaspoon ground ginger or 1 tablespoon fresh ginger
2 Ruby Red grapefruits, peeled and in sections
1 orange, peeled and in sections
1 tablespoon regular ginger
2 teaspoons raspberry vinegar or red wine vinegar

Season chicken with pepper. In a bowl, combine grated orange peel, juice, soy sauce, ginger and 2 tablespoons of the honey. Coat chicken and let stand for 5 minutes. In another bowl, combine grapefruit and orange sections, regular ginger, and vinegar and set aside. Arrange chicken in baking pan and pour marinade over chicken. Bake in a preheated oven at 450 degrees for 20 minutes or until done. Remove chicken and keep warm. Combine fruit mixture with pan juices, pour over chicken and serve.

Sue Clark

POULTRY

Maureen's Italian Chicken

4 boneless, skinless chicken breasts
½ cup Italian bread crumbs
¼ cup grated Parmesan cheese
⅛ teaspoon salt
½ cup Italian salad dressing, fat free
Cooking oil spray

Pour bread crumbs, Parmesan cheese, and salt into a zip lock bag and shake to mix. Take 1 chicken breast and coat completely with salad dressing. Place in bag, close tightly and shake to coat chicken. Coat the rest of the chicken. Place in a baking dish that has been sprayed with cooking oil spray. Bake at 400 degrees for 15 minutes. Take chicken out and spray chicken with cooking oil spray. Cook 5 to 10 minutes more till done.

Joan Moon

Tandoori Chicken

4 boneless, skinless chicken breasts

Marinade:
1 tablespoon paprika
1 teaspoon MSG, optional
1 teaspoon coriander
1 teaspoon salt
½ teaspoon onion powder
¼ teaspoon garlic, cayenne, and cinnamon
⅛ teaspoon chili powder
Dash turmeric
½ teaspoon cardamom, optional
¼ cup corn oil
2 tablespoons water
2 tablespoons lemon juice

Combine all marinade ingredients and marinate chicken breasts overnight or at least several hours. Broil 6 to 7 minutes each side, but don't overcook. Serve with pita bread or rice.

Elaine DeSouza

Country Captain Chicken

1 chicken, cut in serving pieces, or 6 skinless chicken breasts
¼ cup flour
1 teaspoon salt
½ teaspoon pepper
3 tablespoons vegetable cooking oil
1 medium onion, chopped
1 large bell pepper, chopped
1 clove garlic, minced
3 teaspoons curry powder
1 (28 ounce) can peeled tomatoes
½ cup raisins

Combine flour, salt and pepper in a plastic bag. Dredge the chicken in the flour and sauté in a Dutch oven in hot oil until browned. Remove from oil and set aside. Add onion, bell pepper, garlic and curry to remaining oil and sauté until onion is translucent, about 5 minutes. Add tomatoes and raisins and mix well. Return chicken to pan; turn to coat all pieces completely. Cover and simmer for 45 minutes for chicken breasts or 1 hour for 1 chicken. Serve over hot steamed rice.

Ellen Limitone

Country Cajun Chicken Fricassée

½ chicken, cut in pieces
2 tablespoons olive oil
1 cup chopped onions
3 cloves garlic
½ cup green bell peppers
½ cup red bell peppers
½ cup mushrooms
1 tablespoon parsley
½ cup water

Brown the chicken in a cast iron pot in olive oil. Add onions, garlic, green and red peppers. Stir about 5 minutes, then add ½ cup water, let simmer about 10 to 15 minutes. Add parsley and mushrooms, let simmer 10 minutes. Add a little water only if needed. Serve with rice. Use Tabasco sauce as needed.

Ruth H. Guidry

POULTRY

Stir-Fried Chicken with Cashews and Green Onions

1 egg white
1 tablespoon plus 1 teaspoon cornstarch
2 tablespoons soy sauce, reduced sodium
1 pound boneless, skinless chicken breasts, cut in cubes
1 teaspoon sugar
¼ cup chicken broth
1 tablespoon dry sherry
½ cup unsalted cashews
3 tablespoons peanut oil or sesame oil
⅓ cup sliced green onions
¼ teaspoon crushed red pepper flakes

Mix together egg white, 1 tablespoon cornstarch, and 1 tablespoon soy sauce in small bowl. Add chicken, stir to coat all pieces and let stand 15 minutes. Stir together sugar, chicken broth, sherry, the remaining cornstarch and soy sauce in a small bowl until smooth. Sauté cashews in 1 tablespoon oil in a large skillet or wok over medium heat until lightly browned. Remove and reserve. Drain chicken mixture in a strainer. Heat remaining 2 tablespoons oil in skillet. Add chicken; stir fry over medium-high heat until browned on all sides, stirring constantly. Add green onions and pepper flakes; stir fry 30 seconds longer. Stir chicken broth mixture again. Add to skillet along with cashews and cook until mixture is bubbly and thickened. Yields 4 servings.

Note: This is a quick and easy, low cholesterol meal that has become our favorite.

Gretchen Nakayama

Chicken in Wine

1 large chicken, cut in serving pieces
¾ cup dry white wine
¼ cup oil
¼ cup soy sauce
1 tablespoon brown sugar
2 tablespoons water
1 teaspoon ginger
¼ teaspoon oregano
3 cloves garlic

Place chicken in baking dish skin side down. Mix remaining ingredients and pour over chicken. Bake at 375 degrees for 1½ hours, turning once.

Eileen Donovan

Chicken Sherry

12 chicken breasts, boneless and skinless
Paprika and pepper to taste
1 can reduced fat cream of mushroom soup
2 (3 ounce) cans sliced mushrooms, drained
1 cup nonfat plain yogurt
¾ cup sherry

Season chicken breasts with paprika and pepper on both sides. Place in a large casserole dish. Combine remaining ingredients in a bowl and pour over chicken. Bake at 350 degrees for 1¼ hours or until chicken is tender. Yields 12 servings.

Faye Foreman

Chicken Cacciatore

3 pounds chicken parts
¼ cup flour
2 teaspoons salt
¼ teaspoon ground black pepper
¼ cup olive oil
3 tablespoons butter or margarine
2 cups diced onions
1 cup or 1 large diced green pepper
2 cloves garlic, pressed
1 (2 pound, 3 ounce) can Italian plum tomatoes
2 bay leaves
1¼ teaspoons oregano leaves, crumbled
1 teaspoon sugar
1 pound fresh mushrooms
1 teaspoon basil leaves, crumbled
Cooked rice

Dredge chicken parts in flour mixed with ½ teaspoon salt and ⅛ teaspoon black pepper. In large skillet, heat 2 tablespoons oil and all the butter. Add chicken; brown well on all sides. Remove chicken to a 13 x 9 x 2-inch baking dish. To skillet, add onion and green pepper. Sauté 5 minutes. Add garlic; sauté one minute more. With slotted spoon, remove vegetables to large saucepan. Add tomatoes, bay leaves, oregano, sugar, remaining salt and pepper.

Bring to boiling point; reduce heat, simmer sauce uncovered 45 minutes, stirring occasionally. Meanwhile, rinse, pat dry mushrooms. Add remaining oil to skillet; heat. Add mushrooms and sauté 3 minutes. Stir mushrooms and basil into sauce during last 5 minutes of cooking time. Pour sauce over chicken. Cover, bake in preheated 350 degree oven 45 minutes or until chicken is tender. Delicious with hot cooked rice or pasta! Serves 4.

Lucille (Max) Ankner

POULTRY

Rosemary Chicken

4 boneless and skinless chicken breasts
⅓ cup olive oil
⅓ cup sherry
1 tablespoon fresh lemon juice
⅓ cup onion, finely chopped
3 cloves garlic, minced
2 teaspoons dried rosemary
Salt and pepper to taste

In a small bowl, whisk together the olive oil, sherry, lemon juice, onion, garlic, rosemary, salt and pepper. Place chicken breasts in a shallow dish and pour marinade over them. Cover and refrigerate for 2 to 4 hours. Chicken may be broiled or grilled, basting with marinade. Yields 4 servings.

Faye Foreman

Chicken Teriyaki

12 chicken thighs

Sauce:
5 tablespoons peanut butter
1 stalk celery, minced
1 small onion, minced
½ cup sweet wine
5 tablespoons soy sauce
1 tablespoon sugar
Sprinkle of MSG, optional

Bone thighs and flatten the meat. Combine sauce ingredients, mix well to blend peanut butter thoroughly. Soak thighs in sauce for 30 minutes or longer. Broil in oven or grill over charcoal, basting 2 to 3 times during cooking.

Leiola Onishi

Herbed Chicken

1 chicken, cut in serving pieces
1 package onion soup mix
½ teaspoon thyme
½ teaspoon basil
½ teaspoon rosemary
½ teaspoon garlic salt
½ teaspoon paprika

Lay chicken in baking dish and sprinkle soup mix and spices over all. Bake at 350 degrees for 1 hour. Easy, delicious and different!

Mary Jane Morgan

Chicken Paprikash

4 chicken breasts
2 tablespoons oil
Salt and pepper to taste
1 tablespoon paprika
¼ cup sherry
¼ cup chicken broth
½ cup low fat sour cream
1 medium onion, minced
Fresh parsley, optional

Brown chicken breasts in oil in deep skillet. Remove from skillet and salt and pepper pieces. Sauté onion in oil until translucent and add paprika. Return chicken to skillet and turn to coat. Add broth and wine; bring to a simmer on low heat and cover. Continue to cook on low for 30 minutes. When ready to serve, remove chicken to serving dish. Add sour cream to skillet, whisk into sauce until smooth and heated through. Pour over chicken and serve. Garnish with parsley if desired.

Note: Serve with buttered noodles, green vegetables or salad. No fat sour cream can also be used.

Ellen Limitone

Baked Chicken

6 boneless, skinless chicken breasts
1 stick margarine, melted
1 clove garlic, minced
1 cup corn flakes, crushed
1 cup potato chips, crushed

Coat chicken pieces completely with melted margarine. Put flakes and chips in a bag and one piece of chicken at a time to shake and coat well. Bake at 350 degrees in a baking dish for 1 hour.

Shirley Bobo

POULTRY

Baked Chicken

8 to 10 chicken breasts
½ cup Parmesan cheese
1 teaspoon salt
Margarine or butter
1 teaspoon pepper
1 teaspoon garlic
¼ cup parsley
Bread crumbs

Make bread crumbs from bread or rolls using blender. Mix other ingredients except butter and chicken. Melt 1 tablespoon butter for each chicken breast. Dip each breast in butter, then in crumb mixture, coating well. Pour any remaining butter over pieces after placing them in a baking dish. Bake at 350 degrees for 45 minutes or until brown.

Gail Culberson

Oven Fried Chicken

3 to 4 pounds chicken pieces, skinless (optional)
1 tablespoon margarine or butter
⅔ cup Bisquick
1½ teaspoons paprika, optional
¼ teaspoon pepper

Melt butter in 13 x 9 inch baking dish in oven. Combine dry ingredients in bag and dredge chicken pieces. Place in baking dish skin side down and bake in preheated oven at 425 degrees for 25 minutes. Turn and bake another 15 minutes or until done.

Bette Gruber

Oven Fried Chicken

3 pounds chicken, cut up
3 tablespoons flour
¾ teaspoon paprika
¾ teaspoon salt
⅛ teaspoon pepper
¼ cup margarine

Preheat oven to 425 degrees. Wash and dry chicken well on paper towels. Combine flour, paprika, salt and pepper. Coat chicken well with flour mixture. In shallow baking dish, melt margarine. Arrange chicken pieces in pan in single layer. Bake uncovered for 30 minutes. Turn chicken and bake an additional 15 minutes or until brown and tender.

Diann Meriwether

Cheesy Chicken and Ham Bundles

2½ cups water
3 chicken bouillon cubes
6 boneless chicken breasts
½ cup dry sherry
1 (10 ounce) package frozen pastry shells
¼ cup plus 2 tablespoons prepared mustard
¾ teaspoon fines herbes
⅛ teaspoon garlic powder
6 (1 ounce) slices Monterey Jack cheese
6 (1 ounce) slices cooked ham
1 egg white, beaten
Sesame seeds, optional

Combine water and bouillon cubes in a Dutch oven. Heat to boiling, stirring until bouillon is dissolved. Add chicken and sherry and bring to boil again. Cover, reduce heat and simmer about 20 minutes or until tender. Let chicken cool in broth for 30 minutes. Remove chicken and let cool completely. Remove skin. Let pastry shells thaw to room temperature, about 30 minutes. Combine mustard, fines herbes, and garlic powder. Spread about 1 tablespoon mustard mixture over each chicken piece. Wrap a cheese slice and a ham slice around each chicken piece and set aside. Roll out each pastry shell to an 8 inch circle. Place a chicken piece, seam side down, in the center of each pastry circle. Bring side of pastry to overlap in center; moisten with water and pinch together. Fold up ends of pastry; moisten and pinch together. Place each pastry wrapped piece, seam side down, on an ungreased baking sheet. Brush with egg white and sprinkle with sesame seeds. Chill for 30 minutes. Preheat oven to 450 degrees and place chicken in oven. Reduce heat to 400 degrees and bake for 30 minutes or until golden brown. Makes 6 servings. Very nice for company and special occasions.

Diana Plasse

Boned Chicken Breasts with Parmesan

2 large whole chicken breasts (¾ pound each)
½ cup flour
Salt and freshly ground pepper to taste
¼ teaspoon grated nutmeg (fresh)
2 eggs
1 cup fresh bread crumbs
¼ cup grated Parmesan (from wedge of Parmesan cheese)
5⅓ tablespoons margarine (⅓ cup)
4 lemon slices

Skin and bone chicken breasts; wet fingers and dampen breasts, place between waxed paper, and beat lightly until flat. Mix flour, salt, pepper, and nutmeg. Beat eggs gently. Mix bread crumbs and Parmesan. Dip chicken into flour, then eggs, then bread-Parmesan. Place chicken in hot margarine and cook until golden brown for 10 to 15 minutes. Transfer to hot platter and top with lemon slice. Delicious!

Lucille (Max) Ankner

POULTRY

Chicken Noodles

2½ to 3 pounds stewing chicken, cut in pieces
2 tablespoons oil
1 clove garlic
1 piece fresh ginger, 1 inch long
4 cups water
1 stalk green onion

1 pound vermicelli noodles, soaked in hot water and cut in 3 inch pieces
1 teaspoon salt
¼ teaspoon pepper
1 tablespoon soy sauce
1 tablespoon ajinomoto
2 eggs

Fry garlic and ginger in oil until brown. Take out garlic and ginger; add chicken and fry until lightly browned. Add water and cook until chicken is tender, about 2 hours over medium heat. Add vermicelli and seasonings and cook 10 minutes longer. Beat the eggs slightly. Add chopped green onions, salt and pepper. Pan fry in thin sheets. Cut in small squares and add to chicken and noodles.

Leiola Onishi

Chicken Tetrazzini

1 chicken, boiled and deboned, reserve broth
½ cup mayonnaise
1 cup chopped celery
½ cup chopped onion
½ cup chopped bell pepper
1 small can of mushrooms, drained

1 can cream of mushroom or cream of chicken soup
1 small can pimentos, optional
1½ cups grated cheese
1 (12 ounce) package spaghetti

Sauté celery, onion and bell pepper in a small amount of chicken broth. Cook spaghetti in remainder of chicken broth and drain. Combine spaghetti, chicken, mayonnaise, celery, onion, bell pepper, mushrooms, soup and pimentos. Place in a large baking dish, cover and bake at 350 degrees until hot and bubbly, about 30 minutes. Sprinkle grated cheese over top and return to oven until cheese melts. If mixture seems too dry, add chicken broth before baking. Can be made ahead and refrigerated.

Betty Machalec

Ducks - Southern Style

2 ducks
½ stalk celery
1 bunch green onions
1 large white onion
4 cloves garlic
1 bell pepper
Salt, red pepper, black pepper
Flour

Salt and pepper the ducks heavily, inside and out, and rub in by hand. Place ducks in cast iron Dutch oven, breast side up, and sprinkle more black pepper, salt and red pepper on them. Using a sieve, sprinkle ducks with flour until well coated. Chop fine the celery, onion tops, white onion, garlic and bell pepper. This can be put in a blender with a small amount of water and blended to a puree. Pour around the duck. Pour water in the pot to cover ducks, being careful not to wash off the flour. Cover and put in a 450 degree oven for exactly 2 hours. Do not uncover while cooking.

Denise Gunn

Sweet-Sour Roast Duck

1 (4 to 5 pound) duck
2 tablespoons Hoi sin sauce
1½ teaspoons salt
1 teaspoon red food coloring, optional

Sweet and sour sauce:
¼ cup brown sugar
½ cup pineapple juice
1 tablespoon vinegar
2 tablespoons cornstarch
3 drops Tabasco sauce
2 tablespoons toasted sesame seeds
Gravy from roasting pan

Rub salt inside and outside of duck. Mix Hoi sin and food coloring inside and outside and let duck stand for 30 minutes. Roast duck at 275 degrees for 3½ hours. Cut duck in serving pieces. Combine sugar, juice, vinegar and the gravy of the roasted duck in a saucepan. Boil briskly and add cornstarch. Add Tabasco sauce to taste. Pour sauce over roasted duck, sprinkle with sesame seeds and serve.

Leiola Onishi

POULTRY

Pheasants à la Candlelight

2 pheasants
1 cup fat, bacon is best
1 can mushroom soup
2 cups sour cream
1 garlic clove, minced
Flour, salt, pepper, paprika
½ cup white wine, Taylor's White Port

Cut pheasants in serving portions. Combine flour and spices and dredge pieces. Brown in fat over low heat. Place pheasants in casserole. In separate pan, mix 3 tablespoons fat, soup, sour cream, paprika and garlic. Heat and mix well. Pour over pheasants, cover and bake at 325 degrees for 1½ hours. Add wine during the last 15 minutes of baking time.

Editor's Note: Bacon fat gives extra flavor to this recipe, however, an oil of your choice may be used.

Carolyn Thompson

Quick and Easy Chicken

1 frying chicken, cut up
1 package Lipton onion soup mix
1 can whole cranberry sauce
1 bottle Russian dressing with honey

Place chicken in baking dish. Combine rest of ingredients and pour over chicken. Bake at 375 degrees for 40 minutes. Even better the second day.

Michelle Wolk

Sterling is a fixed ration by law of 92½ percent pure silver and 7½ percent hardening alloy.

SEAFOOD

Shrimp with Spanish Sauce over Pasta

1 medium onion, chopped
1 green bell pepper, chopped
1 garlic clove, minced
2 bay leaves
1 teaspoon thyme
Salt and pepper to taste
1 (28 ounce) can peeled tomatoes
½ cup white wine
1 pound raw peeled and deveined large shrimp
1 pound spaghetti or linguine
2 tablespoons olive oil

Heat olive oil over medium heat in large skillet. Sauté onion, bell pepper, garlic until onion is translucent. Add peeled tomatoes, bay leaves, thyme, wine and simmer 15 minutes, breaking up tomatoes. Add salt and pepper to taste. Bring heat to medium high, add shrimp and cook until pink, approximately 5 minutes. Cook pasta according to directions on the package, drain and serve with shrimp and sauce spooned over the top. Yields 4 servings.

Note: Can be made ahead and shrimp added when ready to serve.

Ellen Timitone

Fay's Shrimp Casserole

1 pound shrimp, cleaned and cooked
1 can cream of mushroom soup
4 hard-boiled eggs, chopped
4 ounces American cheese, cubed
1 small can chopped asparagus, drained
1 small can green peas, drained
12 to 14 Ritz crackers, crushed
1 cup milk

Lightly butter a 2 quart baking dish. Spread light layer of cracker crumbs over the bottom. Next, layer the chopped egg, cheese, peas, and asparagus. Mix the shrimp with the condensed cream of mushroom soup and spread on as the top layer. Add pepper to taste. Sprinkle remaining cracker crumbs over top and dot with butter. Add the 1 cup of milk just before baking. Use fork tine holes to help milk sink in. Bake at 350 degrees for 30 minutes or until bubbly and golden brown. Casserole can be assembled a day ahead, covered and refrigerated until time to bake. Yields 8 to 10 servings.

"Pete" Davie

SEAFOOD

Shrimp Divine

1 box wild rice, "original"
1 can mushroom soup
2 teaspoons chopped green pepper
1 tablespoon lemon juice
½ teaspoon dry mustard
1 small can mushrooms
1 pound cleaned and cooked shrimp
½ cup grated cheddar cheese
2 tablespoons melted butter
½ tablespoon Worcestershire sauce
¼ tablespoon pepper

Combine all ingredients and pour into a 1½ quart baking dish. Bake at 375 degrees for 40 minutes or until bubbly.

Jean Whitten

Shrimp Creole

2 pounds raw, cleaned shrimp
1 cup minced onion
1 celery stalk, minced
1 green bell pepper, minced
1 (15 ounce) can tomatoes
1 bay leaf
Salt and pepper to taste
1 (6 ounce) can tomato paste

Sauté in a small amount of olive oil onion, celery, green pepper and bay leaf until brown. Add tomatoes and tomato paste and simmer for 30 minutes. Add shrimp and cook until shrimp are pink, about 15 minutes. Serve over cooked rice.

Note: This was my grandmother's recipe.

Eileen Donovan

Cajun Stir Fry Shrimp

2 cups deveined shrimp
1 tablespoon olive oil
1 cup chopped white onion
¼ cup green bell pepper, chopped
¼ cup red pepper, chopped
2 cups sliced, cooked okra

Sauté peppers and onion in 1 tablespoon olive oil. Add two cups okra and ½ cup water. Let cook 10 minutes. Add shrimp and cook an additional 10 minutes. Serve with rice. Serve over rice with Tabasco sauce.

Ruth H. Guidry

Louisiana Crawfish Casserole

2 tablespoons low fat margarine
1 cup chopped onion
¾ cup chopped green bell pepper
1 clove garlic, mashed
1 can low fat cream of mushroom soup
3 cups cooked crawfish tails
3 cups cooked rice
1 tablespoon chopped parsley
1½ tablespoons lemon juice
1 teaspoon salt
Black and red pepper to taste
2 slices bread, crumbled
½ cup skim milk
Paprika

Sauté together onion, green pepper and garlic in low fat margarine. Combine with remaining ingredients and pour into a 2 quart casserole dish that has been sprayed with cooking oil spray. Sprinkle paprika over top and bake at 350 degrees for 30 minutes. If desired, sprinkle with low fat or non fat cheddar cheese five minutes before removing from oven. Yields 4 servings.

Faye Foreman

Crawfish Etouffée

1 stick low fat margarine or butter
1½ cups chopped onions
1 cup chopped green onions
2 pounds crawfish tails
2 tablespoons parsley, dried or fresh
2 cups water
3 teaspoons cornstarch
Dash of red pepper
Salt and black pepper to taste

Sauté onions in margarine until they are translucent. Add crawfish tails and cook for 15 minutes over medium heat. Add water and green onions and cook 15 minutes more. Add seasonings. Dissolve cornstarch in water and add to crawfish. Add parsley and cook an additional 5 minutes. Serve over hot steamed rice. Yields 4 servings.

Faye Foreman

To tell when a fish is cooked throughout, it should be tested with a fork. Fish, when done, flakes into its natural divisions. If you cook a whole fish or a large piece of fish, probe the center of the thickest part of the fish to test for doneness.

SEAFOOD

Orange Roughy Fillets with Grapefruit Brûlée

1 medium red grapefruit
1 tablespoon Grand Marnier or other orange flavored liquor
4 (3 to 6 ounces) orange roughy fillets
2 tablespoons brown sugar
¼ teaspoon ground cinnamon
2 tablespoons vegetable oil

Peel and section grapefruit, setting aside ¼ cup juice. Combine grapefruit sections and liquor. Cover and let stand about 30 minutes. Arrange fillets in a 10 x 6 x 2 inch greased baking dish. Spoon reserved ¼ cup juice over the fillets. Bake uncovered at 400 degrees until fish flakes easily when tested with a fork (about 10 to 15 minutes). Arrange grapefruit sections over the fillets. Combine the brown sugar and cinnamon. Sprinkle evenly over the grapefruit and fillets. Broil 6 inches from the heat until sugar begins to caramelize. Serve immediately. Yields 4 servings.

Fisherman's Supper

1 pound fish fillets
1 cup sliced zucchini
1 cup thinly sliced carrots
1 cup sliced red onion, separated into rings
¼ cup butter or margarine, melted
¼ teaspoon salt
¼ teaspoon pepper
2 teaspoons minced garlic

Preheat oven to 375 degrees. Place fish into baking dish. Layer vegetables over fish. Stir remaining ingredients together and pour over fish and vegetables. Cover and bake 20 to 25 minutes. Makes 4 servings.

JoAnne Moore

Fish, by nature, is tender and free of tough fibers that need to be softened by cooking. Heat firms the delicate protein in much the same way that an egg firms when cooked. Like an egg, fish becomes tough and dry when overcooked.

Glazed Red Snapper

4 (6 ounce) pieces red snapper
1 onion, chopped
1 red pepper, cut in strips
16 ounces orange juice
1 jar green olives with pimento
3 lemons, wedged
1 teaspoon coriander
1 teaspoon butter
1 tablespoon cilantro
1 tablespoon cornstarch

In a heavy skillet, sauté chopped onion, strips of red pepper. Add one-half of the orange juice, 2 lemons, one-half jar olives, and 1 teaspoon butter for five minutes with fish laying on top. Put contents of skillet in oven for 12 to 15 minutes at 400 degrees. When done, remove fish, and combine cornstarch with remaining orange juice and add to mixture in skillet; add coriander and cilantro. This makes a nice glaze to be poured over the fish. I take the rest of the olives and serve with sweet corn. Garnish with lemon wedges.

Rod Holloway

Red Snapper Provençale

2 tablespoons vegetable oil
2 tablespoons olive oil
1½ pounds dressed, whole red snapper
½ cup dry white wine
¼ teaspoon salt
½ teaspoon chopped thyme
¼ teaspoon pepper
1 bay leaf
1 large tomato, chopped
⅔ cup sliced mushrooms
⅓ cup coarsely chopped green pepper
⅓ cup coarsely chopped onion
2 tablespoons chopped fresh parsley
1 clove garlic, minced

Coat a large non-stick skillet with the vegetable oil. Add olive oil. Place over medium high heat until hot. Brown the snapper. Add the wine, salt, thyme, pepper, and bay leaf and bring to a boil. Reduce heat, cover and simmer until fish flakes easily when tested with a fork. Remove and discard the bay leaf. Transfer fish and vegetables that have been lightly sautéed to a serving platter, using a slotted spoon and keep warm. Simmer liquid in skillet until reduced to ⅓ cup. Pour over fish and serve immediately. Yields 3 servings.

To keep raw fish fresh and odorless, rinse with fresh lemon juice and water, dry thoroughly, wrap in plastic wrap or air tight bags and refrigerate.

PASTA

Best Ever Macaroni and Cheese

1 (12 ounce) package macaroni, cooked as directed

¼ pound sliced cheddar cheese

Sauce:
2½ tablespoons flour
2½ tablespoons butter
½ pound sharp cheddar cheese

2 cups milk
1 teaspoon pepper

Melt butter over low heat, add milk and flour, stirring until sauce thickens. Add cheese, until it melts. Set aside.

Cracker topping:
12 Ritz crackers   2 tablespoons butter

Melt butter over low heat, add crumbled Ritz crackers and mash and stir about 5 minutes, careful not to burn them.

In a large baking dish, alternate layer of cooked macaroni, layer of sliced cheese, layer of sauce and repeat. Sprinkle crackers on top. Place dish on lower rack of oven and bake at 325 degrees for 30 minutes. I put a small piece of foil on top to prevent crackers from burning.

Jenny Hosford

Lasagna

1½ pounds ground meat
½ cup flour
1 large onion, chopped
1 large bell pepper, chopped
1 (15 ounce) can tomatoes
1½ packages Lawry's spaghetti mix
1 tablespoon oregano basil leaves

Parsley flakes
Seasoning salt
1 carton small curd cottage cheese
1½ cups grated mozzarella cheese
8 ounces Philadelphia cream cheese, softened

Brown ground meat. Add ½ cup flour and brown lightly. Add onion, bell pepper, tomatoes, Lawry's spaghetti mix, and seasonings. Simmer for 20 to 30 minutes. Cook noodles according to package directions. In separate bowl, combine cottage cheese, mozzarella cheese, and cream cheese. In a 9 x 13 inch baking dish, layer sauce, noodles, and cheese mixture. Sprinkle generously with Parmesan cheese. Bake at 300 degrees for 1½ hours.

Diann Meriwether

Lasagna

8 ounces lasagna noodles
1 onion, chopped
3 cloves garlic, minced
1 pound ground turkey
2 (6 ounce) cans tomato paste
1½ cups water
1 tablespoon parsley, minced
1 teaspoon oregano
1 teaspoon basil
½ teaspoon fennel
2 teaspoons salt
2 eggs, beaten
8 ounces cottage cheese or ricotta
12 ounces mozzarella cheese, grated
¼ cup grated Parmesan cheese

Cook noodles according to package directions and drain. Brown turkey meat, onion, and garlic in a small amount of cooking oil. Stir in tomato paste, water, parsley, salt and spices. Simmer for 10 minutes. In a separate bowl blend cottage cheese and eggs. In a 9 x 13 inch baking dish spread a thin layer of sauce. Top with half the noodles, all of the cottage cheese mix and half the mozzarella cheese. Cover with half the remaining meat sauce and all the remaining noodles. Top with remainder of meat sauce and mozzarella. Sprinkle with Parmesan cheese. Bake at 350 degrees for 35 to 45 minutes or until hot and bubbly. Let stand for 10 minutes before serving.

Eileen Donovan

Mexican Chicken Lasagna

1 package lasagna noodles
3½ cups salsa mix
1 package taco seasoning, stirred into the salsa
1 pound raw chicken breast meat, cut up
1 (16 ounce) can black beans
1½ cups combination of Monterey Jack and cheddar cheese
1 (4 ounce) can chopped green chilies
15 ounces ricotta cheese
1 egg

Mix ricotta cheese and egg together. In 9 x 13 inch baking dish, pour 1 cup salsa over the bottom. Cover with a layer of dry noodles. Add half the chicken pieces, half the black beans, and all of the green chilies. Spread with half the ricotta cheese mixture. Sprinkle with half the grated cheese. Add another cup of salsa and layer remaining noodles, chicken, beans and ricotta cheese. Cover with remaining salsa and grated cheese. Bake at 340 degrees for 40 minutes.

Note: This is from a dear friend, Phyllis Pettijohn.

Anci Waugh

PASTA

Beefy Mexican Lasagna

1 pound ground beef
1 (16 ounce) can whole tomatoes, dice
1 (1½ ounce) package Durkee taco seasoning mix
1 (12 ounce) carton cottage cheese
1 (2.8 ounce) can Durkee French fried onions
6 ounces grated cheddar cheese
2 eggs, slightly beaten
12 (6 inch) flour or corn tortillas
1 fresh tomato, chopped
Shredded lettuce

Brown ground beef and drain. Add canned tomatoes and taco seasoning. Simmer uncovered for 5 minutes. Stir in ½ can French fried onions. In bowl, combine cottage cheese, 2 cups cheddar cheese, and eggs. In a greased 8 x 12 inch baking dish, place 3 tortillas on bottom of dish and overlap 6 tortillas around sides of baking dish. Spoon meat mixture evenly in dish. Top with 3 tortillas and add cheese mixture. Bake uncovered at 350 degrees for 45 minutes. Sprinkle with remaining cheese. Add remaining onion to center of casserole and bake an additional 5 minutes. Before serving, arrange tomatoes and lettuce around edge of casserole. Serves 9.

Aquila Freeman

Lazy-Day Lasagna

6 ounces lasagna noodles
¼ teaspoon oregano
1 (15 ounce) jar spaghetti sauce with meat
1 cup small curd cottage cheese
6 ounces mozzarella cheese, sliced

Cook noodles according to package directions. Combine oregano with spaghetti sauce. In greased 6 x 10 inch baking dish, alternate layers of noodles, cottage cheese, mozzarella, and sauce, using sauce for top layer. Bake at 375 degrees for 30 minutes. Makes 4 servings.

Ginny O'Connor

Experts call pasta the perfect food. Pasta is low in calories and an excellent source of complex carbohydrates and fiber. It's also a good source of B vitamins.

Almost Fat Free Lasagna

1 (8 ounce) package of lasagna noodles
2 medium eggplants
3 sliced portobello mushrooms
1½ pounds ground turkey
2 (30 ounce) jars of fat free spaghetti sauce
1 cup water
12 ounces shredded mozzarella cheese, fat free
1 cup grated Parmesan, fat free
3 eggs
5 large cloves garlic, crushed
22 ounces fat free ricotta cheese
½ cup fresh parsley, minced

Bake eggplants at 400 degrees for 20 minutes. Let cool, peel and slice in thin pieces. Brown ground turkey. Add spaghetti sauce, water, garlic, salt, pepper, and spices to taste. Lightly sauté mushroom slices using cooking oil spray. In separate bowl, mix half of mozzarella cheese, eggs, ricotta cheese, Parmesan cheese, and parsley. In a 9 x 13 inch baking dish, spread a thin layer of meat sauce mixture. Lay dry, uncooked lasagna noodles over sauce. Layer meat sauce, eggplant slices, mushrooms, cheese mixture and lasagna to top of dish. Cover with foil and cook at 350 degrees for 45 minutes. Remove foil, add rest of shredded mozzarella cheese and bake for an additional 15 minutes. Let cool for 10 minutes before serving. This can be made into vegetarian lasagna by omitting turkey and adding additional eggplant and mushrooms.

Adele Buchman

Cheese-Stuffed Pasta Shells

24 jumbo pasta shells
1 (15 ounce) carton reduced fat ricotta cheese
4 ounces shredded mozzarella cheese
1 cup frozen green peas
2 green onions, thinly sliced
1 teaspoon dried basil leaves
¼ teaspoon black pepper
¼ teaspoon garlic powder
1 (24 ounce) jar spaghetti sauce
Parmesan cheese, freshly grated

Cook pasta shells according to package directions; drain and set aside. In a medium bowl, combine ricotta, mozzarella, peas, onions, basil, pepper and garlic powder. Pour one-half spaghetti sauce in a 13 x 9 inch baking dish. Stuff each cooked pasta shell with a heaping teaspoon of cheese mixture, Place shells on sauce in baking dish. Pour remaining half of spaghetti sauce over top and sprinkle with Parmesan cheese. Microwave on high for 6 to 8 minutes or until heated through. Rotate half way through cooking time. Can be frozen.

Merline Fogtman

Multicolor Pasta

1 pound multicolor spring
   pasta
¼ cup olive oil
3 teaspoons coarse black
   pepper
1 pinch hot peppers
½ cup onions, chopped
2 cloves garlic, pressed

Cook pasta. Sauté onions in olive oil. Squeeze garlic over onions and add peppers; cook for 1 minute. Pour over hot cooked pasta and serve.

Anci Waugh

Tony Marsietti

1 pound dry pasta, penne,
   shells, bowties, etc.
1 pound ground meat
1 medium onion, chopped
1 clove garlic minced
1 (4 ounce) can mushrooms
1 (6 ounce) can tomato paste
1 (8 ounce) can tomato sauce
8 ounces cheddar cheese,
   grated
2 tablespoons sherry
Salt and pepper to taste
Grated Parmesan cheese

Cook pasta in salted boiling water and drain well. Brown ground meat, onion, garlic, and mushrooms. Drain any excess oil and add tomato sauce, tomato paste, ½ of grated cheese, and salt and pepper. Mix well and add to pasta. Pour into large greased baking dish. Bake at 350 degrees for 20 minutes. Pour sherry over top and stir. Sprinkle remaining cheese on top and bake until cheese melts. Serve with grated Parmesan on the side.

Ellen Limitone

Macaroni and Cheese

2 cups elbow macaroni,
   cooked
1 package Pioneer nonfat
   gravy mix
2 cups nonfat cheddar
   cheese, grated

Add cheddar cheese to hot macaroni and stir. Prepare gravy mix according to the package directions and add to the macaroni and cheese. Quick and easy!

Betsy Payne

Baked Spaghetti

1 cup chopped onion
1 cup chopped green bell
  pepper
1 tablespoon margarine
1 (28 ounce) can tomatoes
  with liquid, cut up
1 (4 ounce) can mushroom
  pieces, drained
1 (2¼ ounce) can sliced ripe
  olives, drained
2 teaspoons dried oregano
1 pound ground beef, browned
  and drained
12 ounces of spaghetti,
  cooked and drained
2 cups shredded cheddar
  cheese
1 (10 ounce) can condensed
  cream of mushroom soup
¼ cup water
¼ cup grated Parmesan
  cheese

In a large skillet, sauté onion and green pepper in margarine until tender. Add tomatoes, mushrooms, olives, and oregano. Add ground beef. Simmer uncovered for 10 minutes. Place half of the spaghetti in a greased 9 x 13 inch baking dish. Top with half of the vegetable mixture. Sprinkle with 1 cup of cheddar cheese. Repeat layers. Mix the soup and water until smooth; pour over all and sprinkle with Parmesan cheese. Bake uncovered at 350 degrees for 30 to 35 minutes or until heated through. Yields 12 servings.

Note: This is different spin on spaghetti and is great for pot luck dinners. Also freezes well.

Janice LeBlanc

One-Pot Spaghetti

4 ounces uncooked spaghetti
½ pound ground meat
1 tablespoon cooking oil
1 large onion, chopped
2 (8 ounce) cans tomato sauce
1½ cups water
1½ teaspoons salt
Pepper to taste
1 teaspoon sugar
Grated cheese

Cook onion in oil until soft. Add ground meat and brown. Add tomato sauce, salt, pepper, water, and sugar. Simmer for a few minutes and add spaghetti a little at a time, stirring it into the sauce and keeping it separated. Cover tightly and simmer for 20 to 30 minutes. Stir once toward end of cooking time. Serve with cheese. Makes 4 servings. Makes a good quick meal with a salad and garlic bread.

Ginny O'Connor

Best Yet Spaghetti

2 pounds chicken gizzards, or substitute 1¼ pounds ground meat, browned
4 stalks celery, chopped
3 medium onions, chopped
1 bell pepper, chopped
½ bunch fresh parsley, chopped
3 (15 ounce) cans tomato sauce
1 (31 ounce) can whole tomatoes
1 (15 ounce) can mushrooms
4 cloves garlic, mashed
3 tablespoons olive oil
1 teaspoon basil
1 teaspoon Italian seasoning
2 bay leaves
½ tablespoon Tony Chachere's Creole seasoning
½ tablespoon salt

In a 5 quart pot, sauté celery, onions, bell pepper, and garlic in olive oil. Do not burn. Chop canned tomatoes and add with liquid to pot. Add tomato sauce, meat, and remaining ingredients. Simmer over low heat for 3 hours, stirring occasionally to prevent sticking. Cook until gizzards are very tender. Serve over favorite spaghetti or pasta shells. Sprinkle generously with Parmesan or Romano cheese.

Note: Before we were married, when my husband first took me home to meet his family, this is what his mother served. It was a family favorite. After we married, I wanted to learn how to make it. As Mrs. Morgan had no recipe, I had to watch as she cooked it and write down the ingredients. Everyone we first serve this to is shocked to see the gizzards and then amazed at how tasty they are.

Mary Jane Morgan

Spaghetti Olé

6 ounces uncooked spaghetti
1 cup picante sauce
1 (28 ounce) can chopped tomatoes
1 pound lean ground meat
1 (6 ounce) can tomato paste
½ cup chopped onion
1½ teaspoons cumin powder
1 teaspoon garlic salt
1 tablespoon cooking oil
1 teaspoon oregano

Brown meat and onion in oil and drain. Add all ingredients except spaghetti and simmer uncovered for 15 minutes. Cook spaghetti according to package directions. Serve with Parmesan cheese.

Billie Menn

Black Beans and Pasta

1 cup dried black beans
1 to 2 tablespoons olive oil
1 large onion, chopped
2 cloves garlic, mashed
2 (14 ounce) cans low salt chicken broth
1 (28 ounce) whole tomatoes, cut up with liquid
2 teaspoons honey
¼ teaspoon black pepper
2 tablespoons red wine
1 tablespoon salsa
1 cup uncooked elbow macaroni
1 large red pepper, chopped
2 green onions, chopped
2 tablespoons cilantro leaves, chopped

Cover beans with water, cover and bring to boil for 2 minutes. Turn off heat, let stand for 1 hour and drain. In a 5 quart saucepan heat oil and sauté onion and garlic for about 3 minutes. Add beans and broth and bring to a boil. Cover and simmer for 1½ hours. Add tomatoes with liquid, honey, pepper, wine, and salsa. Simmer covered for 15 minutes. Cook pasta according to package directions and drain. Add pasta and red peppers to soup and simmer 5 minutes. Sprinkle each serving with green onions and cilantro. Makes 10 servings.

Ruth Kirk Soloff

Light and Healthy Pasta Sauce

1 pound Roma tomatoes, chopped
2 cloves garlic, minced
8 large basil leaves, minced
¼ cup Italian parsley, chopped
2 teaspoons olive oil
Grated Romano or Parmesan cheese

Combine all ingredients and let sit at room temperature while pasta cooks. Toss with hot pasta. For variation, heat sauce and add 1 cup chopped spinach leaves. Simmer 5 minutes. Toss with ¼ cup grated mozzarella and pasta.

Anci Waugh

Pasta con Pomodora Crema

2 cups Roma tomatoes,
  chopped
2 tablespoons garlic, minced
½ cup slivered pancetta or
  proscuitto

¼ cup heavy cream
1 bunch basil leaves cut
  en chiffonade
Pinch of crushed chili peppers

Cook the tomatoes with the garlic until most of liquid is gone. Add the meat and cream. Simmer until thick and add seasonings. Serve over fresh, hot pasta.

Editor's Note: Chiffonade — Wash and dry the leaves. (The drier the leaves, the better the separation and presentation of the garnish.) Pile five or ten leaves on top of each other, lining them up as you would stack cards. Roll the pile lengthwise to create a "cigar". Using a very sharp knife, slice the "cigar" across like a jelly-roll, very thinly. When it is completely sliced, fluff the sections to separate — you now have a wonderful, fragrant chiffonade for flavor or garnish.

Anci Waugh

Ira's Special Pasta Sauce

3 tablespoons olive oil
¼ cup onions, diced
½ cup black olives, diced
2 (16 ounce) cans Italian
  plum tomatoes, chopped,
  drain liquid and set aside

4 tablespoons capers
3 cloves garlic, minced
1 small can anchovy fillets

In a 6 quart pan, heat olive oil and add diced onions. Sauté until translucent. Add chopped tomatoes, black olives, capers, garlic, and anchovies. Bring to a slow simmer, stirring constantly to prevent sticking. Simmer for approximately 30 minutes or until thick. Add the liquid from the tomatoes if it gets too thick. Serve over angel hair pasta. Serves 2 to 4.

Elaine Doubrava

VEGETABLES

VEGETABLES

Laredo Ranch Beans

2 cups pinto beans, washed and soaked
8 cups water
½ pound salt pork
1 green bell pepper, finely diced
2 onions, finely diced
1 medium can tomatoes
1 clove garlic, mashed
¼ teaspoon dry mustard
¼ teaspoon chili powder
½ teaspoon MSG powder, optional
Worcestershire sauce to taste
Salt and pepper to taste

Combine all ingredients. Add Worcestershire sauce, salt and pepper to taste. Simmer over low heat until done.

Gaylene Adams

Scalloped Corn

4 ears of fresh corn
¼ cup chopped onion
¼ cup chopped green pepper
2 tablespoons margarine
2 tablespoons flour
1 teaspoon salt
Dash of pepper
½ teaspoon paprika
¼ teaspoon dry mustard
¾ cup milk
1 egg, slightly beaten
⅓ cup cracker crumbs
1 tablespoon melted margarine

Clean and cook corn ears. After cooling, cut enough corn from ears to measure 2 cups. Preheat oven to 350 degrees. In a large skillet, sauté onions and green pepper in 2 tablespoons of margarine until tender. Remove from heat and stir in flour and seasonings. Heat over low heat, stirring until mixture is bubbly. Remove from heat and gradually stir in milk. Heat to boiling, stirring constantly for 1 minute. Stir in egg and corn and pour into an ungreased 1 quart casserole dish. Combine cracker crumbs and 1 tablespoon margarine. Sprinkle over corn mixture and bake at 350 degrees uncovered for 30 to 35 minutes.

Jeanette Nolen

To get the corn silk off the ear of corn, brush downward with a paper towel.

Copper Pennies

2 pounds of carrots cut in circles
Salt
1 small green bell pepper, chopped
1 medium onion, cut in thin rings
1 teaspoon prepared mustard
1 (10¾ ounce) can condensed tomato soup
½ cup cooking oil
1 cup sugar
¾ cup vinegar
1 teaspoon Worcestershire sauce

Cook carrots in salted water until tender. Drain carrots and layer them with green pepper and onion in a serving dish. Blend Soup, oil, sugar, vinegar, mustard, Worcestershire Sauce, and salt to taste. Pour over vegetables and cover dish with foil or plastic wrap. Refrigerate overnight for the best flavor. Use a slotted spoon to serve.

Elizabeth Henson

Sweet-Sour Carrots

5 cups sliced carrots
1 (10 ounce) can cream of tomato soup, undiluted
½ cup salad oil
¾ cup vinegar
1 tablespoon prepared mustard
1 medium onion, chopped
1 medium green pepper, chopped
Dash Worcestershire sauce

Cook carrots in salted water until tender; drain and set aside. Combine remaining ingredients, and cook until onion and pepper are tender; add carrots. Place in a covered dish and chill overnight. Serves: 10.

Mabel E. Lucas

VEGETABLES

Potato Casserole

6 medium potatoes, baked firm
½ cup grated cheddar cheese
16 ounces sour cream

1 bunch chopped green onions
Salt and pepper to taste

Cool and cut potatoes into pieces. Combine all ingredients and refrigerate for at least 3 hours. Bake at 350 degrees for 30 minutes. If you make this the day before, bring to room temperature and bake at about 275 degrees for 30 minutes.

Gaylene Adams

Eggplant Parmesan

1½ pounds eggplant, cut into ¼ inch pieces after boiling
½ cup bread crumbs
½ pound mozzarella cheese, thinly sliced or grated
Parmesan cheese

1 pound ground turkey or beef
Garlic salt and pepper to taste
2 teaspoons oregano
3 small cans tomato sauce
1 small can mushrooms

Boil eggplant until done, cut into pieces and set aside. Sauté ground meat in skillet, stir in garlic salt, pepper, tomato sauce, and mushrooms. In a 13 x 9 inch baking dish, add alternate layers of meat mixture, eggplant, Parmesan cheese, oregano, and mozzarella. Bake in preheated oven at 350 degrees for 30 minutes until bubbly and cheese is melted. Serves 4 to 6.

Elaine Doubrava

Cashew Yam Bake

1 cup salted cashew nuts
2 tablespoons butter
¼ cup sugar
¼ cup frozen orange juice concentrate
2 tablespoons butter
1 teaspoon cinnamon
1 teaspoon salt
2 (29 ounce) cans yams, drained

Sauté nuts in butter until brown. Reserve.

In a small saucepan combine sugar, orange juice, butter, cinnamon, and salt. Heat until sugar and butter melt. Place yams in a 1-quart casserole dish. Pour sauce evenly over the yams. Sprinkle nuts on the top. Bake uncovered at 375 degrees for 15 minutes. Serves 6.

Sharon Kiel Gutormson

Sweet-Sour Cabbage

1 head cabbage (about 2 pounds), coarsely shredded
½ teaspoon salt
3 tablespoons water
6 tablespoons white vinegar
3 tablespoons sugar

Combine cabbage, salt and water in a 2 quart casserole. Cover with a glass lid or plastic wrap. Cook in microwave 15 to 18 minutes at high, or until crisp tender. Stir twice. Add mixture of sugar and vinegar to crisp tender cabbage, mix well. Cook in the microwave for 1 to 2 minutes on high or until tender. Serves: 8.

Mabel E. Lucas

VEGETABLES

Baked Potatoes

1 bag OreIda O'Brien potatoes
8 ounces sour cream
1 can mushroom soup
½ cup shredded cheese

Mix frozen potatoes which have been separated, sour cream and mushroom soup together. Top with shredded cheese. Bake at 350 degrees for 45 minutes.

Janice Schwausch

Roasted Onions

(Roasting makes them sweet!)

3 medium red onions

Preheat oven to 400 degrees. Place onions in a baking pan (leave the exterior layers on the onions). Roast until tender, but not mushy. This may take up to 1 hour, check frequently after 30 minutes. Stick with fork to test. If goes in easy, onions are done. When cool enough to handle, remove skin, cut into eighths or chunks and serve.

Ethel Ankner

Hominy

2 cans white hominy, drained
1 can Ro-Tel tomatoes, drained
1 can mushroom soup
¼ pound melted Velveeta cheese
1 cup Frito chips, crushed

Mix hominy, tomatoes, mushroom soup, and Velveeta cheese. Pour over crushed Fritos in baking dish. Bake at 400 degrees until fluffy.

Barbara Gibbs

Start with cold water and cook any vegetable that grows under the ground, such as potatoes, beets, carrots, etc. Start with boiling water and cook any vegetable that grows above ground such as corn, peas, beans, greens, etc.

VEGETABLES

Baked Corn

1 can whole corn, undrained
1 can cream style corn
1 cup sour cream
1 stick margarine, melted
1 package Jiffy corn bread mix

Mix well place in 9 x 13 inch greased pan. Bake 25 to 35 minutes at 375 degrees, sprinkle with grated cheese; return to oven and melt cheese.

Barbara Gibbs

Corn Casserole

1 can whole kernel corn, drained
1 can cream corn
1 cup sour cream
1 (4 ounce) can green chilies, chopped
2 eggs, beaten
1 stick butter or margarine, mixed well with eggs
1 small box Jiffy cornbread mix

Mix all ingredients together in 7 x 9 inch pan and bake 60 minutes at 350 degrees.

Sarah Keith

Corn Casserole

1 (17 ounce) can cream corn
½ cup sliced celery
¾ cup American cheese (pieces)
2 eggs, well beaten
1 cup milk
¼ teaspoon paprika (on top of corn)
1 cup cracker crumbs
¼ cup sliced onion
1 teaspoon salt
2 tablespoons butter, melted parsley

Mix all ingredients, pour in well greased casserole. Bake 50 minutes at 350 degrees. To double add one can of whole corn.

Jean Whitten

VEGETABLES

Rice-Stuffed Eggplant

⅔ cup green peppers, chopped
⅔ cup celery, chopped
1 cup onions, chopped
2 tablespoons butter
½ cup rice
1 large eggplant
1 (1 pound 13 ounce) can tomatoes
1½ teaspoons salt
⅛ teaspoon pepper
1 teaspoon sweet basil
2 teaspoons Worcestershire sauce
Grated cheese

Sauté green peppers, celery and onions in butter; push vegetables to one side. Add rice; sauté until golden brown, stirring occasionally. Cut eggplant in half; scoop out pulp, leaving ½ inch shell; chop pulp and add to rice mixture. Stir in tomatoes and seasonings. Simmer, covered, for 20 minutes or until rice is tender; turn into eggplant shells. Bake in preheated 350 degree oven for 1 hour. Sprinkle with cheese; bake until cheese is melted. Serves: 5-6.

Helen L. Kainer

Fresh Tomato Tart

1 (9 inch) tart shell, fully baked
4 to 5 firm ripe tomatoes, sliced ½ inch thick
1 teaspoon salt
¼ pound Swiss cheese, coarsely grated
Freshly ground black pepper
2 tablespoons fresh basil, finely cut
5 scallions, coarsely chopped including greens
2 tablespoons Parmesan cheese
2 tablespoons bread crumbs
1 tablespoon butter, cut into bits

Sprinkle tomato slices on both sides with the salt. Place on a rack to drain for 30 minutes. Pat dry with paper towels. Spread Swiss cheese evenly in the tart shell. Arrange the sliced tomatoes so that they cover the cheese completely. Season evenly with a liberal grinding of pepper and scatter the basil and scallions over the top. Combine Parmesan with the bread crumbs, sprinkle the mixture evenly over the filling and dot the top with butter bits. Bake the tart 30 minutes in the upper shelf of a 325 degree oven. Delicious served cold, hot or at room temperature. Serves: 6.

Judy Durand

Baked Sweet Potatoes

2 medium yams
3 eggs
2½ cups milk
2 cups sugar

1 teaspoon cinnamon
½ cup rum or bourbon
(optional)
½ cup sliced almonds

Peel and grate yams into milk, beat eggs, add sugar gradually. Add cinnamon and almonds. Bake uncovered at 350 degrees for 2 hours. Before serving, pour liquor over and light for flame effect!

Sue Simmers

Broccoli Casserole

1 (16 ounce) package frozen chopped broccoli
1 (10¾ ounce) can condensed cream of mushroom soup
1 egg (equivalent egg substitute)
½ cup low fat, no-cholesterol mayonnaise

½ cup grated cheddar cheese
1 small onion, chopped
½ teaspoon bottled hot red pepper sauce
12 round buttery crackers, crushed

Cook and drain broccoli. Preheat oven to 350 degrees. Combine soup, egg, mayonnaise, cheese, onion and hot sauce in a medium mixing bowl. Place a small amount of mixture in a 1½ quart casserole. Add well drained broccoli and pour remaining sauce on top. Top with crushed crackers. Bake 30 minutes or until bubbly. Makes 6 servings.

Dolores Kennedy

VEGETABLES

Rice Pilaf

¼ cup butter or margarine, melted
1 can French onion soup, undiluted
1 can beef consommé soup, undiluted
1 cup regular rice, uncooked
1 (4 ounce) can mushrooms, drained

Preheat oven to 350 degrees. Combine in greased 1½ quart casserole. Cover and bake for one hour. Yields 4 to 6 servings.

Kathy Lopez

Sweet Potato and Carrot Crisp

2½ pounds of sweet potatoes
2 pounds of carrots
¾ cup orange juice
2 tablespoons liquid honey

2 tablespoons butter
2 teaspoons cinnamon
2 cloves garlic, minced
1 teaspoon salt

Topping:
1½ cups fresh bread crumbs
½ cup chopped pecans
⅓ cup butter, melted

1 tablespoon chopped fresh parsley

Peel and cube sweet potatoes and carrots; in large pot of boiling salted water, cook for about 20 minutes or until very tender; drain. Puree in food processor or blender, in batches if necessary, adding orange juice, honey, butter, cinnamon, garlic and salt; spoon into greased 13 x 9 inch baking dish. Topping: Combine bread crumbs, pecans, butter and parsley. Sprinkle over casserole. Cover and bake in 350 degree oven for 20 minutes; uncover and bake for 30 minutes or until heated through. Makes 8-10 servings.

Marilyn Robinson

Spiced Acorn Squash

6 acorn squash, about 1 pound each
¾ teaspoon cinnamon
¾ teaspoon ginger
¼ teaspoon mace
1 tablespoon brown sugar
6 tablespoons low fat butter substitute, melted
1 tablespoon apple cider vinegar

Preheat oven to 350 degrees. Split each squash in half lengthwise; scoop out and discard seeds and fiber from centers. Slice a piece from the underside of each half so it rests flat. Place cut sides up, in a shallow baking dish. Mix spices together; sprinkle over squash. Sprinkle with brown sugar. Combine melted butter substitutes with vinegar; drizzle over squash. Cover pan tightly with foil and bake for 1¾ hours. Remove foil; baste with juices from cavities. Return to oven for 10 minutes. Serves 12.

Annette Carr

Eggplant and Zucchini Casserole

Oil for frying
2 Spanish onions, diced
2 green peppers, cut into chunks
2 medium eggplants, peeled and cut into cubes
8 small zucchini, cut into cubes
1 (28 ounce) can plum tomatoes
¼ cup brown sugar (or more to taste)
salt and pepper

Fry onion and green pepper in generous amount of oil until transparent, not brown. Add eggplant and zucchini, and cook until transparent. Add tomatoes, lots of salt and pepper. Add brown sugar to taste. Cook until vegetables are tender and liquid has disappeared, about 40 minutes. Place in oiled 9 x 13 inch casserole dish.

Topping:
1 cup bread crumbs
½ pound margarine, melted
2 cloves of garlic, crushed
Ground almonds or Parmesan cheese, optional

Preheat oven to 350 degrees. Combine topping ingredients and place over vegetables. Bake until bubbly.

Marilyn Robinson

VEGETABLES _____

Great Grated Potatoes

Peel and grate potatoes (desired amount). Spray heavy skillet with Pam. Fry potatoes at medium heat, turning them frequently.

Jeanette Dent

Ro-Tel Potatoes

6 to 8 medium potatoes

Slice and boil for about 5 minutes or until tender.

Mix together:

1 medium onion, chopped
1 green pepper, chopped
1 can Ro-Tel tomatoes
1 can cream of mushroom soup

1 pound Velveeta (or other) cheese, grated
½ stick margarine, melted

Pour over potatoes in casserole dish and bake 30 to 40 minutes in 350 degree oven or until potatoes and peppers are tender.

Betty Baker

Broccoli with Rice

2 tablespoons salad oil
½ cup chopped onions
½ cup chopped celery
1 package frozen chopped broccoli

1 can cream of chicken soup
¾ cup milk
1 cup water
1 (8 ounce) jar Cheese Whiz
1 cup instant rice

Sauté onions and celery lightly in salad oil on low heat. Add frozen broccoli, cover and steam for 10 minutes. Add remaining ingredients; cover and bring to boil. Pour into well buttered baking dish and bake uncovered for 40 minute at 350 degrees.

Nancy Hughes

Black Bean Cakes with Spicy Vegetable Sauce

1 small can sweet potatoes
1 can black beans, rinsed and drained
1 red pepper, minced
2 green onions, chopped
¼ cup fresh cilantro, chopped
¼ cup lime juice
1½ teaspoons cumin
1½ teaspoons crushed red pepper flakes
2 egg whites
½ cup flour
2 tablespoons cornmeal
olive oil cooking spray
¾ cup V-8 juice
pinch of cayenne pepper
2 tablespoons fat free sour cream

Drain sweet potatoes and place in blender. Set aside. In a large bowl, mash beans. Stir in peppers, green onions, 2 tablespoons of the cilantro, 2 tablespoons of the lime juice, cumin, red pepper flakes and egg whites. Form into patties. Combine cornmeal and flour in a bowl. Coat the patties in the mixture and place on a baking sheet. Spray lightly and bake for 10 to 15 minutes at 450 degrees. Back to the blender, add to sweet potatoes the remaining lime juice, V-8 juice, cayenne and cilantro. Warm over low heat in a saucepan. Pour over patties and top with a dollop of sour cream.

Sue Clark

Bean Gravy

1 (16 ounce) can Great Northern beans, rinsed and drained
1 tablespoon finely chopped onion
¾ cup vegetable broth or water
Pinch of black pepper and garlic powder
½ cup nutritional yeast

Blend all ingredients in a food processor or blender until smooth. Place in a small saucepan and heat until hot and bubbly. Excellent over biscuits or meat!

Gail Greenberg Kirk

Tarragon added to melted butter makes a nice sauce for fresh seafood or vegetables.

Bean and Cheese Casserole

2 cans long green beans, drained
½ stick butter
2 cans mushroom cream soup
2 cups grated American cheese
1¼ cups milk
bread crumbs

Mix soup and butter, cheese, and milk to make a sauce. In a baking dish make one layer of beans and sprinkle with bread crumbs. Spread cheese sauce over top. Bake at 350 degrees for 30 minutes.

Jean Whitten

Ratatouille with Olive Oil

1 small eggplant, cut into 1 inch cubes (skin on)
1 medium red onion, diced
3 cloves of garlic, finely minced
½ teaspoon cinnamon
¼ teaspoon black pepper
1 cup dry white wine
8 plum tomatoes, coarsely chopped
1 medium zucchini, sliced
1 small green or red bell pepper, diced
½ cup tomato puree
1 tablespoon fresh basil, finely minced
1 tablespoon olive oil

In a large pot, combine eggplant, onion, garlic, cinnamon, black pepper and wine. Simmer covered at medium temperature for 10 minutes or until eggplant begins to soften. Add the tomatoes and simmer uncovered for 5 minutes. Add the zucchini and bell pepper and simmer for another 5 minutes. Stir in the tomato puree, basil and olive oil. Heat through and serve over pasta.

Gail Greenberg Kirk

Corn Casserole

1 can cream style corn
1 egg
½ cup milk
2 tablespoons flour
3 tablespoons sugar
3 tablespoons butter

Mix together. Pour into casserole (buttered or sprayed with Pam). Dot with butter. Bake at 350 degrees for 1 hour.

Anna Belle Baugus

VEGETABLES

Almost French Fries

4 baking potatoes, unpeeled, cut into strips

salt and black pepper to taste

Preheat oven to 450 degrees. Lightly oil a baking sheet or spray with a non-stick cooking spray. Arrange potatoes on prepared sheet in a single layer. Sprinkle with salt and pepper. Bake potatoes until crisp, turning several times about 25 minutes.

Gail Greenberg Kirk

Squash and Okra Casserole

3 or 4 large squash, sliced
1 cup okra, sliced
2 teaspoons sugar
½ cup cream of wheat or cream of rice cereal
1 teaspoon salt
1 teaspoon sweet basil

1 can cream of chicken soup
1 cup milk
6 eggs (can omit part of yolks)
Pam
2 cups sliced mushrooms
2 cups grated colby cheese
1 cup Durkee onions

Preheat oven to 400 degrees for the first 20 minutes, then reduce to 375 degrees for remaining baking time. Mix in large bowl, or toss, squash, okra, cream of wheat, salt, sweet basil and sugar. Spray a large baking dish with Pam, then pour the mixed ingredients into the baking container. Combine cream of chicken soup, milk and eggs, mixing well and pour over squash and okra mixture. Cover with foil and bake until squash is almost tender (45 minutes) and add colby cheese or your favorite cheese and top with Durkee onions. Bake uncovered until cheese has melted and is brown as you desire. Can substitute potatoes for squash, etc.

Delores Box

VEGETABLES

Creole Tomatoes

6 ripe tomatoes
2 green bell peppers
2 onions
Butter

Paprika
Salt
2 tablespoons hot water

Peel and cut tomatoes in thick slices. Cut onions and peppers in thin slices. Place in baking dish in layers. Dot each layer with butter and sprinkle with paprika and salt. Add hot water and bake at least 40 minutes in 350 degree oven. Before tomatoes are done, make a hard sauce.

Hard Sauce:
2 heaping tablespoons butter, melted
2 heaping tablespoons flour
½ cup canned milk

½ cup milk
Salt
Paprika

Cook in double boiler until very thick. Season with salt and paprika. When tomatoes are cooked, pour juice into hard sauce. Mix well and pour over tomatoes. Serve immediately.

Shirlee Nicholson

Mexican Grits

3 cups water
1 teaspoon salt
¾ cup grits
¾ stick margarine

½ pound Velveeta cheese
2 eggs, well beaten
1 (4 ounce) can green chilies, chopped

Mix water, salt and grits. Cook until thick. Add other ingredients. Mix well and bake at 350 degrees for 30 minutes.

Diann Meriwether

VEGETABLES

Patio Beans

4 cups pork and beans
¾ cup catsup
1 cup chopped onion
1 cup Dr. Pepper
1 tablespoon prepared mustard
3 or 4 slices bacon

Mix all ingredients excluding bacon. Pour into greased 2 quart casserole dish. Cut bacon into 2 inch lengths and arrange on top. Bake for 2 hours at 350 degrees.

Diann Meriwether

Sunshine Carrots

7 to 8 medium carrots
1 tablespoon brown sugar
1 teaspoon cornstarch
¼ teaspoon ground ginger
¼ cup orange juice
2 tablespoons butter
Salt
Orange twist
Parsley

Bias slice carrots ½ inch thick; cook until tender and drain. In a small saucepan, combine sugar, cornstarch, ginger and dash of salt. Add orange juice. Cook, stirring constantly until thick and bubbly. Boil for 1 minute. Remove from heat; stir in butter. Pour over hot carrots, tossing to coat. Garnish with orange twist and parsley. Serves 6.

Editor's Note: Instead of cooking in water and draining, cook carrots in 1 cup of orange juice, or enough to cover, then remove carrots, add rest of ingredients and cook down to desired consistency. Pour over carrots and serve.

Diann Meriwether

Cheese Carrots

2 cans sliced carrots
½ package flavored croutons
1 stick butter
¼ to ⅓ pound Velveeta cheese

Drain carrots. Put all ingredients in baking dish and place in oven. Bake for 20 to 30 minutes at 350 degrees stirring 2 or 3 times until cheese and butter are melted. Save a few croutons to garnish on top 5 minutes before done.

Note: Very good even for people who don't like carrots. Handed down to me from members of South Main Baptist Church.

Diann Meriwether

VEGETABLES

O'Brien Potato Ring

2 tablespoons fine, dry bread crumbs
¼ teaspoon paprika
Butter flavored vegetable cooking spray
½ cup chopped green bell pepper
½ cup chopped red bell pepper
½ cup chopped onion

6 medium baking potatoes, peeled and cut into 1 inch pieces
½ cup water
⅔ cup skim milk
1 tablespoon plus 1 teaspoon margarine
½ teaspoon salt
¼ teaspoon pepper
carrot curls, optional

Combine bread crumbs and paprika; set aside. Coat a microwave safe 1½ quart ring mold with cooking spray; sprinkle with bread crumb mixture, and set aside. Combine bell peppers and onion in a bowl; cover with heavy duty plastic wrap. Microwave at high 3 to 4 minutes or until tender; let stand, covered. Combine potato and ½ cup water in a 3 quart casserole; cover with heavy duty plastic wrap and vent. Microwave at high 20 to 25 minutes or until tender, stirring every 5 minutes. Let stand, covered, 3 minutes. Add milk and next 3 ingredients. Mash potatoes. Stir in bell pepper mixture. Spoon into prepared mold; pack tightly. Cover with wax paper; microwave at high 4 to 6 minutes. Let stand, covered, 2 minutes. Unmold onto a serving platter. Garnish with carrot curls, if desired. Yields 6 (1 cup) servings.

Annette Carr

Roasted Root Vegetables

4 cups (8) carrots peeled, quartered, cut into 4 inch lengths
1½ pounds (6 medium) red potatoes, scrubbed, cut into wedges

2 cups (12 large) shallots peeled, trimmed and cut in half lengthwise
1½ tablespoons olive oil
½ teaspoon freshly ground black pepper
1 to 2 teaspoons balsamic vinegar

Lightly coat vegetables in olive oil. Roast vegetables at 425 degrees on the lowest oven rack for about 1 hour. Toss with balsamic vinegar and transfer to a serving dish. Serves 6.

Ruth Kirk Soloff

VEGETABLES

Eggplant Casserole

1 medium eggplant, cubed
1 stick margarine
1 medium onion, chopped
1 (16 ounce) can tomatoes
2 level tablespoons chili powder
Salt and pepper to taste
1 bag regular size Fritos
grated cheese

Sauté onion and eggplant in margarine. Add tomatoes, chili powder, salt and pepper to taste. Keep in mind the Fritos will be salted. Simmer until eggplant is tender. Alternate layers of Fritos and eggplant mixture in baking dish. Top with grated cheese and bake in moderate oven at 350 degrees until cheese is melted.

Elly Wells

Spicy Pinto Beans

2 pounds dried pintos or red beans
ham hock, ham bone or smoked turkey bones
2 to 3 green onions
2 fresh hot peppers
salt
pepper

Wash pinto beans thoroughly. Place in a large container and cover with fresh water. Soak beans 3 hours. Rinse beans and place in a large pot (5 quart or larger). Cover with water about 4 inches above beans. Add meat/bones, salt and pepper to taste, green onion, and hot peppers. Turn on low and cook 6 hours or longer—the longer the better! Add water as required. Beans are done when there is a rich brown broth and beans are tender. Beans are even better as leftovers and they freeze well!

Note: This recipe works well with white beans or butterbeans. Add a yellow onion for a sweeter taste. Add a little ground beef or turkey for a change. I call these chili beans. My mother served this with cornbread. I often serve them with rice.

Liz Kuntz

VEGETABLES

Potato Wedges

4 medium russet potatoes, unpeeled, cut in large wedges
1 tablespoon vegetable oil
¼ teaspoon ground black pepper
⅛ teaspoon salt
2 cloves minced garlic, optional

Place potatoes in a large bowl of cold water. Let stand for 15 minutes. Preheat oven to 425 degrees. Spray a baking sheet with non-stick cooking spray. Drain potatoes in a colander; spread on a paper towel. Cover with a second layer of paper towels. Press down on towels to dry potatoes. Transfer potatoes to a large, clean bowl. Sprinkle with oil, pepper and salt. Toss gently. Arrange potatoes in a single layer on baking sheet.

Bake potatoes for 20 minutes. Use spatula to turn potatoes. Sprinkle with garlic. Bake until golden, about 20 minutes, turning the pan at least once during this time.

Note: These are great as a side dish or as a late night snack food. Really crunchy!

Anna Bell

Maquechou (pronounced "Mock-shoo")

12 ears corn
1 large onion, chopped
1 medium bell pepper, chopped
¼ cup cooking oil
2 to 3 pods garlic, minced
1 whole tomato, peeled and chopped, optional
Salt
Red and black pepper to taste

Shuck corn, remove silk and rinse thoroughly. Cut corn off cobs. Make one cutting if kernels are small and two cuttings if kernels are large. Scrape cob if you like creamy maquechou. Place cooking oil in the bottom of a heavy pot, to avoid sticking. Add all other ingredients and cook slowly on low heat, stirring occasionally until onions are transparent. If corn is dry, add a small amount of water to reach desired consistency. Season to taste.

Note: To prepare a large amount for freezer, follow the recipe above and cook corn in oven at 350 degrees until onions are transparent. Cool, place in containers and freeze. You will probably need to add salt when you thaw and serve maquechou.

This is a Cajun recipe for preparing fresh corn for the freezer.

Ann Gilliam

Italian Artichoke Hearts

3 (14 ounce) cans artichoke
  hearts
2 eggs
½ cup milk
1½ cups Progresso bread
  crumbs

¾ cup grated Romano or
  Parmesan cheese
6 tablespoons olive oil
salt to taste

Drain artichoke hearts. Mix eggs and milk in one bowl. Mix bread crumbs and cheese in a second bowl. Lightly grease bottom of pan with some of the olive oil. Now, roll artichokes in egg mixture, then in bread crumbs, then put in pan turned up. Do all hearts. When finished, drizzle olive oil over each heart and salt to taste. Bake uncovered 30 minutes in 300 degree oven.

Note: This is a holiday favorite for our family. It's been made for four generations in Bobby's family and now my family has started to enjoy it also.

Mary Jane Morgan

Sweet Potato Soufflé

3 cups sweet potatoes,
  cooked, drained, mashed
½ cup Egg Beaters
½ cup sugar

¼ cup liquid Butter Buds
½ cup milk
½ teaspoon salt
1 teaspoon vanilla

Topping:
½ cup brown sugar
⅓ cup flour

¼ cup liquid Butter Buds
½ cup pecans

Mix first 7 ingredients. Pour in baking dish sprayed with Pam. Mix topping ingredients and sprinkle over potatoes. Bake at 350 degrees for 35 to 40 minutes.

Note: This dish tastes like sweet potato pie and is a low fat version of a Thanksgiving favorite.

Henrietta Hall

VEGETABLES

Cucumber Vegetable Side Dish

2 cups yogurt, plain, drained overnight in coffee filter or cheesecloth
4 whole cucumbers
2 tablespoons caraway seeds
2 tablespoons white vinegar
1 teaspoon freshly ground pepper

Cut in half and seed the cucumbers. Grate them and place in colander with a heavy weight, like a bowl of water, for 1 hour. Then combine with yogurt, caraway seeds, vinegar and pepper (Yogurt should be like sour cream by now). Serve with cold or warm pork, or by itself as a salad.

Hanna Drahotova (Babicka)

Tzimmes

vegetable cooking spray
6 cups (about 2 pounds) sweet potatoes, peeled, thinly sliced
6 cups (about 1½ pounds) Rome apples, unpeeled, thinly sliced
1⅓ cups carrots, thinly sliced
1 cup small pitted prunes, halved
¼ cup unsweetened orange juice
¼ cup honey
2 tablespoons brown sugar
2 teaspoons grated orange rind

Coat a 13 x 9 x 2 inch baking dish with cooking spray. Layer half of potato, apple, carrot, and prunes in dish, overlapping slices. Repeat procedure with remaining potato, apple, carrot and prunes. Combine orange juice and remaining ingredients; pour over potato mixture. Cover baking dish with aluminum foil; cut 8 (1 inch) slits in foil. Bake at 350 degrees for 1 hour and 30 minutes or until tender. Yield: 12 servings (1 cup each).

Annette Carr

Yellow Squash Casserole

3 cups cooked yellow squash, drained
1 large onion, chopped, cooked with squash
1 package Mexican cornbread mix
1 (15 ounce) can cream style corn
1 egg, beaten
⅓ cup sugar
½ stick butter, melted
salt and pepper to taste
cracker crumbs, buttered, optional

Cook squash with onion until tender, drain and mash. Add remaining ingredients. Mix well. Pour into well greased casserole dish and bake at 350 degrees for 40 to 45 minutes until firm. Top with buttered cracker crumbs if you like.

"Delicious." This is very good!

Glennie Janssen

Red Cabbage

1 (3 pound) head red cabbage
2 green apples, peeled and chopped
1 onion, finely chopped
¼ cup sugar
¼ cup vinegar
2 tablespoons bacon fat
1 teaspoon salt
freshly ground black pepper

Shred cabbage. Put in saucepan with apples, onion, sugar, vinegar, bacon fat, salt and pepper and ½ cup boiling water. Bring to a boil, reduce heat, cover and simmer for 1 hour, stirring occasionally. Serves 6.

Brigette Bosarge

VEGETABLES

Sylvia's Casserole

2 (8 ounce) cans green beans, drained
1 (14 ounce) can quartered artichoke hearts, packed in water, drained
1 cup Italian-style bread crumbs
½ cup olive oil
1 teaspoon garlic powder
½ cup grated Parmesan cheese
½ teaspoon salt
½ teaspoon pepper
2 tablespoons lemon juice
vegetable cooking spray

Toss all ingredients in large bowl and mix well. Spray large casserole with cooking spray and spoon mixture into it. Bake for 30 minutes in 350 degree oven.

Ellen Limitone

Confetti—Wild Rice Toss

1 (6 ounce) package long grain and wild rice with seasonings
½ cup French's creamy spread mustard
¼ cup olive oil
1½ cups red and green peppers
½ cup green onion

Cook rice, omit butter. Combine all ingredients. Mix well. Chill before serving.

Great summer side dish.

Kelly Jo Myers-Madison

Fresh Peas in Velvet Sauce

2 pounds fresh peas
1 (1¼ ounce) envelope chicken gravy mix
1 cup water
1 tablespoon brown sugar
1 tablespoon prepared yellow mustard

Shell peas. Cook, covered, in small amount of salted water about 10 minutes, until tender; drain. Stir in contents of envelope of gravy mix, water, brown sugar, and mustard. Cook over medium heat, stirring occasionally, until sauce comes to a boil. Serves 4 to 5.

Ethel Ankner

VEGETABLES

Quick Spinach and Artichoke Casserole

1 (14 ounce) can artichoke hearts, drained, cut in half
2 (10 ounce) packages frozen, chopped spinach, cooked, drained
1 (8½ ounce) package cream cheese, softened
1 stick butter, softened
1 (8 ounce) can water chestnuts, chopped, optional
salt and pepper to taste
½ cup seasoned Italian bread crumbs
2 tablespoons butter or margarine

Arrange artichoke halves in 9 inch square baking dish. Mix remaining ingredients, except bread crumbs and butter. Pour over artichoke hearts. Cover with bread crumbs and dot with butter. Bake uncovered at 350 degrees for 30 minutes. Serves 6. May be prepared ahead of time and frozen.

Janet Jones

Spinach Artichoke Casserole

1 can artichokes
2 packages frozen chopped spinach
1 (8 ounce) package cream cheese
2 tablespoons butter
¾ cup bread crumbs

Cut artichokes in pieces and place in the bottom of an 8 inch square or round pan. Cook spinach according to package directions. Melt cream cheese and add butter. Mix well. Drain spinach. Mix well with cheese. Place cheese and spinach mixture on top of artichokes. Sprinkle top with bread crumbs. Bake at 350 degrees for 15 minutes.

Fern Hull

Citrus Okra

¼ cup butter or margarine
2 tablespoons chopped onion
6 tablespoons concentrated grapefruit juice, thawed
⅛ teaspoon pepper
1 grapefruit, peeled and sectioned
2 (10 ounce) packages frozen whole okra

In saucepan over low heat, melt butter. Add onion and cook until tender. Stir in undiluted grapefruit juice and pepper. Heat. Stir in grapefruit sections. Meanwhile, cook okra according to package directions. Drain and turn into serving dish. Pour grapefruit sauce over okra. Serves 6.

Sharon Kiel Gutormson

Sweet Potato Casserole with Praline Topping

3 large eggs
6 cups (5 pounds) fresh sweet potatoes, boiled, drained, peeled and mashed
⅔ cup granulated sugar

⅔ cup butter or margarine, melted
⅓ cup heavy cream
1 teaspoon vanilla
½ teaspoon ground nutmeg
½ teaspoon allspice

Topping:
1 cup light brown sugar, packed
⅓ cup all-purpose flour
1 cup pecans, finely chopped

⅓ cup butter or margarine, cut in small pieces
pecan halves

Heat oven to 350 degrees. Grease a 2 quart baking dish. Beat eggs in a large bowl. Stir in potatoes until blended. Add sugar, margarine/butter, cream, vanilla and spices and mix well. Spread evenly in prepared baking dish.

Topping: Mix sugar, flour and nuts in a medium sized bowl. Work in butter with hands until well blended. Sprinkle evenly over potato mixture. Bake at 350 degrees for 60 to 70 minutes until topping is browned and bubbling. Garnish with pecan halves. Makes 12 servings.

This recipe gets rave reviews!

Diana Plasse

Baked Yams Supreme

2 pounds fresh yams
½ cup and 2 teaspoons melted butter
4 large apples, peeled and sliced thin

¾ cup light brown sugar
½ cup slivered almonds
½ cup Grand Marnier
½ cup mandarin orange sections

Boil yams with their jackets on until almost tender. Drain and let cool. Butter an ovenproof, 10-inch baking dish. Peel and slice yams. Put a layer of yams in dish, then a layer of apples, and sprinkle with sugar. Continue until yams, apples, and sugar are used up. Sprinkle top with almonds. Let ½ the melted butter dribble through the layers. Pour Grand Marnier over top layer gently. Cook in a 400 degree oven for about 35 minutes. Use balance of butter to lightly sauté the mandarin oranges; arrange on top before serving. Serve hot with poultry, ham, or lamb. Serves 6.

VEGETABLES

Spicy Vegetable Couscous

1 to 2 tablespoons olive oil
½ cup yellow squash, diced
½ cup zucchini, diced
½ cup red onion, diced
1 clove garlic, minced
1 can chick peas, drained and rinsed
½ teaspoon ground cumin
½ teaspoon curry powder
½ teaspoon dried red pepper flakes
pepper to taste
2 to 3 cups couscous, cooked according to package directions
¼ cup fresh parsley, chopped

Heat oil, sauté vegetables, onion and garlic for 5 minutes. Stir in chick peas and spices. Gently fold in cooked couscous. Cook until hot about 8 minutes. Garnish with parsley.

Note: You may also heat this in the oven. Preheat oven to 350 degrees. Pour mixture into casserole; dot with low fat butter substitute. Bake about 15 minutes. Serves 4 as side dish or 2 for main dinner dish.

Ruth Kirk Soloff

Hash Brown Potato Casserole

2 pounds frozen hash brown potatoes, thawed
2 cups (8 ounces) shredded sharp cheddar cheese
2 cups sour cream
1 (10¾ ounce) can cream of chicken soup
⅔ cup chopped onion
⅔ cup butter or margarine, melted
¾ teaspoon salt
¼ teaspoon black pepper
2 cups corn flakes, crushed

Preheat oven to 350 degrees. Stir together potatoes, cheese, sour cream, soup, onion, ⅓ cup of the butter, salt and pepper in a large bowl. Pour into buttered, shallow 3 quart baking dish. Mix the remaining ⅓ cup butter with corn flakes in a small bowl. Sprinkle over potato mixture. Bake 40 to 45 minutes or until hot and bubbly. Let stand 10 minutes before serving. Serves 8 to 12.

Diana Plasse

VEGETABLES

Squash Casserole

1½ pounds yellow squash
1 teaspoon salt
2 eggs, separated
10 crackers, crumbled
1 medium onion, diced

3 tablespoons butter
1 cup grated medium cheddar cheese
dash pepper

Slice squash; cook with a small amount of water and salt until tender. Drain and mash. Mix butter, cheese, onion and egg yolks. Beat egg whites until stiff. Add squash to butter, cheese, onion and egg yolk mixture. Fold in egg whites and cracker crumbs. Place in a greased casserole dish and bake at 350 degrees for 45 minutes. Yields 4 to 6 servings.

Note: Even those who believe they don't like squash will be won over by this recipe.

Diana Plasse

Marinated Vegetables

1 cauliflower, cooked and chilled
1 pound fresh mushrooms, slightly sautéed and chilled
2 packages frozen artichoke hearts, cooked and chilled

2 packages frozen regular-cut green beans, cooked and chilled
2 packages frozen asparagus, cooked and chilled
2 packages frozen green limas, cooked and chilled
1 can sliced beets, chilled

Marinade:
½ cup tarragon vinegar
2 teaspoons salt
2 teaspoons sugar
2 tablespoons dried fines herbes

¼ teaspoon cayenne
1 cup vegetable oil
½ cup chopped fresh parsley

Combine vegetables in large bowl. Pour marinade over vegetables. Marinate, covered, overnight in refrigerator. Drain off excess marinade.

Lucille (Max) Ankner

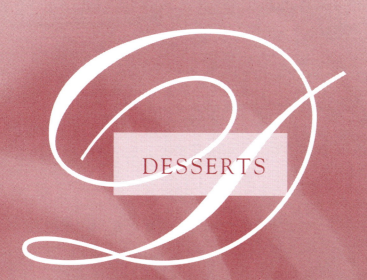

DESSERTS

DESSERTS

Death by Chocolate

Brownie mix
1 package Jell-O chocolate mousse pudding
Chopped pecans
6 Skor's (toffee candy bars) - crushed
1 (16 ounce) container Cool Whip

Make a pan of brownies. Cool. Cut in half and crumble half of brownies into large trifle bowl. Prepare mousse pudding mix according to package directions and spread half of it over the brownies. Add thin layer of pecans, half of the Skor's and half of the Cool Whip. Layer again and sprinkle remaining pecans on top of last layer of Cool Whip. Voilà!

Maxwell Miller Suarez

Frosted Pineapple Squares

½ cup sugar
3 tablespoons cornstarch
¼ teaspoon salt
1 egg yolk, slightly beaten
1 (1 pound 14 ounce) can pineapple, crushed
1 package active dry yeast
3¾ to 4¼ cups unsifted flour
1 teaspoon sugar
½ cup milk
½ cup water
1 cup (2 sticks) corn oil margarine
4 egg yolks (at room temperature)
Confectioners' sugar

Mix ½ cup sugar, cornstarch and salt together in saucepan. Stir in slightly beaten egg yolk and undrained pineapple. Cook over medium heat, stirring constantly, until mixture comes to a boil. Set aside to cool. In a large bowl thoroughly mix 1⅓ cups flour, 1 teaspoon sugar and dissolved Active Dry Yeast. Combine milk, water, and margarine in a saucepan over low heat until liquids are warm. (Margarine does not need to melt. Gradually add to dry ingredients and beat 2 minutes at medium speed with electric mixer, scraping bowl occasionally. Add egg yolks and ½ cup flour or enough flour to make a thick batter. Beat at high speed 2 minutes turning bowl occasionally. Stir in enough additional flour to make a soft dough. Divide dough in half. Roll out ½ the dough on floured board to fit the bottom of ungreased 15½ x 10½ x 1 inch jellyroll pan. Spread with cooled pineapple filling. Roll remaining dough large enough to cover filling. Seal edges together. Snip surface of dough with scissors to let steam escape. Cover; let rise in warm place, free from draft, until doubled in bulk, about 1 hour. Bake in moderate oven (375 degrees) about 35 to 40 minutes or until done. Let cake cool in pan. While warm, sprinkle with confectioners' sugar. Cut into squares to serve.

Judy Durand

DESSERTS

Peachy Cobbler

2 cups sliced peaches
   (canned or fresh)
2 tablespoons lemon juice
   (optional)
1 cup brown sugar
1 teaspoon cinnamon
   (if needed)
¾ cup flour
2 teaspoons baking powder
¾ cup milk
½ cup sugar
¼ teaspoon salt
⅓ cup margarine (melted)

Put drained peaches in 10 inch square baking dish. Pour on lemon juice, sprinkle on brown sugar and cinnamon. In a bowl, mix flour, sugar, baking powder and salt. Add milk, beat until smooth. Pour over fruit and brown sugar. Drizzle melted butter over batter. Bake at 350 degrees about 35 minutes. (Instead of peaches you can use any berries, even strawberries.)

Helen L. Kainer

Cream Cheese-Chocolate Cupcakes

1 (8 ounce) package cream
   cheese, softened
1 egg
⅓ cup sugar
⅛ teaspoon salt
1 (16 ounce) package
   chocolate chips
¾ cup chopped pecans
1 package dark chocolate
   cake mix

Mix cream cheese, egg, sugar and salt with a fork or hand mixer. Add chocolate chips and nuts and set aside. Prepare cake mix according to package directions. Line a muffin pan with paper liners or grease and flour well. Fill cups about ⅓ to ½ full of cake batter. Top each cupcake with a tablespoon of the cream cheese mixture. Bake at 350 degrees as directed on the cake mix package.

Leslie LeVack

DESSERTS

Ginger Snaps and Cream Cheese

1 (8 ounce) package non-fat cream cheese, softened
2 tablespoons skim milk
3 tablespoons chopped crystallized ginger
2 tablespoons toasted almonds, chopped
1 box gingersnaps

Combine cream cheese and milk. Beat at medium speed with an electric mixer until mixture is smooth. Stir in ginger, cover and chill. Sprinkle with chopped almonds and serve with gingersnaps. Yields 1 cup.

Nancy Maranto

Fudge Chews

2 tablespoons margarine
3 cups or 1½ (6 ounce) packages semi-sweet chocolate chips
1 (14 ounce) can sweetened condensed milk
1 cup all-purpose flour
1 cup chopped pecans
1 teaspoon vanilla

Preheat oven to 325 degrees. Melt margarine over low heat. Add chips and stir until melted. Add milk and mix well. Add flour, mixing thoroughly. Stir in nuts and vanilla. Remove from heat. Drop small teaspoonfuls of dough on greased baking sheet. Bake 10 to 12 minutes. Yields 4 dozen cookies.

Kathy Lopez

Chocolate stains can be removed with a paste of borax and water.

Apple Butter Squares

½ cup butter or margarine
1 cup sugar
3 eggs
2½ cups sifted flour
1½ teaspoons baking soda
1 teaspoon cinnamon

½ teaspoon ground cloves
½ teaspoon nutmeg
½ teaspoon salt
1 cup buttermilk
1 cup apple butter

Beat butter and sugar until fluffy. Add eggs one at a time, beating well after each addition. Add the sifted dry ingredients alternately with the buttermilk. Fold in the apple butter, blending well. Pour in well greased 9 inch square pan and bake at 350 degrees for 50 minutes.

Victoria LeBlanc Guidry

Pumpkin Squares

2 cups pumpkin
1 cup sugar
1 teaspoon salt
1 teaspoon ginger
1 teaspoon cinnamon

½ teaspoon nutmeg
1 cup chopped nuts
½ gallon vanilla ice cream, softened
36 gingersnap cookies

Combine pumpkin, sugar, salt and spices. Add nuts. In a chilled bowl, fold pumpkin mixture into ice cream. Line the bottom of a 13 x 9 x 2 inch dish with half of the gingersnap cookies. Top with half of the ice cream mixture. Cover with a layer of gingersnaps and the remaining ice cream. Freeze until firm, about 5 hours. Cut into squares and serve with whipped cream and nuts. Yields 18 servings.

Nadeen McClellan

DESSERTS

Gingerbread

½ cup shortening
½ cup sugar
3 eggs, beaten
2½ cups all purpose flour
1½ teaspoons baking powder
½ teaspoon baking soda
½ teaspoon salt
1 teaspoon ginger
1 teaspoon cinnamon
¼ teaspoon cloves
1 cup cane syrup
1 cup boiling water
1 cup chopped nuts, optional

Sift together all dry ingredients. Cream shortening and sugar until fluffy. Add eggs, then dry ingredients, alternately with the syrup and water. Add nuts if desired. Beat enough to mix thoroughly and pour into well greased 12 x 8 inch pan and bake at 350 degrees for 40 to 45 minutes. Serve warm with whipped cream.

Victoria LeBlanc Guidry

Hello Dolly Bars

½ cup melted margarine
1½ cups graham cracker crumbs
1 cup semi-sweet chocolate chips
1½ cups coconut
1 cup butterscotch chips
1 can sweetened condensed milk
½ cup chopped pecans or walnuts

Layer in the order listed in a 13 x 9 inch baking dish. Bake in a 350 degree preheated oven for 25 minutes. Cool thoroughly before cutting into squares. Yields 2½ dozen squares.

Kathy Lopez

Cherry Crunch

2 cups Bisquick mix
⅔ cup sugar
¾ teaspoon cinnamon

1 egg, beaten
⅓ cup margarine
1 can cherry pie filling

Preheat oven to 400 degrees. Melt margarine. Mix all ingredients except pie filling. Dough will be crumbly. Press ⅔ of dough into 8 x 8 inch baking dish. Cover with cherry pie filling. Sprinkle remainder of dough on top of filling. Bake at 400 degrees for 30 minutes or until golden brown.

Ginny O'Connor

Français Parfait

A cluster of good friends
1 package frozen raspberries

1 gallon Blue Bell vanilla ice cream
Chambord raspberry liqueur

Invite at least a half dozen old pals. Thaw out the raspberries. Scoop three reasonable scoops of vanilla ice cream into a stunning ice cream dish for each person. Pour whatever raspberries and liqueur you desire. Add more liqueur to your pals' dishes if you are worried about the state of your house, hair, or whatever. After two or three shots, they won't care if you are wearing rags and live in a dump.

Busy Day Cheese Cake

1 (8 ounce) package cream cheese, softened
2 cups milk

1 package lemon instant pudding mix
1 (8 inch) graham cracker crust

Blend cream cheese with ½ cup milk. Add remaining milk and pudding mix to cream cheese mixture. Beat slowly with egg beater, just until well mixed. About 1 minute. Do not over beat. Pour at once in cracker crust. Sprinkle with graham cracker crumbs lightly over top. Chill 1 hour. Will serve 8 people. Cooked pudding will not give good results with this recipe.

Victoria LeBlanc Guidry

DESSERTS

Banana Split

2 cups graham cracker crumbs
⅓ cup melted margarine

4 cups powdered sugar (sifted, no lumps)
2 eggs
1 cup margarine

Pour over graham cracker crumbs.

1 large can crushed pineapple (drain well)

4 bananas, sliced
1 cup chopped pecans

Mix graham crackers with ⅓ cup margarine; press into 9 x 13 inch pan. Bake at 350 degrees for 8 minutes. Cool. Mix for 15 minutes powdered sugar, eggs and 1 cup margarine until smooth and thick. Pour onto graham crackers. Layer crushed pineapple, sliced bananas and pecans over mixture. Top with 10 ounces Cool Whip. Garnish with cherries. Chill overnight.

Bette Gruber

Pumpkin Swirl Cheesecake

2 cups vanilla wafer crumbs
¼ cup melted margarine
2 (8 ounce) packages light Neufchâtel cream cheese, softened

¾ cup sugar
1 teaspoon vanilla
3 eggs
1 cup canned pumpkin
¼ teaspoon ground nutmeg

Combine crumbs and margarine, press onto bottom and sides of 9 inch springform pan. Combine Neufchâtel cheese, ½ cup sugar and vanilla, mix at medium speed in electric mixer until well blended. Add eggs one at a time, mixing well after each addition. Reserve 1 cup cheese mixture; add pumpkin, remaining sugar and spices to remaining cheese mixture. Mix well. Layer half of pumpkin mixture and half cheese mixture over crust, repeat layers. Cut through batter with knife several times for marble effect.

Bake at 350 degrees for 55 minutes. Loosen cake from rim of pan. Serve chilled. Makes about 10 to 12 servings.

Anita L. Bell

Neiman Marcus Bars

1 yellow cake mix
1 stick butter, melted

1 egg, beaten

Topping:
1 box powdered sugar
3 eggs, beaten

8 ounces cream cheese

Combine cake mix, butter and egg; press in 9 x 13 inch greased and floured cake pan. (Do not use mixer).

Topping: Beat 5 minutes with mixer and pour on top of cake. Bake 10 minutes at 350 degrees, then bake another 30 minutes at 325 degrees.

Betsy Payne

Strawberry Dessert Roll

4 eggs
¾ cup granulated sugar
½ teaspoon vanilla

¾ cup cake flour
1 teaspoon baking powder

Filling:
1 pint whipping cream
   (do not use Cool Whip)
3 tablespoons sugar

1½ cups sliced or diced strawberries

Cake: Separate the eggs. Beat egg yolks until thick; gradually add sugar and vanilla. Beat egg whites until almost stiff. Gradually add ½ cup sugar and beat until very stiff. Fold in yolks, then fold in sifted dry ingredients. Spread the batter evenly into a waxed paper lined jellyroll pan. Bake in moderately hot oven (375 degrees) for 12 minutes or until cake springs back when touched. Loosen edges of cake and turn into towel sprinkled with powdered sugar. Peel off waxed paper quickly, but carefully. While cake is warm, lay a piece of waxed paper on it. Roll cake quickly with paper inside. Wrap towel with powdered sugar and cool cake on rack.

Filling: When cake is cool unroll and remove waxed paper. Whip 1 pint of whipping cream, take out ¾ cup whipping cream and add the 3 tablespoons sugar to the sliced strawberries. Spread this mixture on cake; roll like jellyroll. Spread remaining whipped cream over cake roll. Put whole strawberries down middle of roll; put in refrigerator. Use a quart of strawberries, saving the large strawberries for down the middle of the roll. I serve this when strawberries are in season. You can use frozen strawberries, well drained!

Virginia Sattler

DESSERTS

Strawberry Shortcake

1¾ cups all-purpose flour
2 tablespoons granulated sugar
1 tablespoon baking powder
½ teaspoon grated orange peel

3 tablespoons unsalted butter or margarine, cut into pieces
¾ cup skim milk

Filling:
2 pints fresh strawberries, sliced
1 tablespoon orange juice

1 tablespoon granulated sugar
vanilla non fat yogurt

Cake: Preheat oven to 450 degrees. Spray a baking sheet with non-stick coating. In a large bowl, sift together the flour, sugar, and baking powder. Stir in the orange peel. Using a pastry blender, cut the butter into the flour mixture until coarse crumbs form. Quickly stir in the milk until a soft dough forms. On a lightly floured surface roll out dough to a ½ inch thickness. Cut out biscuits (approximately 2½ inches in diameter). Gather trimmings, re-roll and cut out more biscuits. Place on prepared baking sheet. Bake until golden, about 12 to 15 minutes. Place biscuits on a wire rack to cool slightly.

Filling: In a large bowl, combine strawberries, orange juice and sugar. Mix well.

Split warm biscuits in half horizontally. Place bottom half on individual plates. Top with some filling. Cover with biscuit tops. Serve with remaining filling, garnish with yogurt.

Editor's Note: You may want to use a 12 ounce coffee can or larger biscuit cutter to make shortcakes 3-4 inches in diameter. You may also roll to ¾ inch thickness for larger shortcake.

Anna Bell

Enjoy angel food cake instead of high fat cakes made with butter and shortening.

DESSERTS

Blackbottom Cupcakes

1 (8 ounce) package cream cheese
1 egg, unbeaten
⅓ cup sugar
⅛ teaspoon salt
1 (6 ounce) package semi-sweet chocolate morsels
1 cup chopped pecans
1½ cups all-purpose flour

1 cup sugar
¼ cup powdered cocoa
1 teaspoon baking soda
½ teaspoon salt
1 cup water
⅓ cup salad oil
1 teaspoon vinegar
1 teaspoon vanilla

Cake: Preheat oven to 350 degrees. Cream together the cream cheese, egg, sugar, and ⅛ teaspoon salt. Fold in the chocolate morsels and pecans. Set aside. In a mixing bowl, combine the flour sugar, cocoa, soda and ½ teaspoon salt. In a separate bowl, mix together the water, oil, vinegar and vanilla. Add this liquid mixture to the dry ingredients. Mix well. Fill each cup ⅓ full and then drop a spoonful of the cream cheese mixture on top. Bake at 350 degrees for 20 to 25 minutes.

Mary Uhle

Miniature Cheesecakes

2 dozen Nabisco vanilla wafers
2 (8 ounce) packages Philadelphia cream cheese
¾ cup sugar

1 teaspoon vanilla
1 teaspoon lemon juice
2 eggs
1 can cherry pie filling

Put paper liners in muffin tins. Place vanilla wafer in each. Mix softened cream cheese in bowl. Gradually add sugar, lemon juice and vanilla. Beat in eggs, one at a time until light and fluffy. Spoon into liners. Bake at 375 degrees until set (about 15 minutes). Cool. Do not remove liners. Top each cheesecake with 1 tablespoon cherry pie filling. Refrigerate until ready to serve. Can also use lemon pudding, blueberry pie filling or one can crushed pineapple with vanilla pudding for topping. Serves 24.

These are very easy to make and taste delicious. My girls whip these out in no time. On the 4th of July, I do 12 with cherry and 12 with blueberry filling - looks very patriotic!

Mary Jane Morgan

DESSERTS

Strawberry Omelet Supreme

6 eggs
3 tablespoons orange juice
½ teaspoon salt
Dash pepper

2 tablespoons butter or margarine
Fluffy Strawberry Sauce
Strawberries for garnish

Beat together eggs, orange juice, salt and pepper until frothy. In 10-inch omelet pan, melt butter over medium heat, tilting pan to coat sides. When butter begins to brown, add egg mixture to pan. Stir eggs gently, sliding bits of set eggs to sides. Allow eggs to set. As eggs become firm lift edges occasionally, tilting pan so that liquid egg in center runs under set portion. Cook until bottom of omelet is golden brown and eggs are set to desired doneness. Fold in half and turn out onto plate. If making more than one omelet, keep warm in 200 degree oven. Serve with Fluffy Strawberry Sauce and garnish with strawberries. Makes 1 omelet or 2 to 3 servings.

Fluffy Strawberry Sauce

¾ cup mashed strawberries
2 tablespoons powdered sugar
3 tablespoons orange liqueur

1½ teaspoons flour
½ cup heavy cream, whipped
¼ teaspoon vanilla

In 1-quart saucepan combine mashed berries and sugar. Combine liqueur and flour to form a paste; stir into berries. Cook over low heat until hot and thickened. Fold in whipped cream and vanilla. Serve immediately over omelet. Makes 1½ cups or enough for 3 (10-inch) omelets.

Note: To use frozen strawberries, drain, and omit sugar.

Sharon Kiel Gutormson

Orange Coconut Balls

6 ounces vanilla wafers
½ box powdered sugar
¼ cup soft margarine

½ cup orange juice concentrate
½ cup flaked coconut
½ cup finely chopped nuts

Crush vanilla wafers into fine crumbs. Add other ingredients, except coconut. Form balls and roll in coconut. Freeze or chill overnight.

Diann Meriwether

Eggs separate most easily if they are very cold. Whites, however, should be beaten at room temperature.

Date Pinwheel

Dough:
½ cup light brown sugar
½ cup white sugar
½ cup soft margarine
1 egg or substitute egg
¼ teaspoon salt
1½ cups flour
1 teaspoon baking powder
1 teaspoon vanilla

Filling:
½ pound dates (chopped)
¼ cup sugar
¼ cup water
¼ cup grated orange rind (optional)
½ cup pecans
1 teaspoon vanilla

Mix dough ingredients and chill. Blend and cook chopped dates, sugar, water, grated orange rind, pecans and vanilla until well blended and as smooth as possible. Cool before spreading. Take dough and divide into several balls. Roll dough out to about ⅛ to ¼ inch thick. Spread filling thinly on top of dough. Roll up and place wrapping paper around roll and put rolls into freezer. Next day remove one roll at a time from freezer and slice ¼ inch thick. Place cookies on greased cookie sheet about 2 inches apart. Bake at 375 degrees for 15 - 20 minutes until only light brown.

Special tip: I have made these rolls as much as 2 months ahead and baked as needed. When storing this long, put into a sealed bag. Usually I make up to six batches at a time because of all the work involved. These are a special treat for anyone that loves dates.

Yvonne E. Constantino

Sugar-free Ice Custard

¾ envelope unflavored gelatin
1 quart half and half
2 eggs, separated
¼ teaspoon salt
2 tablespoons Sucaryl
2 tablespoons vanilla extract

Sprinkle gelatin over ½ cup of half and half. Set aside. Beat egg yolks, salt and 1 cup of half and half together in saucepan, cook, stirring constantly over medium heat until mixture thickens slightly and coats the spoon. Remove from heat at once. Add softened gelatin and stir until dissolved. Blend in remaining half and half. Pour into freezer canister and chill. Add Sucaryl and vanilla just before freezing. Beat egg whites until stiff. Fold into custard.

Elizabeth Henson

DESSERTS

Snickers Frozen Bars

2 cups vanilla ice milk
1 small package sugar-free chocolate pudding mix
¼ cup chunky peanut butter
½ cup Lite Cool Whip
1½ ounces Grape Nuts

Mix all of the above ingredients. Press into 9 x 9 inch pan. Cover and freeze.

Elizabeth Henson

Poached Pear Gratin

8 medium firm, ripe pears, peeled (about 3½ pounds)
4 cups unsweetened apple cider
⅔ cup low-fat sour cream
⅓ cup vanilla low-fat yogurt
¾ teaspoon vanilla extract
¼ cup firmly packed brown sugar

Place pears upright in a large Dutch oven. Pour apple cider over pears; bring to a boil. Cover; reduce heat and simmer 8 minutes or until tender. Remove from heat. Let stand, covered, 2½ hours. Remove pears. Cut each pear in half lengthwise; remove core. Place pears, cut side down, on a cutting board; cut lengthwise into ¼ inch slices. Keeping slices together, place 2 pear halves, cut side down, into each of 8 individual serving dishes. Press gently to fan slices. Set aside. Combine sour cream, yogurt and vanilla; stir well. Spoon 2 tablespoons sour cream mixture over each serving and sprinkle with brown sugar. Place dishes on a baking sheet. Broil 3 inches from heat 1½ minutes or until sugar melts. Makes 8 servings.

Note: Remaining poaching liquid may be used in a pear-apple cider. (Pear-Apple Cider - see page 219).

Annette Carr

DESSERTS

English Trifle

3 cups fruit of your choice, fresh or frozen (thawed)
12 Hostess Twinkies
3 cups whipping cream
1 cup butterscotch schnapps

In large glass bowl, crumble 4 Twinkies; cover with 1 cup of fruit. Drizzle one-third cup of liqueur. Cover with one cup whipping cream. Repeat the layers two more times. Decorate with fruit and a sprig of mint. Refrigerate overnight if possible, or 4 to 5 hours at the least.

Hilary Cobb

Strawberry Dips

1 quart fresh strawberries with stems
1 cup sour cream
Powdered sugar

Dip strawberries in sour cream; coat with powdered sugar. About 6 servings.

JoAnne Moore

Strawberries 'N Cream Chillout

1 package low-calorie whipped topping mix
½ cup skim milk
½ teaspoon strawberry extract
3 cups strawberries, quartered
2 cups club soda
6 packages of Equal
6 dashes of bitters
1 teaspoon lemon juice
10 ice cubes
8 fresh strawberries

Prepare whipped topping according to package directions, but substitute milk for water and strawberry extract for vanilla extract. Puree the strawberries in a blender. Add club soda. Add the rest of the ingredients except fresh strawberries. Blend on high until creamy and smooth. Serve with a generous dollop of whipped topping. Garnish with fresh strawberries. Add liqueur or brandy, if desired.

DESSERTS

Pistachio Salad

1 (8 ounce) container Cool Whip
1 small package pistachio instant pudding
1 (20 ounce) can crushed pineapple, partially drained
1 cup coconut (optional)
1-1½ cups miniature marshmallows
½ cup pecans

Combine Cool Whip and pudding. Fold in remaining ingredients and refrigerate.

Dorothy E. Schuchardt

Glazed Apple Slices

½ cup cranberry juice
⅛ teaspoon ground allspice
⅓ cup light brown sugar
3 large apples, cored and thinly sliced

In a large skillet, combine cranberry juice, brown sugar, and allspice. Stir over low heat until brown sugar dissolves and mixture boils. Add apple rings. Simmer uncovered over low heat for 30-40 minutes or until apples are tender. Spoon syrup over apples during cooking. Serve hot with ice cream or French toast. Serves 4.

Deby Koudelik

Cream Puffs

½ cup butter
1 cup water
⅛ teaspoon salt

1 cup all-purpose flour
4 eggs

Heat in heavy saucepan. Heat to boiling. Gradually stir in flour and beat until ball forms in center of pan. Take pan off heat and let stand for 5 minutes. Add eggs, one at a time, beating vigorously after each addition. Beat until thick and smooth. Shape batter into 12 mounds and place 2 inches apart on a well oiled baking sheet. Bake for 15 minutes at 450 degrees. Reduce heat to 375 degrees. Bake another 20-25 minutes until moisture beads disappear. Cool on rack.

Filling:
1 pint heavy cream
1 teaspoon vanilla

½ cup confectioners' sugar

In a chilled bowl, beat cream. Gradually add sugar and vanilla when cream begins to thicken. Continue beating until stiff. Split cooled puffs open and spoon in cream filling. Sprinkle tops with confectioners' sugar.

Maxwell M. Suarez

Puppy Chow

1 large box of Crispix
1 stick margarine
12 ounces crunchy peanut
   butter

12 ounces of chocolate chips
1 box of powdered sugar

Melt margarine, peanut butter and chocolate chips on medium heat. Pour cereal into large mixing bowl. Pour melted mixture over top. Empty box of powdered sugar into grocery bag. Dump coated cereal into paper bag and shake until all pieces are coated. Place on wax paper. Store in sealed containers.

Maxwell M. Suarez

DESSERTS

Brown Sugar Pudding

1 cup brown sugar
2½ cups water
1 cup flour
2 teaspoons baking powder

½ cup sugar
2 tablespoons butter
½ cup raisins

Combine sugars and 2 cups water in saucepan. Boil 10 minutes. Add butter and put into 1½ quart dish. Combine flour, baking powder, raisins and ½ cup water. Pour this batter into the syrup (do not stir). Bake 25 minutes at 400 degrees.

My great-grandmother brought this recipe with her during the Civil War into the Indian territory around 1885. Even during the depression years and later, we loved it!

Shirlee Nicholson

Poached Pears

1 Bartlett pear
4 dried apricot halves, finely chopped

¼ cup finely chopped walnuts or pecans
⅓ cup orange juice

Peel pear and cut in half lengthwise. With a small sharp knife, cut out the core and stem. If the half won't sit flat, cut a small piece from bottom. Mix together the apricots and nuts. It will be gooey. Fill the cavity and stem of the pear halves with the mixture. Place in a shallow microwave dish. Pour orange juice over top. Bake at full power for about 2 minutes or until pears may be easily pierced with a fork. Place on individual dishes and pour juice over top. Garnish with a sprig of mint at the stem end. Serves 2.

Georgie McIrvin

DESSERTS

Pretzel Salad

First layer:
2 cups crushed pretzels
1 cup melted butter
1 tablespoon sugar

Second layer:
1 envelope of Dream Whip
¾ cup sugar
8 ounces softened cream cheese

Third layer:
2 cups pineapple juice
1 (6 ounce) package of strawberry Jell-O
1 large package of sliced frozen strawberries

Mix first layer ingredients and pat into 9 x 13 inch glass dish. Bake 10 minutes at 350 degrees and cool. Mix Dream Whip according to directions. Blend in cream cheese and sugar, beat well. Spread over cooled first layer. Heat pineapple juice to boiling and dissolve Jell-O. Stir in frozen strawberries. Cool, then spread over second layer. Chill at least 2 hours before serving.

Diann Meriwether

Tassies

8 ounce cream cheese
½ pound of butter or margarine
2 cups flour

Cream together cream cheese and margarine. Add flour gradually until soft. Line each cupcake pan with mixture in a ball the size of a walnut.

Filling:
3 eggs, slightly beaten
1½ cups brown sugar
1 cup chopped walnuts
3 tablespoons melted butter
2 tablespoons vanilla

Stir all ingredients and then add 1 cup of chopped nuts. Fill pans ¾ full (1 teaspoon). Bake at 350 degrees for 25 minutes. Makes 48.

Wanda Szot

DESSERTS

Apple Pudding

1½ cups sugar
2 eggs, beaten
3 cups chopped apples
1 cup flour
4 teaspoons baking powder
¾ teaspoon cinnamon
½ cup nuts
pinch of salt

Mix together sugar, eggs and apples. Combine flour, baking powder, cinnamon, salt and nuts and add to sugar mixture. Put into ungreased 9 inch square pan. Bake 30 minutes at 350 degrees. Serves 6.

Nancy G. Brown

Oranges, Provençal Style

½ cup sugar
½ cup water
½ cup orange juice
1 cinnamon stick
pinch of cloves
Grand Marnier or Grenadine
Orange zest
Oranges

Bring the sugar and water to a boil and cook to soft ball stage. Remove the zest from 2 oranges with zester or cut into julienne strips. Place in syrup and boil for 1-2 minutes. Remove and drain on wax paper or plate. Sprinkle with sugar. Add orange juice and spices to remaining syrup and simmer for 5 minutes. Remove from heat and add Grand Marnier. Peel 1 orange per person, removing the white pithy part. Slice into flowers or slices. Pour syrup over oranges. Garnish with mint sprigs, etc.

Anci Waugh

DESSERTS

Rice Pudding

1 cup rice (cooked and
   drained)
3 eggs, beaten
1 teaspoon vanilla
Dash of almond extract
⅓ cup oil

⅓ cup sugar
juice from 1 orange
1 apple, grated (optional)
1 teaspoon salt
handful of raisins (optional)

To rice, add all ingredients. Taste, if not sweet enough, add a little more sugar. Bake in 8 x 8 inch or 9 x 9 inch pan about 1 hour at 350 degrees until brown on top.

Aviva Hoffman

Sugarless Apricot Delights

1 cup coconut
1 cup dried apricots
½ cup chopped dates
½ cup golden raisins

½ cup currants
⅔ cup walnuts or pecans
1 tablespoon orange juice (if
   necessary)

Using a food processor, finely chop the coconut, then spread it on a double layer of paper towels. Then process each item listed above, one at a time and put it into a large bowl. Using a large wooden spoon, mix thoroughly. Pinch a piece of the mixture to see if it will hold together. If not, add the orange juice. Dip out by teaspoon and mold into round balls. Roll each ball lightly through the coconut until coated. Place on serving dish. May be refrigerated overnight, but is not necessary. Makes about 50.

Georgie McIrvin

DESSERTS

Blueberry, Cherry or Strawberry Dessert

3 egg whites
1 cup sugar
½ cup chopped pecans
1 large container Cool Whip
½ teaspoon baking powder

10 soda crackers
1 teaspoon vanilla
1 can pie filling (favorite flavor)

Beat egg whites and baking powder until stiff but not dry. Gradually add sugar. Crush the crackers and add pecans. Fold the crackers and pecans into the egg white mixture and add vanilla. Bake in slightly greased 9 x 13 inch cake pan at 300 degrees for 45 minutes. Cool completely. Spread ½ the Cool Whip on the Crust. Spread pie filling over this and top with the other half of the Cool Whip. Sprinkle with nuts. Refrigerate, but serve the same day.

Deby Koudelik

Fudge Pie

1 cup sugar
8 tablespoons melted butter
2 eggs
dash of salt

5 tablespoons cocoa
1 teaspoon vanilla
½ cup chopped pecans

Mix sugar and melted butter. Beat until creamy. Add eggs, flour, salt, cocoa and vanilla. Beat well. Stir in pecans. Bake in a greased 8 inch pie pan for 30 minutes at 300 degrees. Do not over cook. Great topped with vanilla ice cream.

Bobbie Walters

Dark Chocolate Fudge

4 cups sugar
6 ounces evaporated milk
1½ sticks of margarine
2 tablespoons corn syrup
1 tablespoon cocoa powder
12 ounce package of chocolate chips
1 teaspoon vanilla extract
1 (7 ounce) jar of marshmallow creme

Spray pan well with cooking spray. Stir sugar, milk, margarine, corn syrup and cocoa powder together and boil to 234 degrees or soft ball in cold water. Stir occasionally with wooden spoon. When done, add chocolate chips, vanilla and marshmallows cream. Stir well and spread in pan.

Mabel E. Lucas

Peanut Butter Fudge

3 cups sugar
1 cup brown sugar
1 stick margarine
½ can evaporated milk
2 tablespoons corn syrup
1 (10 ounce) package peanut butter chips
6 ounces creamy or chunky peanut butter

Mix together sugars, margarine, milk and corn syrup and boil to soft ball stage or 234 degrees. Stir often with wooden spoon. Remove and stir in peanut butter chips and peanut butter. Mix well and beat until it loses its gloss and spread in a greased pan.

Mabel E. Lucas

DESSERTS

Buttermilk Fudge

½ cup butter (1 stick)
2 cups sugar
1 cup buttermilk
1 teaspoon soda

2 teaspoons Karo corn syrup
1 cup chopped pecans
1 teaspoon vanilla

Mix soda in buttermilk and let stand a few minutes. Mix all ingredients except nuts. Cook until soft ball stage and add nuts. Beat until firm. Pour in buttered pan.

Ruby McAbee

Melt-Aways

1 stick margarine
½ cup peanut butter
6 ounces chocolate chips

8 cups Rice Chex cereal
2 cups powdered sugar

Combine margarine, peanut butter and chocolate chips. Melt in microwave. Mix well. Pour melted ingredients over the cereal and stir until coated. Put powdered sugar in large bag and add the coated cereal mix. Shake until coated. Place mixture in refrigerator for 2 hours. Store in airtight container.

Mary Uhle

Heavenly Hash

2½ pounds milk chocolate
9 ounces slivered almonds

26 ounces miniature marshmallows

Break chocolate into blocks and place in top pan of double boiler. Water temperature should be about 150 degrees. Stir chocolate. When chocolate reaches 120 degrees, remove from heat. Place pot on towel and stir in almonds. Fold in marshmallows in 8 ounce increments. When marshmallows are coated, pour mix into a metal tray (1-1½ inches deep; lined with foil). Bump tray a few times to remove bubbles and spread mixture evenly. Refrigerate covered about 2 hours before cutting. It is important to keep stirring the entire time candy is being made.

Fern Hull

DESSERTS

Best Fudge You Ever Ate

2 tablespoons butter or
  margarine
⅔ cup evaporated milk
1⅔ cups sugar
½ teaspoon salt

2 cups miniature
  marshmallows
1½ cups semi-sweet chocolate
  chips
1 teaspoon vanilla
½ cup chopped walnuts

Combine butter, milk, sugar and salt in a saucepan over medium heat. Bring to a boil. Cook 5 minutes, stirring constantly. Start timing when mixture starts to bubble around edge of pan. Remove from heat. Stir in marshmallows, chips, vanilla and nuts. Stir vigorously for 1 minute until the marshmallows melt and blend. Pour into 8 inch buttered square pan. Cool thoroughly. Cut into squares.

Gailyn Malone

Fudge

2 cups sugar
6 tablespoons cocoa
2 tablespoons white Karo
  syrup
3 tablespoons butter

⅔ cup milk (or ⅓ cup
  evaporated milk and ⅓ cup
  water)
1 teaspoon vanilla
½ cup chopped nuts

Mix sugar, milk, cocoa and Karo; bring to a boil rather slowly, stirring until well blended. Boil to soft ball stage (238 degrees). Add butter but don't stir in. When lukewarm add vanilla and beat until the shine goes away and the fudge will hold its shape when dropped from a spoon. Add nuts. Spread in buttered pan and cut when hard. This is my mother's recipe. It is delicious!

Eileen Donovan

Vanilla flavor evaporates when it is boiled. Add vanilla to candies and desserts after they have been removed from heat.

Pumpkin Cake

2 cups sugar
1 cup oil
4 eggs (part could be substituted with Egg Beaters)
1 teaspoon salt
dash of cinnamon

3 cups flour
2 teaspoons baking soda
2 teaspoons baking powder
2 cups pumpkin mix (Libby's)
Nuts, raisins, chocolate chips, etc., can be added if desired

Beat sugar, oil, and eggs well together. Slowly add other ingredients. Add flour and pumpkin mix - alternately. Add nuts, raisins, chocolate chips, etc., if desired. Bake in greased pan 1 hour at 350 degrees.

This was handed down from my sister-in-law. It is easy to make. I bake it in a loaf pan or tube pan. Also good for muffins. It is more like a pumpkin bread. With additional flour, I make cookies.

Aviva Hoffman

Blueberry Lemon Cake

1 package lemon cake mix
1 stick margarine
1 cup packed brown sugar

1 (20 ounce) package frozen blueberries, thawed and drained

Preheat oven to 350 degrees. Melt margarine in 13 x 9 inch baking dish. Sprinkle brown sugar evenly in dish. Arrange blueberries over the sugar mixture. Prepare cake mix as directed on the package. Spread the batter over the fruit. Bake 45 to 55 minutes. Let stand for 5 minutes before serving.

Kathy Lopez

Seven Minute Icing

3 egg whites
2¼ cups sugar
7½ tablespoons cold water
2¼ teaspoons light corn syrup
½ teaspoon cream of tartar
1 teaspoon vanilla

Beat all ingredients except vanilla with a hand mixer over boiling water for 7 minutes. Add vanilla and spread on your favorite cake or cupcakes.

Shirlee Nicholson

Cajun Day Syrup Cake

½ cup butter or margarine
1 cup sugar
3 eggs
2 cups dark syrup
1 cup milk
4 cups flour
2 teaspoons baking soda
½ teaspoon cinnamon
½ teaspoon ground cloves
½ teaspoon nutmeg

Cream butter and sugar. Add eggs, syrup, and milk. Sift flour with baking soda and spices, stir into the other mixture. Pour into a greased and floured 9 x 12 inch baking dish. Bake at 400 degrees 45 to 55 minutes. May be served with lemon sauce but is delicious plain.

Note: This is an old but popular recipe used at bake fairs and family get-togethers in south Louisiana.

Jan LeBlanc

CAKES

Pound Cake

1 cup butter or margarine
2 cups cake flour or regular flour
2 cups sugar
1 teaspoon vanilla
5 eggs

Cream butter and sugar together. To this mixture, add 1 egg at a time, then add flour and vanilla and beat well. Pour into greased and floured loaf pan and bake at 350 degrees about 45 to 50 minutes or until toothpick inserted in center comes out clean.

Victoria LeBlanc Guidry

Chocolate Fudge Cake

1 box chocolate cake mix
1 (8 ounce) container Cool Whip
1 can Hershey Hot Fudge (not chocolate syrup)
Grated chocolate

Prepare cake mix according to package directions. Cool. Mix Hershey's Hot Fudge with 1 to 2 tablespoons of water to spread easier. Spread over cake; top with Cool Whip. Grate chocolate over top. Chill several hours.

Bette Gruber

Do not substitute liquid oil for solid butter or margarine in a recipe for cake. The texture will be poor because air will not be beaten in with the adding of the fat.

Oatmeal Cake

1 cup oatmeal
1½ cups boiling water
½ cup margarine
1 cup white sugar
1½ cups brown sugar
2 eggs
1⅓ cups flour
½ teaspoon salt

1 teaspoon baking soda
½ teaspoon nutmeg
1 teaspoon cinnamon
½ cup margarine, melted
¼ cup evaporated milk
1 teaspoon vanilla
1 cup coconut flakes
1 cup chopped pecans

Combine the oatmeal, boiling water, and ½ cup margarine and let stand for 20 minutes. Add 1 cup white sugar, 1 cup brown sugar and 2 eggs and beat well. In a separate bowl, combine the flour, salt, baking soda, nutmeg, and cinnamon and beat into the oatmeal mixture until well mixed. Pour into a greased 9 x 13 inch baking dish and bake at 350 degrees for 30 minutes. For the topping mix the melted margarine, evaporated milk, ½ cup brown sugar, vanilla, coconut flakes, and pecans. When cake is done, spread the topping on immediately and broil for a few minutes until brown and bubbly.

Eileen Boren

Turtle Cake

1 package German chocolate cake mix
1 cup milk chocolate morsels
1 cup chopped pecans

1 stick butter/margarine
½ cup canned milk
1 pound Kraft caramels
1 can milk chocolate frosting

Prepare cake mix as directed. Grease/flour pan (9 x 13 inch). Pour ½ cake mix into pan. Bake 15 minutes. Remove from oven, spread on mix chocolate morsels and pecans. In saucepan, melt butter, caramels and canned milk. Heat medium - stir constantly. Add mixture to partially baked cake. Pour remainder of cake mix over caramel. Bake 30 minutes. Cool. Spread 1 can milk chocolate frosting over top of cake. Very rich - cut in small servings.

Bette Gruber

Mississippi Mud

1 package dark chocolate cake mix
3½ ounces shredded coconut
½ cup chopped pecans
7 ounces marshmallow creme
1 can dark chocolate frosting
1-2 tablespoons milk or water

Prepare mix as directed and then fold in coconut and pecans. Mixture will be thick. Pour into greased/floured 9 x 13 inch pan. Bake at 350 degrees for 30 to 45 minutes.

Spread marshmallow mixture over hot cake immediately when removed from oven. Cool thoroughly. Thin chocolate frosting with 1 to 2 tablespoons milk or hot water. Top with chocolate icing.

Bette Gruber

Piña Colada Cake

1 white cake mix
¼ cup oil
4 large eggs
1 package Jell-O instant coconut cream pudding mix, 4 serving size

½ cup water
⅓ cup rum, water or pineapple juice
½ cup shredded coconut

Icing:
1 (8 ounce) can crushed pineapple with juice
⅓ cup rum, water or pineapple juice
1 package Jell-O instant coconut pudding

1 (9 ounce) container Cool Whip
2-3 tablespoons coconut for garnish

To make cake, combine cake mix, oil, eggs, pudding, water, Rum and coconut. Beat 4 minutes at medium speed. Pour into greased/floured 9 x 13 inch pan. Bake at 350 degrees 30 to 40 minutes. Cool.

Icing: Blend together pineapple and pudding mix and rum. Fold in Cool Whip. Frost cake. Sprinkle coconut over cake. Refrigerate several hours before serving. Enjoy! Also can be made layered using 9 inch pans. Bake at 350 degrees for 25 to 30 minutes. Cool in pan 15 minutes; remove; cool.

Bette Gruber

Microwave Mississippi Mud Cake

1 cup butter or margarine
2 cups granulated sugar
½ cup unsweetened cocoa powder
4 large eggs

2 teaspoons vanilla extract
1½ cups all-purpose flour
¼ cup walnut or pecan pieces, chopped coarsely
¼ teaspoon salt

Frosting:
½ cup miniature marshmallows
½ cup butter or margarine
½ cup milk

¼ cup unsweetened cocoa powder
¼ teaspoon vanilla extract
1 (16 ounce) box confectioners' sugar

To make cake, put butter in large mixing bowl. Microwave on high 1 or 1½ minutes until melted. Stir in sugar and cocoa powder. Add eggs and vanilla, beat vigorously until well blended. Stir in flour, nuts and salt. Let the batter rest 10 minutes. Pour into an 11 x 7½ inch baking pan. Place on a plastic trivet or inverted saucer in microwave oven. Microwave on medium 9 minutes, rotating dish after 3 minutes. Shield the corners of the dish with small triangles of foil (don't let triangles touch each other or sides of oven). Microwave on high 3 to 5 minutes, rotating dish ½ turn once, until top is mostly dry with a few moist spots and pick inserted near center comes out clean. Sprinkle marshmallows evenly over top of cake. Let stand about 5 minutes until marshmallows are slightly melted. To make the frosting, put butter in large bowl, Microwave on high 30 to 60 seconds until melted. Stir in milk, cocoa powder and vanilla. Add sugar, beat vigorously until smooth. Spread over marshmallows. Let stand on flat heatproof surface 30 minutes until slightly warm, or cool completely and serve at room temperature. Makes 16 servings with a lot of calories and fat. Cake is gooey served warm or at room temperature, but fudgy when cold.

Mabel E. Lucas

CAKES

Chocolate Cherry Cake

1 package fudge cake mix
1 (21 ounce) can cherry pie filling
Frosting:
1 cup sugar
5 tablespoons butter or margarine
1 teaspoon almond extract
2 eggs, beaten

⅓ cup milk
1 (6 ounce) package semi-sweet chocolate pieces

Preheat oven to 350 degrees. Spray Pam into a 13 x 9 inch glass pan. In a large bowl, combine first 4 ingredients. By hand, stir until well mixed. Pour into pan. Bake 25 to 30 minutes.

Frosting: In small saucepan, combine sugar, butter and milk. Boil, stirring constantly, 1 minute. Remove from heat, stir in chocolate pieces until smooth. Pour over warm cake and cool completely.

Sharlene Farrar

Carrot Cake

2 cups grated carrots
2 cups sugar
1½ cups Wesson oil
½ to 1 cup chopped nuts
4 eggs (beaten)
Frosting:
1 box confectioners' sugar
1 (8 ounce) package cream cheese
3½ cups flour
1 teaspoon baking soda
1 teaspoon cinnamon
1 teaspoon salt
1 teaspoon baking powder

2 tablespoons margarine or butter

Mix grated carrots, sugar, and oil. Then add the nuts and eggs, mix thoroughly. Add flour one cup at a time with spices. Pour contents into a tube pan and bake at 450 degrees for 45 minutes. Cool before removing from pan.

Frosting: Mix confectioners' sugar, cream cheese and margarine/butter until creamy or smooth.

Jean Whiten

Poppy Seed Cake

1 package yellow cake mix
½ cup oil
4 eggs
1 teaspoon almond extract
Glaze:
1½ cups powdered sugar
1 teaspoon almond extract

1 small package instant
 vanilla pudding
4 tablespoons poppy seeds
1 cup hot water

Juice of 1 lemon, or 2
 tablespoons "Real Lemon"

Mix cake mix with pudding. Add oil and almond extract. Add eggs one at a time, hot water, and poppy seeds. Bake in greased Bundt pan at 350 degrees for 35 to 40 minutes.

Glaze: Mix powdered sugar, lemon juice, and almond extract while cake is baking. Spoon glaze onto cake while hot.

Great with milk or coffee.

Betty Dickey

Chocolate Sheet Cake

2 cups flour, sifted
2 cups sugar
1 cup water
½ cup shortening
½ cup margarine
¼ cup cocoa
Frosting:
4 tablespoons cocoa
½ cup margarine
6 tablespoons milk

½ cup buttermilk
1 teaspoon vanilla
1 teaspoon baking soda
1 teaspoon cinnamon
½ teaspoon salt
2 eggs, beaten

1 package powdered sugar
1 teaspoon vanilla
1 cup chopped nuts

Grease and flour sheet cake pan. Boil water, shortening, margarine, cocoa in a saucepan. Add flour and sugar to boiled mixture. In another bowl combine beaten eggs, buttermilk, vanilla, soda, cinnamon and salt. Add flour, sugar and the boiled mixture. Bake at 400 degrees for 20 minutes.

Frosting: Using "same ole pan," combine cocoa, margarine and milk and heat to boiling. Add powdered sugar, vanilla and nuts. Beat until smooth. Frost cake warm from the oven.

Ruby McAbee

CAKES

Milky Way Cake

8 Milky Way bars
2 sticks margarine
2 cups sugar
4 eggs

2½ cups flour
½ teaspoon baking soda
1¼ cups buttermilk
1 cup chopped nuts

Icing:
2½ cups sugar
1 cup evaporated milk
6 ounces chocolate chips

1 cup marshmallow cream
1 stick margarine

To make cake, melt candy bars and one stick margarine; set aside. Cream sugar and one stick margarine. Add eggs. Mix soda with buttermilk and add alternately with flour. Add melted candy and margarine mixture. Add pecans. Blend all well. Bake in a tube pan at 325 degrees for 70 minutes or until done.

Icing: Cook sugar and milk to soft ball stage. Add chocolate chips, marshmallow cream and margarine. Stir until all is melted.

JoAnne Moore

Diabetic Apple Cake

1⅓ cups unsifted flour
2½ teaspoons baking powder
6 packages of Equal or Sweet & Low
1 teaspoon cinnamon
⅓ cup margarine (softened)

½ cup egg substitute
½ teaspoon vanilla
½ cup skim milk
½ cup raisins
4 cups peeled sliced apples

Combine flour, baking powder; stir to blend; set aside. Blend 1 package of sugar substitute and cinnamon; set aside. Cream margarine and remaining 5 packages of sugar substitute; beat in egg substitute and vanilla. Beating on low speed, alternately add dry ingredients and milk, beginning and ending with dry ingredients. Fold in raisins and 1 cup chopped apples. Pour batter into greased 8 x 8 x 2 inch pan. Arrange the 3 cups of sliced apples on batter in rows. Sprinkle with sugar substitute and cinnamon. Bake at 375 degrees for 1 hour or until done. Cool cake in pan.

Note: This is for a person who is diabetic, has heart problems, people with cancer or anyone on a special diet. My late husband was a diabetic, and I made this cake a lot.

Virginia Sattler

CAKES

Delicious Chocolate Cake

2 cups flour
2 cups sugar
2 sticks margarine
1 cup water

4 tablespoons cocoa
2 eggs
½ cup buttermilk
½ teaspoon baking soda

Icing:
1 box powdered sugar
3 tablespoons cocoa
1 stick butter

6 tablespoons milk
1 cup chopped pecans

To make cake, mix flour and sugar together in a large bowl. Melt butter or margarine and mix with water and cocoa. Bring it to a boil and pour over flour and sugar mixture. Mix with a spoon, not a mixer. Add eggs, buttermilk and soda. Mix together and bake in a greased 9 x 13 inch pan at 350 degrees for 25 to 30 minutes.

Icing: Melt butter and add sugar, cocoa and milk. Heat until good and hot and then add 1 cup chopped pecans. Pour hot icing over cake while cake is still hot.

Diann Meriwether

Earthquake Cake

1 cup coconut
1 cup pecans
1 box German chocolate cake
  mix

1 (8 ounce) package cream
  cheese
1 stick margarine
1 box powdered sugar

Grease pan and spread coconut over bottom of 9 x 13 inch pan. Spread pecans over coconut. Prepare cake mix per directions on box and spread over pecan layer. Mix cream cheese, margarine and sugar until soft. Drop by dollops on cake. Do not mix. Bake in 350 degree oven for 45 to 50 minutes. May be served slightly warm. Really, really ugly cake, but it is very, very delicious!

Suzanne Garnett

Mom's Pound Cake

6 eggs
1 cup shortening
3 cups sugar
3 cups flour

½ teaspoon salt
¼ teaspoon baking soda
1 cup buttermilk
2 teaspoons vanilla

Separate egg yolks from whites. Beat egg whites until stiff and set aside. Cream shortening and sugar. Add egg yolks and mix. Sift flour, salt and soda. Add alternately with buttermilk and vanilla. Fold in egg whites. Bake in greased tube pan for 1 hour and 10 minutes in a 350 degree oven.

Odell Cross

Orange Cake

1 cup shortening
2 cups sugar
1½ cups buttermilk
1 teaspoon baking soda
2 tablespoons grated orange rind

4 cups flour
4 eggs
1 package dates
1 cup nuts

Sauce:
1 cup orange juice
2 cups sugar

2 tablespoons orange rind

To make cake, cream shortening and sugar. Add baking soda to buttermilk and set aside. Add eggs to cream mixture. Next add flour and buttermilk alternately to cream mixture. Add orange rind, dates and nuts. Bake in greased tube pan for 1 hour in a 350 degree oven.

Sauce: Combine orange juice, sugar and orange rind and cook until thick syrup. When cake is done, pour sauce over cake and keep it in pan until cooled. Remove.

Odell Cross

Died-and-Went-to-Heaven Chocolate Cake

1¾ cups all-purpose flour
1 cup white sugar
¾ cup unsweetened Dutch-process cocoa powder
1½ teaspoons baking soda
1½ teaspoons baking powder
1 teaspoon salt

1¼ cups buttermilk
1 cup packed light brown sugar
2 large eggs, lightly beaten
¼ cup canola oil
2 teaspoons vanilla extract
1 cup hot strong black coffee

Icing:
1 cup confectioners' sugar
½ teaspoon vanilla extract

1 or 2 tablespoons buttermilk or low fat milk

Preheat oven to 350 degrees. Lightly coat a 12 cup Bundt pan with non-stick cooking spray. Dust pan with flour - shake out excess. In a large mixing bowl, whisk together flour, white sugar, cocoa, baking soda, baking powder and salt. Add buttermilk, brown sugar, eggs, oil and vanilla; beat with an electric mixer on medium speed for 2 minutes. Whisk in hot coffee until completely incorporated. (The batter will be quite thin) Pour the batter into prepared pan. Bake for 35 to 40 minutes or until cake tester inserted in center comes out clean. Cool the cake in pan for 10 minutes; remove from pan and let cool completely.

Icing: In a small bowl, whisk together confectioners' sugar, vanilla and enough buttermilk or low fat milk to make a thick but pourable icing. Set cake on serving plate and drizzle icing over top. Serves 16.

This cake has only 4 grams of fat per serving with icing and is so good, we eat it without the icing!! Also, instead of dusting pan with flour, I use cocoa - it makes a prettier cake.

Ruth Kirk Soloff

Two egg whites can be substituted for each whole egg in many baking recipes.

CAKES

Coconut Pound Cake

1 cup butter
½ cup shortening
2½ cups sugar
5 eggs
3 cups flour

½ teaspoon baking powder
1 cup cream of coconut
   (Coco-Lopez)
1 teaspoon grated lemon rind
1 teaspoon vanilla

Cream butter and shortening, gradually adding sugar, beating until light and fluffy. Add eggs, beating well after each addition. Combine flour and baking powder. Add to creamed mixture, alternating with cream of coconut, beginning and ending with flour mixture. Stir in lemon rind and vanilla. Pour batter into a greased and floured 10 inch tube pan. Bake at 350 degrees for 1 hour and 15 minutes or until wooden toothpick inserted comes out clean. Cool in pan for 10 to 15 minutes. Remove from pan and cool on rack.

This is a great morning or afternoon treat with coffee or tea. A perfect dessert by itself or it can be "dressed" with fruit and whipped cream or spread with jam. Super moist.

Elly (Memaw) Wells

Cowboy Coffee Cake

2½ cups flour
2 cups brown sugar

1 teaspoon salt
⅔ cup margarine

Combine and mix until crumbly; reserve ½ cup.

2 teaspoons baking powder
½ teaspoon baking soda

½ teaspoon cinnamon
½ teaspoon nutmeg

Add to crumbly mixture and mix thoroughly.

1 cup buttermilk

2 eggs, well beaten

Add to batter and mix well. Pour into greased and floured 9 x 13 x 2 inch cake pan. Sprinkle with remaining crumbly mixture. Bake 25 to 30 minutes in a 375 degree oven.

Great anytime, especially delicious during the Christmas holidays.

Betsy Payne

Angel Food Cake

1½ cups egg whites (11 to 12 eggs)
1 teaspoon cream of tartar
½ teaspoon salt

1¼ cups cake flour
1¾ cups sugar
1 teaspoon vanilla extract
¼ teaspoon almond extract

Frosting:
⅓ cup soft butter
a pinch of salt
3 cups sifted Imperial 10X powdered sugar

¼ cup milk or cream
1½ teaspoons vanilla extract

Cake: Beat egg whites until frothy, add cream of tartar and continue beating until whites will peak, but not dry. Add flavoring. Sift flour. Measure and sift together with sugar and salt 9 times. Fold in dry ingredients as rapidly as possible. Pour into ungreased tube pan and bake at 325 degrees for one hour or until cake shrinks from side of pan. Remove from oven, turn upside down and allow to cool. Cut from pan and frost.

Frosting: Cream butter, salt and 1 cup powdered sugar until light and fluffy. Add remaining sugar and milk alternately, blending until smooth and of spreading consistency. Add vanilla.

Note: My Grandmother, Elsie Bogs Rolmuto, always topped this cake with a "nest" of green coconut and jelly beans as a special treat on Easter Sunday.

Cindy Caulking Bouse

Birthday Cake

9 egg whites
1 cup butter
3 cups sugar
2 teaspoons vanilla

4 cups flour
1½ cups milk
1 heaping teaspoon baking powder

Filling:
1 can crushed pineapple
1 tablespoon flour
3 egg yolks

Juice of ½ lemon
1½ cups sugar
lump of butter

Cake: Cream butter and sugar until fluffy. Sift flour and then measure. Sift 3 more times. On last sift, add baking powder. Add to butter and sugar; alternately with milk and vanilla. Beat egg whites until stiff and fold into batter. Bake at 325 degrees in 3 greased and floured cake pans.

Filling: Mix pineapple, flour, egg yolks, lemon juice, sugar and butter together and cook in double boiler until thick. Let cool.

Shirlee Nicholson

CAKES

1-2-3-4 Cake

1 cup butter
2 cups sugar
3 cups flour *
4 eggs

Secret to success ingredients: (what any fool should know)
3 teaspoons baking powder
1 cup milk
2 teaspoons flavoring (vanilla, lemon, almond, etc.)

* This recipe pre-dates already sifted flour. You will have to sift or stir the flour to fluff it before measuring.

Cream butter and sugar with electric mixer for 8 minutes. Mix baking powder with flour. Add eggs to butter/cream mixture one at a time, alternating with flour. Add flavoring. Mixture will resemble whipped cream. Pour into well greased cake pans. This makes three 9 inch layers or one large pound cake. Bake at 350 degrees until fingerprints are not left when pressed lightly in the center. Cool in the pan 5 minutes, then turn out to completely cool. Frost as desired.

This recipe has been in my family for five generations now. My grandmother used it with sliced bananas between the layers. Chocolate icing was my mother's favorite. I made a five tier wedding cake for my daughter with it. My grandsons like it plain, hot from the oven. It was always called 1-2-3-4 cake, but was never written down. I only knew the 1-2-3-4 part when I first married. I tried it twice, but 1-2-3-4 does not make cake. When I asked my mother what was wrong, her answer was "any fool knows..." and gave me the balance of the recipe. My grandsons call this "1-2-3-4 and what any fool knows."

Georgie McIrvin

Gooey Butter Cake

1 box yellow cake mix
1 stick margarine, melted
2 eggs
1 box powdered sugar (reserve ¾ cup for top)
2 eggs
1 (8 ounce) package cream cheese, softened

Beat together eggs with cake mix and margarine. Spread mixture into a well greased 9 x 13 inch pan. Mix together sugar, eggs and cream cheese until smooth. Spread mixture on top of dough. Sprinkle sugar on top. Preheat oven to 350 degrees. Bake cake for 40 minutes. Cake will puff up and then go down almost flat when cool. It's really good!

Mary Uhle

CAKES

Chocolate Cake

½ cup real butter
2½ cups sugar
3 egg yolks
1 cup chopped nuts
4 squares melted chocolate
1½ cups milk

2 teaspoons vanilla
2 cups cake flour
2 teaspoons baking powder
¼ teaspoon salt
3 egg whites, beaten stiff

Icing:
½ cup real butter
½ cup coffee cream
2 squares melted chocolate

1 teaspoon vanilla
1 box powdered sugar

Cake: Cream butter and sugar. Add egg yolks and melted chocolate. Sift dry ingredients and add alternately with milk. Last, add egg whites, nuts and vanilla. Bake in 3 cake pans at 350 degrees for 30 minutes.

Icing: Melt butter and chocolate in cream. Add powdered sugar to thicken, about 1 box. Add vanilla, and beat until glossy.

Denise Gunn

Better Than Sex Cake

1 cup flour
1 cup chopped pecans
1 stick of margarine
1 cup sugar
1 container Cool Whip (large)

1 large package cream cheese
2 boxes instant chocolate
  pudding
2 cups milk

Mix flour, pecans and margarine. Press in 9 x 13 inch pan. Bake for 20 minutes at 350 degrees. Let crust cool. Mix sugar, Cool Whip and the cream cheese and spread this on the crust. Mix 2 boxes of instant chocolate pudding with 2 cups of milk, spread pudding on top. (Do not mix this ahead of time!) Top off with left over Cool Whip. Refrigerate until needed. Enjoy!!!!

Rita Michalak

Why egg whites are folded into batters with care: When egg whites are beaten, air is trapped in them. These air bubbles expand when they are heated in the oven and help make the baked product light. It is important to fold the beaten egg whites gently into the batter to retain as much of the air as possible.

CAKES

Oatmeal Cake

1¼ cups boiling water
1 cup quick cooking oatmeal
1 stick margarine
1 cup sugar
2 eggs

1⅓ cups flour
1 cup brown sugar
1 teaspoon soda
½ teaspoon cinnamon

Frosting:
1 stick margarine
1 teaspoon vanilla
¼ cup canned milk

1 cup coconut
½ cup sugar
1 cup chopped pecans

Cake: Pour 1¼ cups boiling water over 1 cup quick cooking oatmeal and 1 stick of margarine. Let stand 20 minutes. Add sugar, eggs, flour, brown sugar, baking soda and cinnamon to oatmeal mixture, stir by hand. Bake in greased and floured 9 x 13 x 2 inch cake pan 35 minutes in a 350 degree oven. While cake is baking, combine: margarine, vanilla, canned milk, coconut, sugar and pecans. Stir and spread on cake and broil until brown.

Betsy Payne

Sock-It-to-Me Cake

1 box butter cake mix
½ cup sugar
4 eggs
½ cup Wesson oil

1 cup (8 ounces) sour cream
3 tablespoons brown sugar
2 teaspoons cinnamon
½ cup finely chopped pecans

Icing:
1 cup powdered sugar
2 teaspoons canned milk

1 teaspoon vanilla

Cake: Cream oil, sugar and cake mix. Add 1 egg at a time, add sour cream and mix, set a side. Mix together brown sugar, cinnamon and nuts, set aside. In a greased and floured Bundt pan pour ½ of the cake mixture. With a spoon tunnel out a space in the mixture to sprinkle cinnamon mixture, then add the other ½ of the cake mixture. Bake 60 to 65 minutes at 325 degrees.

Icing: Mix powdered sugar, canned milk and vanilla together and dribble over cool cake.

Diann Meriwether

CAKES

Light Amaretto Delight Cake

1 (18.5 ounce) package white cake mix (pudding included)
1 (3.4 ounce) package instant pistachio pudding and pie filling mix

1 cup frozen fat free egg product, thawed
1 cup unsweetened applesauce
⅔ cup orange juice
¼ cup amaretto
¼ cup vodka

Glaze:
1 cup sugar
⅓ cup orange juice
3 tablespoons amaretto

½ teaspoon butter flavoring (Butter Buds)
¼ cup non fat vanilla yogurt

Cake: Heat oven to 350 degrees. Spray 12 cup Bundt pan with non-stick cooking spray and coat with flour. In large bowl, combine all cake ingredients. Beat at low speed until moistened, beat 2 minutes at high speed. Pour into prepared pan. Bake at 350 degrees for 45 to 55 minutes or until toothpick in center comes out clean.

Glaze: In medium non-stick saucepan, combine sugar, orange juice and amaretto. Mix. Bring to boil. Reduce heat to medium, boil 1 minute stirring constantly. Remove from heat. Blend in butter buds and yogurt using wire whisk. Using long tined fork, pierce hot cake about 20 times. Slowly pour hot glaze over cake and let stand in pan 30 minutes. Loosen edges and invert on plate. Cool. Wrap and store in refrigerator. Yields 12 to 16 servings.

Henrietta Hall

7-Up Pound Cake

2 sticks (1 cup) margarine
½ cup vegetable shortening
3 cups sugar
5 eggs
3 cups flour

1 can 7-Up
1 teaspoon lemon extract
1 teaspoon vanilla
1 teaspoon butter flavoring

Preheat oven to 325 degrees. Ingredients should all be at room temperature. Cream margarine and shortening with sugar. Add eggs, one at a time, beating well after each. Add flour alternately with 7-Up and flavorings. Bake in greased tube pan at 325 degrees for at least 1 hour.

Zucchini Chocolate Nut Cake

3 ounces unsweetened chocolate (melted and cooled)
3 cups flour
1½ teaspoons baking powder
1 teaspoon baking soda
1 teaspoon salt
4 eggs
3 cups sugar
1½ cups oil (1 cup is enough)
3 cups zucchini
1 cup chopped nuts

Melt chocolate and cool. Sift flour, baking soda, baking powder and salt. Set aside. In large bowl, beat eggs until thick and light. Gradually add sugar a little bit at a time. Add oil and chocolate. Blend well. Add dry ingredients, add zucchini and nuts. Bake in 10 inch tube pan 1 hour and 15 minutes in a 350 degree oven.

Marilyn Robinson

Red Velvet Cake

½ cup Crisco shortening
1½ cups sugar
2 eggs
2 ounces red food coloring
2 ounces water
1 cup buttermilk
2 tablespoons cocoa
2½ cups flour
1 teaspoon salt
1 teaspoon baking soda
1 tablespoon vinegar
1 teaspoon vanilla

Icing:
6 tablespoons flour
1½ cups milk
1½ cups real butter (3 sticks)
1½ cups sugar
1½ teaspoons vanilla

Cake: Cream shortening, sugar and vanilla. Make a paste of cocoa, food coloring and water. Add to first mixture. Add sifted flour and salt to mixture along with buttermilk. Add one egg at a time and beat after each. Add vinegar to soda and fold in mixture. Bake in 2 9-inch pans for 30 minutes at 350 degrees.

Icing: Mix flour and milk and cook until thick, stirring constantly. Cool. Cream butter, sugar and vanilla until fluffy. Add to first mixture and beat until fluffy. Layers of cake may be split in half making a four layer cake.

Bet you can't eat just one slice. Never fail recipe and easy to prepare.

Wanda Wise

Dirt Cake

1 large package Oreo cookies, crushed
1 cup (8 ounces) cream cheese
¼ cup butter
1½ cups (12 ounces) Cool Whip
2¾ cups milk
1 large package vanilla pudding
¾ cup powdered sugar

Cream butter, cream cheese and sugar. Mix pudding and milk. Combine with cream cheese mixture. Fold in Cool Whip. Use clean flower pot with an 8 inch diameter top. Plug hole at bottom with top from Cool Whip. Layer ⅓ amount of crushed Oreo cookies, then ½ cream mixture, ⅓ Oreo cookies, other ½ of cream mixture and final layer of Oreo cookies. Refrigerate overnight.

This is a great recipe when you want to forget the fat and calories and enjoy the chocolate. You can fool someone to believing it is a real flower. Buy a artificial flower from a store and put in cake. I did that to my sister-in-law, and she thought I brought her an Easter Lily Plant.

Joy Caka

Date Nut Cake

1 (8 ounce) package cream cheese
1 cup margarine
1½ cups sugar
1½ teaspoons vanilla
3 eggs
2 cups flour (1¾ cups; then ¼ cup)
1½ teaspoons baking powder
1 cup chopped dates
1 cup chopped pecans

Preheat oven to 325 degrees. Combine cream cheese, margarine, sugar and vanilla. Add eggs, beating well. Add 1¾ cups flour and the baking powder. Toss remaining ¼ cup flour with chopped dates to coat them. Add nuts to mixture and stir well. Grease and flour 10 cup Bundt pan. Spoon batter into pan. Bake 50 to 55 minutes until pick inserted into center comes out clean and top is slightly browned. Remove from pan after it is cool. Can be made into 2 loaves instead of Bundt. Freezes well. Can use raisins instead of dates if preferred.

Elaine DeSouza

CAKES

Dannon Apple Spice Cake

2¾ cups unsifted all-purpose flour
2¼ cups sugar
2½ teaspoons baking soda
1¼ teaspoons baking powder
1 teaspoon cinnamon
½ teaspoon allspice
1 teaspoon salt
¼ teaspoon cloves
1¾ cups applesauce
1¼ cups Dannon plain nonfat yogurt
½ cup cholesterol-free egg substitute
⅓ cup vegetable oil
1 cup raisins

Glaze:
1½ cups Dannon plain nonfat yogurt
3 tablespoons light brown sugar, packed
1 teaspoon vanilla extract

In a large bowl, thoroughly combine flour, sugar, baking soda, baking powder, cinnamon, allspice, salt and cloves. Add applesauce, yogurt, egg substitute and oil; blend well using spoon. Stir in raisins. Pour into greased and floured 12 cup Bundt or 13 x 9 inch pan. Bake at 325 degrees for 50 to 60 minutes or until toothpick inserted in middle comes out clean. Cool 15 minutes. Loosen cake from sides of pan with knife. Invert onto plate. Cover loosely with foil or wax paper. Cool completely. Slice and serve with Quick Yogurt Glaze.

In small bowl, combine Dannon plain nonfat yogurt, light brown sugar and vanilla extract. Beat with fork or wire whisk until smooth.

Annette Carr

Chocolate Angel Food Cake

¾ cup sugar
¾ cup cake flour
4 tablespoons cocoa

Sift flour, sugar and cocoa together 4 times. Set aside.

1½ cups egg whites (12 eggs)
1½ teaspoons cream of tartar
¼ teaspoon salt
1½ teaspoons vanilla
¾ cup sugar

Beat egg whites, cream of tartar, vanilla and salt enough to hold up in soft peaks and is glassy. Add remaining ¾ cup sugar to whites, 2 tablespoons at a time, beating after each addition. Sift about ¼ of flour mixture over whites. Fold in remaining flour by fourths. Bake in ungreased tube pan at 375 degrees for 40 minutes. Invert pan and cool.

Paulene Harp

Hummingbird Cake

3 cups all-purpose flour
1 teaspoon baking soda
½ teaspoon salt
2 cups sugar
1 teaspoon cinnamon
3 eggs, beaten
¾ cup vegetable oil

1½ teaspoons vanilla extract
1 (8 ounce) can crushed
   pineapple, undrained
1 cup pecans
1¾ cups bananas, mashed
½ cup chopped pecans

Frosting:
½ cup butter or margarine,
   softened
1 (8 ounce) package cream
   cheese, softened

1 (16 ounce) package
   powdered sugar, sifted
1 teaspoon vanilla extract
½ cup pecans

Cake: Combine first 5 ingredients in a large bowl; add eggs and oil, stirring until dry ingredients are moistened. Do not beat. Stir in vanilla, pineapple, 1 cup pecans and bananas. Pour batter into 3 greased and floured 9 inch round cake pans. Bake at 350 degrees for 23 to 28 minutes or until a wooden pick inserted in center comes out clean. Cool in pans 10 minutes and remove from pans. Let cool completely on wire racks.

Frosting: Cream butter and cream cheese. Gradually add powdered sugar. Beat until light and fluffy. Stir in vanilla. Stir ½ cup pecans into cream cheese frosting. Spread frosting between layers and on top and sides of cake. Yields enough for 1 3-layer cake.

Diana Plasse

Rum Cake

1 package Duncan Hines
   Butter Recipe Golden cake
   mix
1 small package jello instant
   vanilla pudding

½ cup Crisco oil
½ cup water
½ cup rum
4 eggs

Mix and bake in greased and floured Bundt pan for 50 to 60 minutes at 325 degrees.

Sauce:
1 cup sugar
1 stick butter

¼ cup water
¼ cup rum

Boil all ingredients for 3 minutes and pour over baked cake (right from the oven) while it is still in the pan. Let set in the pan for 30 minutes before removing.

Lucille (Max) Ankner

COOKIES

Fudge No-Bake Cookies

2 cups sugar
½ cup cocoa
1 stick margarine
½ cup milk
1 teaspoon vanilla
½ cup peanut butter
1 cup coconut
3 cups quick cooking
   oatmeal, uncooked
½ cup pecans or walnuts

Combine sugar, cocoa, margarine, and milk in a large saucepan. Bring to a boil. Stir in the remaining 5 ingredients and remove from heat. Drop by teaspoonfuls on wax paper and allow to cook until firm. Yields 4 dozen cookies.

Kathy Lopez

The Great Oatmeal Bar

1 cup Crisco shortening
1 cup white sugar
1 cup brown sugar
1 teaspoon vanilla
1½ cups flour
1 teaspoon baking soda
1 teaspoon salt
3 cups oatmeal
Raisins and pecans, optional

Frosting:
5 tablespoons margarine
1½ cups powdered sugar
1 teaspoon vanilla
1-2 tablespoons milk

In a large bowl, mix shortening, sugar, vanilla, flour, baking soda, salt and oatmeal until well blended. Spread mixture into a 12 x 18 x 1 inch jellyroll pan. Bake at 350 degrees for 20 to 30 minutes.

Frosting: Melt margarine, add powdered sugar, vanilla and enough milk to spread. Frost as soon as taken out of oven. Cut in bars.

Eileen Boren

Candy-making is affected by the weather. In a moist, hot climate, it will not harden, however, if you must make candy, cook 2 degrees higher than normal.

Non Fat Oatmeal Cookies

1 cup flour
1 cup oatmeal
½ cup sugar
½ teaspoon salt
½ teaspoon baking powder
½ teaspoon baking soda

1 teaspoon cinnamon
2 egg whites
⅓ cup Karo syrup, light
1 teaspoon vanilla
1 cup raisins

Combine dry ingredients. Add remainder and mix. Spray cookie sheet with Pam. Drop by teaspoon. Cook at 375 degrees for 10 minutes or less. Makes approximately 2 dozen.

Annette Carr

Snickerdoodles

1 cup soft shortening
1½ cups sugar
2 eggs
2¾ cups flour

2 teaspoons cream of tartar
1 teaspoon baking soda
½ teaspoon salt
Cinnamon and sugar mixture

Cream together shortening, sugar and eggs. Sift together flour, cream of tartar, baking soda and salt. Combine both mixtures. Press mixture into a bowl with a lid and chill in refrigerator over night. Remove from refrigerator; spoon a small piece and roll into small balls in palm of your hand. Roll "balls" in a mixture of cinnamon and sugar. Place on ungreased cookie sheet and bake at 350 degrees. Remove before bottoms turn brown. Cool. They will be soft and chewy and melt in your mouth! Makes about 5 dozen.

Handed down from my Aunt Maureen from Scotland. They have always been my favorite cookie. My Aunt died of a brain tumor the year I was diagnosed. She was a dear, brave woman who loved her family. During my treatment, when I needed a lift, this "comfort food" always hit the spot. I'd feel better, think of my Aunt and smile.

Kelly Jo Myers-Madoian

COOKIES

Florence's Toffee-Chocolate Squares

Graham crackers
1 cup dark brown sugar
1½ cups chopped toasted almonds (or 1 cup ground pecans)

1 (11¾ ounce) package milk chocolate chips
1 cup butter

Line a pan (at least 10 x 15 inches in size) with foil on bottom and sides. Line this with separated rectangular graham crackers (not crumbs) placed side by side. Simmer together for three minutes the sugar and butter. Pour mixture quickly over crackers and bake in preheated 400 degrees oven five minutes. Remove from oven. Sprinkle chocolate chips over all, spreading to cover as they melt. Sprinkle almonds or pecans over top. Cool and cut into squares. Makes about 75 squares.

Helen L. Kainer

Cocoa Waffle Cookies

½ cup margarine or butter
¾ cup white sugar
2 eggs
1 teaspoon vanilla
2 tablespoons milk

6 tablespoons cocoa
½ teaspoon cinnamon
1 teaspoon baking powder
1¼ cups flour
Chocolate icing (optional)

Cream margarine or butter and sugar until light and fluffy. Add eggs and vanilla and beat. Add other ingredients and beat together real well. Bake on a hot waffle iron. Drop one small teaspoon of batter for each cookie on oiled waffle iron for one minute. Ice cookies with chocolate icing and put a nut half on top if desired.

Note: These cookies are made for special occasions such as Christmas and bake sales.

Mrs. Virginia Sattler

Fruit Cake Cookies

1½ cups dates, cut up
¼ pound candied red cherries, cut up
¼ pound candied green cherries, cut up
2 slices yellow candied pineapple
3 cups chopped nuts
1 cup flour
1 cup sugar
3 egg whites
1 teaspoon vanilla
¼ teaspoon salt

Mix by hand the cut up fruit and nuts. Mix flour and sugar with fruit and nuts. Beat egg whites real stiff, add salt and vanilla. Pour over fruit mixture. Blend lightly. Drop by teaspoons on greased cookie sheet. Bake at 350 degrees for 15 minutes or until brown.

Ruby McAbee

Ginger Cookies

1⅓ cups oil
2 cups sugar
2 eggs
½ cup molasses
4 cups flour
2 teaspoons ginger
2 teaspoons cinnamon
1 teaspoon salt
4 teaspoons baking soda
Powdered sugar for dipping

Mix oil and sugar thoroughly. Add eggs and beat well. Stir in molasses. Sift dry ingredients together, add and mix. Drop by teaspoonful into powdered sugar and form into balls coated with sugar. Place balls on ungreased cookie sheet 3 inches apart. Bake 12 to 15 minutes at 350 degrees.

Shirlee Nicholson

COOKIES

Pecan Cookies

½ cup margarine
1 cup brown sugar, packed
1 egg, unbeaten
1 teaspoon vanilla
1 cup flour
1 cup chopped pecans

Cream margarine and brown sugar; add egg, vanilla, flour and pecans mixing well between each ingredient. Spread in shallow pan; bake until brown at 325 degrees. Be sure not to cook too long or cookies will be hard. When done, cut into squares.

Diann Meriwether

Oatmeal Cookies

¾ cup shortening, soft
1 cup brown sugar
½ cup sugar
1 egg
¼ cup water
1 teaspoon vanilla
1 cup flour
1 teaspoon salt
½ teaspoon baking soda
3 cups oatmeal
½ cup pecans or raisins
  (optional)

Mix and beat first six ingredients, then add flour, salt, baking soda and oatmeal. Bake on greased cookie sheet at 350 degrees for 10 to 12 minutes.

Diann Meriwether

Coconut Bon-Bons

2 pounds powdered sugar
¼ pound butter, softened
1 can Eagle Brand condensed milk
2 cups chopped pecans

2 cups coconut
12 ounces chocolate chips
4 ounces paraffin or almond bark

Combine powdered sugar, butter, condensed milk, pecans and coconut and mix well. Chill 1 hour. Roll into small balls. In a double boiler, melt slowly chocolate chips and paraffin or almond bark. Dip balls in chocolate mixture and place on wax paper.

Maxwell Miller Suarez

"Forgotten Cookies" or Chocolate Chip Kisser

2 egg whites
⅔ cup sugar
1 teaspoon vanilla
pinch of salt

1 cup broken pecans
1 (6 ounce) package chocolate chips

Preheat oven to 350 - 400 degrees. Beat egg whites until stiff. Blend in sugar and add vanilla and salt. Fold in pecans and the chocolate chips. Drop on shiny side of foil on cookie sheet. Turn oven off. Place cookies in oven until cooled.

Diann Meriwether

'Almost' Fat-Free Brownies

½ cup cake flour
½ cup unsweetened cocoa powder
¼ teaspoon salt
2 egg whites
1 large egg
¾ cup granulated sugar
6 tablespoons unsweetened applesauce
2 tablespoons vegetable oil
1½ teaspoons vanilla extract
1 tablespoon chopped walnuts (optional)

Preheat oven to 350 degrees. Spray an 8-inch square pan with non-stick vegetable coating. In a mixing bowl, combine flour, cocoa and salt. Mix well. Set aside. In a large bowl, whisk together egg whites, egg, sugar, applesauce, oil and vanilla. Blend in flour mixture; do not overmix. Pour batter into prepared pan; sprinkle with walnuts. Bake until a toothpick inserted in center comes out clean, about 25 minutes. Cool for at least 15 minutes before cutting.

Note: I'm usually disappointed with low-fat variations of recipes, but this one is surprisingly good. A plus is that it only takes 10 minutes to make.

Gretchen Nakayama

Instant Candy Cookies

1 stick margarine
1 cup sugar
½ cup milk
¼ cup cocoa
1 teaspoon vanilla
¼ teaspoon salt
½ cup peanut butter
3 cups quick cooking oatmeal
½ cup chopped pecans

Combine butter, sugar, milk and cocoa and heat to boiling. Cook 1 minute. Mix remaining ingredients together. Pour boiling mixture over remaining ingredients and mix quickly. Drop by teaspoons on waxed paper and let stand about 20 minutes. Makes 4-5 dozen.

Diann Meriwether

COOKIES

Cocoons

1½ sticks butter
5 tablespoons sugar
1 teaspoon vanilla
2 cups sifted flour
1 tablespoon water
1 cup nuts
powdered sugar

Cream butter and sugar. Add flour and gradually beat in vanilla, water and nuts. Shape into small crescents. Bake at 350 degrees for 15-20 minutes. Cool and roll in powdered sugar.

Diann Meriwether

Miz' Jeanette's Cocoons

2 sticks margarine or butter
4 heaping tablespoons
  powdered sugar
2 heaping cups of flour
1 tablespoon vanilla
3 cups of chopped pecans

Preheat oven 300 degrees. Put margarine and powdered sugar (one tablespoon at a time), in mixer and cream; Add 1 heaping cup of flour and the vanilla then the other heaping cup of flour. Gradually, add chopped pecans (will be thick). Roll pieces of stiff batter between palms of hands to the size of a small finger - break into pieces 1½ to 2 inches to form cocoon pieces. Put close together (touching) on cookie sheet. Bake for 25-30 minutes; makes 50-60. These should be barely tan when baked. Let cool to lukewarm then sprinkle with powdered sugar. Separate while warm with spatula. These are rich, not sweet and keep well. They go well with sherbet, ice cream and orange ambrosia.

"Pete" Davie

COOKIES

Top-of-the-Range-Cookies

2 packages butterscotch morsels
1 can chow mein noodles
1 cup chopped nuts

Melt candy in double broiler; remove from heat. Fold in noodles and nuts. Mix well. Drop on greased paper.

Diann Meriwether

Nut Coconut Bars

1 cup flour plus 2 tablespoons flour
½ cup butter
1½ cups brown sugar
¾ teaspoon baking powder
2 eggs (beaten)
1 can coconut
1 cup pecans
1 teaspoon vanilla
pinch of salt
¾ cup powdered sugar
1-3 tablespoon lemon juice

Mix 1 cup flour, butter, ½ cup brown sugar and ½ teaspoon baking powder. Spread and pat this in bottom of greased 9 x 13-inch pan. Bake 12 minutes at 325 degrees while blending 1 cup brown sugar, 2 tablespoons of flour, eggs, coconut, pecans, vanilla, ¼ teaspoon baking powder and the pinch of salt. When bottom layer is done, pour egg mixture over it and bake another 25 minutes at 325 degrees. Finally, mix powdered sugar with lemon juice and pour this over baked bars. Cool.

Odell Cross

Hawaiian Kisses (Cookies)

½ teaspoon salt
½ teaspoon baking powder
½ cup flour
1 cup and 2 tablespoons brown sugar
⅔ cup oatmeal
2½ cups grated coconut
½ teaspoon vanilla

Sift together salt, baking powder and flour. Mix with brown sugar. Add oatmeal, coconut, vanilla and blend. Drop by teaspoon onto a greased baking sheet and bake at 400 degrees for 10 - 15 minutes or until lightly browned. Makes 36 cookies.

Leiola Onishi

Coconut Macaroons

2 egg whites
Dash of salt
½ teaspoon vanilla
⅔ cup sugar
1 (3½ ounce) can or 1⅓ cups flaked coconut

Beat egg whites with dash of salt and vanilla until soft peaks form. Gradually add sugar, beating until stiff. Fold in coconut. Drop by rounded teaspoons onto a greased cookie sheet. Bake at 325 degrees about 20 minutes. Makes about 1½ dozen.

Cathy Dean

COOKIES

Starlight Sugar Crisps (Sour Cream Twists)

Dough:
1 package dry yeast
¼ cup lukewarm water
3¾ cups sifted flour (I use self-rising)
1½ teaspoons salt (omit if you use self-rising flour)

1 cup butter
2 eggs (beaten)
½ cup sour cream
1 teaspoon vanilla

Vanilla Sugar:
1½ cups sugar
2 teaspoons vanilla

Dissolve 1 package dry yeast in ¼ cup very warm (not hot) water. Sift together flour and salt if you are not using self-rising flour. Otherwise, just sift the flour. Cut in butter until particles are the size of small peas. Blend in the beaten eggs, sour cream, 1 teaspoon vanilla and the softened yeast. Mix thoroughly. Cover; chill at least 2 hours.

Vanilla Sugar: Mix vanilla sugar by combining 1½ cups sugar with 2 teaspoons vanilla.

To make the cookies: Roll out ½ of the chilled dough on a pastry cloth or board that has been sprinkled with about ½ cup of the vanilla sugar. Roll dough to a size of 16 x 8 inch rectangle. Sprinkle vanilla sugar over the rectangle. Fold one end over and sprinkle with sugar. (This makes three layers). Turn ¼ way around and repeat rolling, sprinkling and folding (9 times). Sprinkle board and dough with additional vanilla sugar as needed. Roll out dough to a 16 x 8 inch rectangle (approximately ¼ inch thick). Cut into 4 x 1 inch strips. Twist each strip 2 or 3 times. Place on ungreased baking sheets. Repeat entire rolling, sprinkling and folding process with remaining dough. Bake in moderate oven (375 degrees) 15 to 20 minutes until golden brown. Remove from pan immediately.

This recipe is a favorite of my daughters who like for me to make it at Christmas time.

Louise M. Mitchell

Grandma's Molasses Cookies

¾ cup shortening
1 cup white sugar
1 egg, beaten
½ cup molasses
½ teaspoon salt
1 teaspoon cinnamon

2 teaspoons baking soda
½ teaspoon cloves
½ teaspoon ginger
2¼ cups flour
Sugar

Cream shortening, sugar and egg. Add the molasses and spices, then add flour. Refrigerate overnight. Make into walnut size balls and roll in sugar, do not flatten. Bake at 325 degrees for about 15 minutes. Makes 3½ dozen.

The grandma in this recipe is my mother, but from the moment she became grandmother, her name changed. These cookies have won many contests for my mother, but the real test is that these are a favorite of friends and family alike. The name used to be Mother's Molasses Cookies.

Yvonne E. Constantino

German Chocolate Dream Bars

½ cup margarine
1 package German chocolate cake mix
2 eggs
1 cup brown sugar, packed
1 cup chopped pecans

1 teaspoon vanilla
2 tablespoons flour
1 teaspoon baking powder
½ teaspoon salt
1 cup flaked coconut

Cut butter into dry cake mix until crumbly. Press evenly in greased and floured 15½ x 10½ x 1-inch jellyroll pan. Bake at 350 degrees for 10 to 12 minutes or until light brown. Beat eggs; stir in remaining ingredients. Spread over baked layer. Bake 12-15 minutes or until topping is golden brown. Run knife around edges to loosen sides. Cool. Cut into bars. Makes about 30 bars.

Diann Meriwether

COOKIES

Rum Balls

2¼ cups vanilla wafer crumbs
1 cup finely chopped pecans
½ cup rum or bourbon
1 cup powdered sugar
3 tablespoons cocoa

2 tablespoons white corn syrup
Finely ground nuts or powdered sugar

Combine crumbs and pecans. Place remaining ingredients in bowl and beat. Pour over dry mixture and blend. Roll into balls about 1 inch in diameter and roll each ball in either finely ground nuts or powdered sugar. Makes 40-60 balls. If balls seem too dry to hold together when rolled in hand, add a bit more corn syrup.

Cathy Dean

Walnut Balls

½ pound margarine
¼ cup sugar
2 cups flour

1 teaspoon vanilla
1 cup walnuts, ground
powdered sugar

Cream lightly margarine and sugar. Add and mix with hands flour, vanilla and the ground walnuts. Chill in refrigerator. Roll into balls and bake on greased cookie sheet (grease only once) at 350 degrees for about 15 minutes. After they are cool, roll in powdered sugar.

Wanda Szot

COOKIES

Chocolate Dipped Chocolate Chip Cookies

4½ cups all-purpose flour
2 teaspoons baking soda
2 teaspoons salt
2 cups butter
1½ cups sugar
1½ cups firmly packed brown sugar
2 teaspoons vanilla
4 eggs
2 cups semi-sweet chocolate morsels
1 cup chopped pecans
1 pound package chocolate almond bark

Preheat oven to 375 degrees. In small bowl, combine flour, baking soda and salt. Set aside. In large mixer bowl, beat butter, sugar, brown sugar and vanilla until creamy. Beat in eggs. Gradually add flour mixture. Stir in semi-sweet chocolate morsels and pecans. Drop by rounded tablespoons onto ungreased cookie sheet. Bake 9-11 minutes. Makes about 2½ - 3 dozen cookies depending on how large you make them. Melt chocolate almond bark in double-boiler. After cookies have cooled, dip them about half way in chocolate and let set. Then enjoy. These cookies are to die for.

Ann Bragg

Texas Ranger Cookies

1 cup shortening
1 cup white sugar
1 cup brown sugar
2 eggs
2 cups corn flakes
2 cups oatmeal (quick or regular, uncooked)
2 cups sifted flour
2 teaspoons soda
1 teaspoon salt
1 teaspoon vanilla

Cream together the shortening and sugars. Add unbeaten eggs and blend. Stir in corn flakes and oats. Gradually add dry ingredients, which have been sifted together, flour, salt and soda. Add vanilla, drop by teaspoonful on lightly greased cookie sheet. Bake at 375 degrees for 8 to 10 minutes or until lightly browned. Makes 6 dozen cookies.

Dorothy Schuchardt

Cranberry Crunch Pie

1 baked 9-inch pie shell
1 (8 ounce) package cream cheese
⅓ cup packed brown sugar
2 tablespoons cornstarch

Walnut Streusel:
⅓ cup flour
½ cup chopped walnuts
3 tablespoons brown sugar

⅛ teaspoon salt
1 (1 pound) can whole cranberry sauce
2 cups (2 large) peeled and chopped tart apples

¼ teaspoon cinnamon
¼ cup chilled butter or margarine

Prepare pie shell. Set aside. In small bowl, beat cheese until soft and creamy and spread in pie shell. Stir together brown sugar, cornstarch and salt. Add cranberry sauce and apple and blend thoroughly. Spoon cranberry mixture on top of cream cheese, spread evenly. To make the streusel, blend flour, walnuts, brown sugar, cinnamon and butter. Rub mixture with fingers to form large crumbs. Sprinkle this mixture on top of cranberry mixture. Bake at 375 degrees for 45 minutes until streusel is golden brown. Cool, then refrigerate and serve chilled. Serves 6-8.

Barbara Nelson

Pecan Crunch Pie

4 ounces egg whites
4 ounces granulated sugar

3 ounces chopped pecans
3 ounces saltine crackers, crushed

Place egg whites and sugar in mixing bowl and beat on high speed for 15 minutes. Fold in pecans and crackers, combining well. Pour into greased pie pan and bake at 350 degrees for 20 to 30 minutes. Let cool and top with whipped cream. Serves 8.

Elizabeth Henson

Favorite Pecan Pie

1 (9 inch) unbaked pie shell
1 cup sugar
1 teaspoon vanilla
1 cup chopped pecans
1 cup dark Karo syrup
3 eggs, slightly beaten

Mix all ingredients together, adding pecans last. Pour into prepared, unbaked 9 inch pie shell. Bake at 350 degrees for 50 to 60 minutes.

Diann Meriwether

Tiny Pecan Tarts

1 (3 ounce) package cream cheese
Filling:
1 egg
1 teaspoon vanilla
¾ cup brown sugar
½ cup butter
1 cup sifted all-purpose flour

⅔ cup coarsely chopped pecans
1 tablespoon melted butter

Combine cream cheese and butter; blend in flour and mix well. Chill about 1 hour. Shape into balls about 1 inch in diameter and press into small-sized, ungreased muffin tins. For the filling, beat egg with wooden spoon; add brown sugar, melted butter and vanilla. Mix well and stir in pecans. Pour carefully into each shell and bake at 350 degrees for 25 minutes. Cool before removing from pan. Makes about 20 tarts.

Diann Meriwether

My Favorite Apple Pie

¼ cup light brown sugar, packed
¼ cup granulated sugar
1 tablespoon flour
1 teaspoon grated lemon peel
¼ teaspoon ground cinnamon
¼ teaspoon ground nutmeg

6 medium baking apples (tart), peeled, cored and thinly sliced
1 cup raisins
1 unbaked, ready made 9 inch pie crust

Glaze: (optional)
1 large egg, beaten
1 teaspoon granulated sugar

Preheat oven to 425 degrees. Spray a 9 inch deep dish pie plate with nonstick vegetable spray. In a large bowl, combine brown sugar, granulated sugar, flour, lemon peel, cinnamon and nutmeg. Mix well. Add apples to sugar mixture, stir until coated; add raisins. Spoon into greased pie plate and place pie crust on top of filling. Trim edges to fit plate. With a sharp knife, cut steam vents in pie crust. To glaze, lightly brush pie crust with beaten egg and sprinkle with sugar. Bake for 35 to 40 minutes until pie crust is golden brown. Cool on a wire rack for 30 minutes and serve warm.

Gretchen Nakayama

Multi-Fruit Pie

2 "Ready Crust" graham cracker 8 inch crust pie shells
1 large can crushed pineapple
1 can tart pitted cherries, drained

1½ tablespoons flour
¾ cup granulated sugar
4 bananas, sliced
1 cup chopped pecans
1 small package of strawberry Jell-O

Combine pineapple, cherries, flour and sugar in a saucepan. Cook over medium heat until thick. Remove from heat; add dry Jell-O and nuts. Cool slightly before adding sliced bananas. Fill the 2 pie shells and refrigerate, allowing to jell. Serve with whipped topping or ice cream.

Note: From a dear friend, Phyllis Pettijohn.

Anci Waugh

Pineapple Sour Cream Pie

¾ cup sugar
¼ cup flour
½ teaspoon salt
1 (#2) can crushed pineapple
1 cup sour cream
1 tablespoon lemon juice

2 slightly beaten egg yolks
1 baked pie shell
2 egg whites
¼ teaspoon cream of tartar
½ teaspoon vanilla

In a heavy saucepan, combine ¾ cup sugar, ¼ cup flour and ½ teaspoon salt. Stir in next 3 ingredients. Stirring constantly, cook until mixture thickens and comes to a boil. Cook 2 minutes and remove from heat. Pour ½ of mixture into a bowl with 2 egg yolks while stirring. Return this to mixture in saucepan, stirring constantly over heat for 2 minutes more. Cool to room temperature. For the meringue, beat 2 egg whites, cream of tartar, and vanilla till stiff. Pour filling in pie shell, cover with meringue and bake at 350 degrees for 12 to 15 minutes.

Odell Cross

Fresh Strawberry Pie

3 tablespoons cornstarch
1 cup sugar
1 cup cold water
2 tablespoons corn syrup

2 tablespoons strawberry Jell-O
1 baked pie shell
1½ pints fresh strawberries
3 drops red food coloring

Cook cornstarch, sugar, water, and corn syrup for 5 to 6 minutes or until thick. Add 2 tablespoons strawberry Jell-O and 3 drops red food coloring. Wash and cut in half the fresh strawberries and place in pie shell. Pour mixture over the berries and chill. Serve plain or with whipped cream.

Yvonne E. Constantino

To prevent juices in pies from cooking out into the oven, place a 4 inch stick of uncooked macaroni upright in the center of the pie.

Frozen Peanut Butter Pie

4 ounces cream cheese, room temperature
1 cup powdered sugar
½ cup of peanut butter
½ cup milk
8 ounces Cool Whip
¼ cup chopped nuts
1 graham cracker pie crust

Mix all ingredients except chopped nuts and pour into pie crust. Sprinkle nuts over top and freeze.

Jane Alexander

Chocolate Pie

⅓ cup sifted flour
1 cup sugar
¼ teaspoon salt
2 (1 ounce) squares unsweetened chocolate
2 cups milk - scalded
3 egg yolks, lightly beaten
2 tablespoons butter
½ teaspoon vanilla
1 baked 9-inch pastry pie shell
3 stiffly beaten egg whites
6 tablespoons sugar

Preheat oven to 350 degrees. Mix flour, sugar and salt in a small mixing bowl and set aside. Melt chocolate squares in scalded milk. Add flour and sugar, mix gradually. Cook over moderate heat, stirring constantly until mixture thickens and boils. Cook 2 minutes and remove from heat. Gradually add egg yolks and cook 1 minute, stirring constantly. Add butter and vanilla and let cool slightly. Pour into baked pastry pie shell and set aside to cool. For the meringue, in a large mixing bowl, beat egg whites at high speed until thick and fluffy. Slowly add sugar and continue beating at high speed for about 15 to 30 seconds. Cover pie with meringue and bake at 350 degrees for 12 to 15 minutes. Let cool and serve.

Betty Orand

In many recipes, cocoa powder can be substituted for chocolate squares to reduce fat.

No Bake Pumpkin Pie

1 (9 inch) graham cracker crust
6 ounces cream cheese, softened
2 tablespoons milk
2 tablespoons sugar
2 cups Cool Whip
1 teaspoon cinnamon
½ teaspoon ginger
½ teaspoon nutmeg
1 cup cold milk
2 packages instant vanilla pudding
1 (16 ounce) can pumpkin

In a large bowl, mix cream cheese, 2 tablespoons milk and sugar until smooth. Using a spatula, gently stir in Cool Whip. Spread mixture over bottom of pie crust. For second layer, in a large bowl, pour 1 cup milk, add pudding mix and whisk until well blended, about 1 to 2 minutes. Mixture will be thick. Stir in pumpkin and spices and whisk, mixing well. Spread over cream cheese layer. Refrigerate at least 3 hours. Garnish with Cool Whip and nuts, if desired.

Bette Bruber

Luscious Lemon Pie

1 cup sugar
3 tablespoons cornstarch
1 tablespoon grated lemon peel
¼ cup margarine
¼ cup lemon juice
1 cup milk
3 egg yolks, slightly beaten
1 cup sour cream
1 baked 9 inch pastry shell
Whipped cream

Combine first 7 ingredients in heavy saucepan. Cook over medium heat until smooth and thickened, stirring constantly. Cover and cool. Fold sour cream into cooled filling and pour into pastry shell. Chill 2 hours before serving. Top with whipped cream if desired.

Diann Meriwether

PIES

Meringue Pie Crust

3 egg whites
½ teaspoon baking powder
1 cup sugar

10 saltine crackers, crushed
½ cup chopped pecans

Beat egg whites with baking powder until thick. Fold in sugar, crackers, and pecans. Bake at 400 degrees for 30 minutes.

Denise Gunn

Never Fail Pie Crust

1½ cups flour
¼ teaspoon salt
¼ cup milk

1 teaspoon sugar
½ cup oil

Mix all ingredients in pie plate and shape into crust. If doubling recipe for two crusts only use ¾ cup of oil.

Helen L. Kainer

About pie pans: A glass pie pan is ideal for baking pies because it absorbs the heat and browns the pastry attractively. Aluminum pie pans can be used, but shiny pans give pies a soggy bottom crust.

When using dark pans or glass — lower oven temperature by 25 degrees.

Extraordinary Extras

EXTRAORDINARY EXTRAS

Wine

1 gallon crushed berries, such as boysenberries or strawberries
½ gallon water
2 pounds sugar

Combine berries and water in a crockery jar. Let stand for 24 hours. Strain and add sugar. Return to jar and let stand 2 days. Strain again, return to jar and let stand for 2 months. Strain again and bottle. During process, keep covered with thick cheesecloth.

Note: This is a 1935 recipe from my father, Walter LeBlanc. In those days, Cajuns made their own wine and shared it with their neighbors (they still do).

Janice LeBlanc

Kahlúa

2 cups water
½ cup instant coffee
4 cups sugar
⅕ vodka
1 vanilla bean

Boil water, add instant coffee and sugar and dissolve completely. Cool completely and add vodka. Pour in a large jar with a tight fitting lid. Cut vanilla bean in thirds and add to jar. Close and let set 30 days or longer.

Janice LeBlanc

Amaretto Liqueur

½ gallon vodka
2 ounces almond extract
1 bottle (⅕) Apricot Cordial
4 cups water
6 cups sugar
48-50 drops caramel coloring

Boil water and sugar until clear. Cool. Add rest of ingredients. Use caramel drops at end to adjust color. Makes 1 gallon & ⅕.

Note: I use Chefmaster Liquid Paste Instant food color - 3127 brown.

Lucille (Max) Ankner

Ola Mae's Wassail

1 gallon apple cider
1 liter bottle Sprite
6 whole cloves
3 to 4 sticks cinnamon,
 2 inches long
1 fresh orange, thinly sliced
1 package of red hots
 cinnamon candy

In a large coffee maker, add the apple cider and Sprite. Place all other ingredients in the top part and percolate.

Ola Mae Davis

Sparkling Pear-Apple Cider

3½ cups reserved poaching
 liquid from Poached Pear
 Gratin, chilled
2½ cups sparkling water,
 chilled
Fresh raspberries (optional)

Combine first 2 ingredients. Stir well and serve over ice. Garnish with raspberries, if desired. Yield: 1½ quarts.

Note: Poached Pear Gratin - see page 162.

Annette Carr

Fruity Punch Delight

1 bottle concentrated
 Delaware Punch
1 small can frozen
 concentrated orange juice
Ginger Ale, to taste

Fix punch according to directions. Add orange juice concentrate (do not dilute) to punch. Add ginger ale to taste.

Nancy Hughes

EXTRAORDINARY EXTRAS

Holiday Punch

46 ounces pineapple juice
6 ounces frozen orange juice
6 ounces frozen lemonade
6 cups water

1 cup sugar
5 ripe, mashed bananas
2 liters 7-Up or Sprite

Using a large container, mix all ingredients except 7-Up. At party time, put in punch bowl, add 7-Up and serve.

Mary Jane Morgan

Soft Pretzels

1 package dry yeast
4 cups flour
¾ teaspoon salt
1½ teaspoons sugar

1½ cups warm water
1 egg, beaten
Coarse ground salt

Preheat oven to 400 degrees. Dissolve yeast in warm water in large bowl. Add salt and sugar. Mix in flour, kneading to make soft, smooth dough. Do not let rise. Cut immediately into smaller pieces. Roll into ropes and shape for pretzels. Place on cookie sheet covered with foil and dusted with flour. Brush pretzels with egg and sprinkle with salt. Bake 15 minutes or until light brown. Makes about 3 dozen.

Note: This was a favorite recipe for my Girl Scout Troop many years ago.

Ginny O'Connor

Sugar and Spice Pecans

¾ cup sugar
1 egg white
2½ tablespoons water
1 teaspoon ground cinnamon
½ teaspoon salt

¼ teaspoon ground allspice
¼ teaspoon ground cloves
¼ teaspoon ground nutmeg
8 cups pecans halves

Combine first 8 ingredients in a large bowl; mix well. Add pecans; stir until evenly coated.

Spread pecans in a greased 15 x 10 x 1-inch jellyroll pan. Bake at 275 degrees for 50 to 55 minutes. Remove to waxed paper while still warm; cool. Store in airtight container. Yield: 9 cups.

Lucille (Max) Ankner

Yorkshire Pudding

2 eggs
1 cup milk
1 cup sifted flour
½ teaspoon salt
¼ cup beef drippings or melted suet

Preheat oven to 450 degrees. Beat eggs with milk. Sift together flour and salt. Stir flour mixture into egg mixture. Beat batter until well blended (smooth - like eggnog). Discard most of fat from pan in which beef was roasted. Heat 11 x 7 inch baking pan and pour in ¼ cup beef drippings. Make sure it's very hot - just short of smoking. Quickly and evenly pour in pudding mixture and close oven door quickly. Bake at 450 degrees for 10 minutes. Reduce oven temperature to 350 degrees and bake 15 to 20 minutes longer or until puffy and delicately brown. Don't keep opening oven door. Cut into squares and serve immediately with roast beef and gravy. Makes approximately 10 to 12 squares.

I most often use a pot roast with potatoes and carrots and onions baked around it. This makes a wonderfully flavored gravy. When I do this, I melt down enough beef suet to equal ¼ cup. I have used margarine in a pinch.

Note: My grandmother from England taught my mother this traditional recipe. When my mother died, I became the only remaining family member to carry on and now I'm teaching my daughter and daughter-in-law. Everybody loves it.

Dorothy Boyle

Nancy's Sweet and Sour Pickles

1 gallon jar of sour pickles
1 (4 pound) bag of sugar
1 small bottle of Tabasco sauce

Drain and throw away juice from pickles. Cut pickles into thick slice chunks. Layer pickles, sugar and Tabasco in original jar. (You have to really force it to get all into the jar.) Seal. Turn pickles every day for 14 days. It will make its own juice. After day 14, pour pickles and juice into smaller containers. They make great gifts for the holidays!

Nancy Hughes

EXTRAORDINARY EXTRAS

Dora's Mother's Waffles

1 cup flour
2 teaspoons Rumford baking powder

1 cup milk
1 egg, beaten lightly
1 tablespoon cooking oil

Combine dry ingredients in bowl. Add rest of ingredients and mix well. Thin with additional milk if needed so it will pour easily. Pour ½ batter onto a preheated non-stick waffle iron, or an iron that has been well seasoned. Cook to desired brownness. When the waffle is done, remove it to a wire rack if it is not to be eaten immediately. Waffles may be reheated in a toaster and can also be frozen.

Note: Waffles can be made with skim milk, egg substitute, and reduced amount of oil. A variation can be made by adding a teaspoon of sugar and small pieces of banana and nuts or add ⅓ cup blueberries. The secret to success of these waffles is the use of Rumford baking powder.

Jo Nogee

A "Home" Made Recipe

Half a cup of friendship

and a cup of thoughtfulness

Creamed with a pinch of tenderness,

Very lightly beaten.

In a great big bowl of loyalty,

Add a cup of faith and hope

And one of charity.

Be sure to add a spoonful each of gaiety and songs,

And also the ability

to laugh at little things.

Moisten with the tears

Of heart-felt sympathy.

Bake in a good natured pan

And serve repeatedly.

Cathy Dean

Squash Pickles

5 pounds yellow and green squash
2 large green bell peppers
2 large onions, white or yellow
1 medium jar of pimentos
¾ cup salt
3⅓ cups white vinegar
2 to 3 cups sugar, depending on your taste
3 teaspoons celery seed
1½ teaspoons mustard seed
1½ teaspoons dill seed

Slice squash, peppers, onions, and pimentos and let stand 1 hour in salt. Rinse in cold water to remove all salt. Combine with remaining ingredients in large pot and bring to a boil. Remove from heat and let cool a few minutes. Seal in sterilized canning jars while hot. Let set in jars about a month before eating. Best when served cold.

Adelene G. Engelbrecht

Spiced Pear Preserves

1⅓ cups sugar
⅓ cup water
2 to 3 cups white vinegar
1¼ sticks cinnamon
12 whole cloves
6 large pears

Boil all ingredients except pears for 20 minutes. Add pears that have been carefully pared and cored. Cook until tender or transparent. Test by piercing with a fork. Seal in canning jars with 1 stick of cinnamon and pierce each peak with 2 cloves.

Note: You can leave the stem on the pears. You can also tint red or green if desired. The extra syrup can be reused. Wonderful on hot biscuits.

Adelene G. Engelbrecht

Tarnish will not harm silver.

EXTRAORDINARY EXTRAS

Apple Butter Recipe

1 gallon apples, peeled, cored, and cut up
1 cup plus 3 tablespoons vinegar
3½ cups brown sugar

In a heavy pot or Dutch oven, combine all ingredients and simmer over low heat until boiled down to about ½ gallon. Use a vegetable oil spray on the pot to help keep the apple butter from sticking. Stir frequently with a wooden spoon to keep the apple butter from sticking and burning. Place in hot sterilized jars and seal.

Note: This is a 1915 recipe from my mother.

Mabel E. Lucas

Cranberry Relish

1 pound fresh cranberries, cleaned and rinsed
1 cup orange marmalade
1 cup sugar
½ cup chopped pecans
1 tablespoon lemon juice

Spread cranberries in a 9 x 13 inch baking dish. Sprinkle sugar over berries, cover with foil and bake at 350 degrees for 35 minutes. Add marmalade, lemon juice, and nuts to cover cranberry mixture and stir well. Cover with foil and bake for an additional 10 minutes. Cool and store in the refrigerator. Makes about 20 servings and keeps in refrigerator well for a week.

Note: A colorful and delicious accompaniment to poultry or game. Don't save this just for the holidays.

Betty Behan

Cranberry Jelly Sauce

1 bag cranberries
3 cups water
2½ cups sugar

Mix berries and water and cook at medium-high temperature until berries are soft and popped, about 15-20 minutes. Mash berries through strainer, discarding hulls. Heat strained berries to a boil and add sugar. Cook until mixture forms a soft ball in cold water on a saucer. Pour mixture into small casserole dish. Cranberry sauce will have a jelly consistency. May be bubbly on top layer. Cooking time takes practice and weather may upset consistency. Cranberries can be frozen until needed.

Debbie Collard

Recipe for the Perfect Honeymoon

Lettuce alone

Carolyn Thompson

Glazed Apples

6 Washington state apples
2 cups water
1 teaspoon butter or margarine
1 cup sugar
½ teaspoon vinegar

Peel and quarter apples. In heavy skillet mix sugar, water and vinegar, add apples and cook slowly over low heat for 1 hour. Turn once. When finished, very little liquid is left and apples will be beautifully glazed. Great with roast pork.

Diana Plasse

Coat the inside of votive candle container on bottom and sides with petroleum jelly for easy removal of candle after burning.

EXTRAORDINARY EXTRAS

Banana Pancakes

¾ cup whole wheat flour
½ cup flour
2 teaspoons baking powder
1 tablespoon sugar
pinch of salt
1¼ cup skim milk
1 tablespoon canola oil
1 cup chopped banana

Combine dry ingredients in bowl. Add milk and oil. Stir until combined. Add banana. Batter will be lumpy. Cook pancakes in a pan coated with no-stick cooking spray. Serve with "light" syrup. Makes 12 pancakes.

Faye Foreman

Cold Grand Marnier Soufflé

1 envelope unflavored gelatin
¼ cup cold water
4 egg yolks
1 cup sugar, divided
¼ cup orange juice
¼ cup Grand Marnier
½ teaspoon salt
1 tablespoon grated orange rind (grating of 1 orange)
6 egg whites
½ pint heavy cream, whipped

Sprinkle gelatin over cold water to soften. In the top of double boiler, mix egg yolks, ½ cup sugar, orange juice, Grand Marnier, and salt. Cook the mixture over simmering water, stirring constantly, until slightly thickened. Remove from heat and stir in the gelatin mixture and grated orange ring. Stir until the gelatin is completely dissolved and let it cool

Beat the egg whites until they hold a soft shape, and gradually beat in ½ cup sugar until the egg whites hold definite peaks. Fold the egg whites and whipped cream gently but thoroughly into the custard mixture. Spoon the soufflé mixture into a prepared dish, and chill until it is firm. Serves 6 to 8. May also be spooned into individual servings such as champagne glasses.

To prepare soufflé dish: Rub it with soft butter and sprinkle with sugar.

Ethel Ankner

Lentil Sauce

1 tablespoon olive oil
1 onion, chopped
1 large garlic clove, mashed
1 teaspoon chopped basil
½ pound tomatoes, peeled and chopped, or 1 (8 ounce) can, drained
½ cup dried lentils
1 tablespoon tomato paste
1¼ cups dry red wine
1¼ cups vegetable stock or water
Sea salt and pepper to taste
Cheese to taste

Heat oil in a medium saucepan and sauté onion for 10 minutes, or until softened and lightly browned. Add garlic, basil, tomatoes, lentils, tomato paste, wine, and stock. Bring to a boil and cover pan. Turn down heat and simmer gently for 45 minutes. Stir occasionally until lentils are tender and reduce to a thick puree. Season to taste and serve over pasta with cheese. Yields 6 servings.

Note: Quick and easy - fits into a busy schedule.

Susan Rafte

Applesauce-Cinnamon Christmas Ornaments

1 cup applesauce
1 cup cinnamon

Mix the two ingredients well and roll out to ¼ inch thick. Cut into different shapes with cookie cutters such as stars, angels, trees and punch a hole in the top of each with a straw or toothpick. Bake in a 200 degree oven for 1½ hours. Thread ribbon through the holes and hang where everyone can smell them. Yields 15 ornaments.

Deby Koudelik

Elephant Stew

1 elephant
1 bushel potatoes
1 bushel carrots
1 bushel onions
10 gallons brown gravy
Seasoning to taste
12 rabbits

Cut elephant into little pieces. This takes approximately 3 months. Add enough gravy to cover. Cook at 450 degrees over an open fire until tender, about 4 weeks. Serves 4,242 - if more are expected, add the rabbits. Add rabbits only if necessary, as most people do not like hare in their stew.

Shirley Murphy

EXTRAORDINARY EXTRAS

French Soap

Soap can be made from any grease such as deer fat, beef suet, lard, bear fat, etc. For this example, we will describe making soap using lard as grease.

Take 10 pounds of lard. If you desire to perfume the lard with flowers, spread the lard about 1 inch thick on wooden boards. Place the boards in a building or shelter outside. Take the blossoms of any strong smelling flowers and stick them into the lard as close together as possible. Do not cover them with lard, just pat them well into the lard. Leave the flower blossoms in the lard for 24 hours, then remove. The lard will have extracted most of the perfume of the flowers. Repeat if you desire a stronger perfume odor.

This is the same method used to make perfume in France. In making perfume, the lard is then distilled to extract the perfume.

If you desire a pine odor to your soap, boil pine needles slightly in soft water and use the water in place of regular soft water as described later.

Take the 10 pounds of lard and place it in a kettle with 2 quarts of soft water or 2 quarts of pine water. Bring to a boil, then remove the kettle and set it aside to cool for 10 to 12 hours over overnight. Any dirt or meat particles will settle out and sink to the bottom of the kettle.

Now take:
4 tablespoons sugar   **6 tablespoons powdered Borax**
2 tablespoons salt   **½ cup ammonia**

Mix these ingredients well in 1 cup of soft water or pine water.

Go outdoors and mix 2 quarts of COLD soft water or pine water into 2 cans of Lewis Lye, in a granite dishpan. **If you use HOT WATER, THE LYE WILL FUME UP AND EXPLODE, CAUSING BURNS AND POSSIBLE BLINDNESS.** The lye will cause the cold water to become hot. Leave the lye and water mixture to cool down to lukewarm. Now take the sugar, salt, borax, and ammonia mixture and pour it into the cool lye and water mixture. Then add the cool lard. Stir well with a wooden paddle. Stir until honey colored. Cut the soap into squares before it becomes completely hard. If you desire the soap in other shapes, place a piece of soap in two-piece wooden or metal molds and squeeze to desired shape.

This soap is very good for face, hand, and body soap as well as for washing dishes and clothes. It floats like Ivory soap.

Note: This recipe came down in my mother's family in southern Louisiana. The early French fur traders and trappers were the best soap makers. They also brought with them the art of extracting perfume to scent the soap.

Shirlee Nicholson

SPECIAL GUIDES

Mass Weight

1 ounce (oz)	=	28	grams (g)
1 pound (lb)	=	450	grams (g)
1 gram (g)	=	.035	ounces (oz)
1 kilogram (kg) or 1000 g	=	2.2	pounds (lbs)

Liquid Volume

1 fluid ounce (fl oz)	=	30	milliliters (ml)
1 fluid cup (c)	=	240	milliliters (ml)
1 pint (pt)	=	470	milliliters (ml)
1 quart (qt)	=	950	milliliters (ml)
1 gallon (gal)	=	3.8	liters (l)
1 teaspoon (tsp)	=	5	milliliters (ml)
1 tablespoon (tbsp)	=	15	milliliters (ml)
1 milliliter (ml)	=	.03	fluid ounces (fl oz)
1 liter (l) or 1000 ml	=	2.1	fluid pints or 1.06 fluid quarts
1 liter (l)	=	.26	gallons (gal)

Common Kitchen Pans

4 cup baking dish:
- 9-inch pie plate
- 8 x 1½-inch layer cake pan
- 7⅜ x 3⅝ x 2¼-inch loaf pan

6 cup baking dish:
- 8 or 9 x 1½-inch layer cake pan
- 10-inch pie plate
- 8½ x 3⅝ x 2⅝-inch loaf pan

8 cup baking dish:
- 8 x 8 x 2-inch square pan
- 11 x 7 x 1½-inch baking pan
- 9 x 5 x 3-inch loaf pan

10 cup baking dish:
- 9 x 9 x 2-inch square pan
- 11¾ x 7½ x 1¾-inch baking pan

12 cup baking dish:
- 13½ x 8½ x 2-inch glass baking pan

15 cup baking dish:
- 13 x 9 x 2-inch metal baking pan

19 cup baking dish:
- 14 x 10½ x 2½-inch roasting pan

SPECIAL GUIDES

Contents of Cans

Size	Avg. Contents
6 oz.	¾ cup
8 oz.	1 cup
No. 1 (picnic)	1¼ cups
12 oz. (vacuum can)	1½ cups
No. 300	1¾ cups
No. 1 tall	2 cups
No. 303	2 cups
No. 2	2½ cups
No. 2½	3½ cups
No. 3	4 cups
No. 5	7 cups
No. 10	12 to 13 cups or 1 gallon

Oven Temperature Chart

Slow — 250° to 325° F.
Moderate — 325° to 400° F.
Hot — 400° to 450° F.
Very hot — 450° F. and above

Equivalent Measures

Dash - less than ⅛ teaspoon
Pinch - approximately ⅙ teaspoon
3 teaspoons - 1 tablespoon
2 tablespoons - ⅛ cup or 1 oz.
4 tablespoons - ¼ cup
5 tablespoons and 1 teaspoon - ⅓ cup
8 tablespoons - ½ cup
12 tablespoons - ¾ cup
16 tablespoons - 1 cup
2 cups - 1 lb. granulated sugar
2 cups - 1 pint
4 cups - 1 quart
2 pints - 1 quart
4 quarts - 1 gallon
8 quarts - 1 peck
4 pecks - 1 bushel
4 ounces - ¼ pound
8 ounces - ½ pound
16 ounces - 1 pound

SPECIAL GUIDES

Equivalent Amounts

almonds	⅘ lb. shelled	1 cup chopped
apples	1 lb.	3 cups sliced
apricots	1 lb.	6 cups cooked
beans, dried	½ lb.	1 cup
butter	1 lb	2 cups
cheese	4 oz.	1 cup
cheese, American	½ lb.	2 cups grated
cheese, cream	3 oz.	6 tbsp.
chocolate	1 oz.	1 square
chocolate morsels	6 oz.	1 cup
crumbs, graham	14 squares	1 cup
crumbs, saltines	28 squares	1 cup
crumbs, bread	2 slices	1 cup
egg whites	8 to 10	1 cup
egg yolks	14 to 16	1 cup
flour	1 oz.	4 tbsp.
flour, all purpose	1 lb.	4 cups sifted
flour, cake	1 lb.	4½ cups sifted
flour, whole wheat	1 lb	3½ cups
lemon juice	1 medium	3 tbsp.
lemon rind	1 medium	1 tbsp. grated
marshmallows	¼ lb.	16
meal	1 lb.	3 cups
meat	1 lb.	2 cups diced
nuts	¼ lb.	1 cup
orange juice	1 medium	⅓ cup juice
orange rind	1 medium	2 tbsp.
pecans	1 lb.	4 cups
potatoes, white	1 lb.	3 medium large
raisins	1 lb.	3 cups
rice	1 lb.	2½ cups raw and 3½-4 cups cooked
spaghetti	7 oz.	4 cups approx.
sugar, brown	1 lb.	2½ cups
sugar, confectioners'	1 lb.	2½ cups
sugar, granulated	1 lb.	2 cups
tomatoes	1 lb	3 medium
walnuts, black	5½ lbs. unshelled	4 cups

SPECIAL GUIDES

Substitutes

If the recipe calls for:	Substitute:
1 teaspoon baking powder	¼ teaspoon baking soda plus ½ teaspoon cream of tartar
1 cup barbecue sauce	1 cup ketchup plus 2 teaspoons Worcestershire
brown sugar	3 parts white sugar to 1 part molasses
1 cup (2 sticks) butter	1 cup margarine OR ⅞ cup vegetable oil or vegetable shortening
1 cup buttermilk	1 cup plain yogurt OR 1 tablespoon vinegar (or lemon juice) plus enough milk to equal 1 cup (let stand 5 minutes) OR 1¾ teaspoons cream of tartar plus one cup of milk
1 ounce chocolate (semisweet)	½ ounce unsweetened chocolate plus 1 tablespoon sugar
1 ounce chocolate (unsweetened)	3 tablespoons unsweetened cocoa plus 1 tablespoon butter or margarine
1 tablespoon cornstarch	2 tablespoons flour OR 2 teaspoons arrowroot (as thickener)
1 cup corn syrup	1¼ cups white OR packed brown sugar plus ¼ cup liquid
1 cup cream (light/20%)	3 tablespoons butter plus enough whole milk to equal 1 cup
1 cup cream (sour)	1 cup plain yogurt OR ¾ cup sour milk, buttermilk, or plain yogurt plus ⅓ cup butter OR 1 tablespoon lemon juice plus enough evaporated milk to equal 1 cup
1 cup cream (whipping)	¾ cup whole milk plus ¼ to ⅓ cup butter
1 cup flour (sifted, all-purpose)	1 cup minus 2 tablespoons unsifted all-purpose flour
1 cup flour (sifted, cake flour)	1 cup minus 2 tablespoons sifted all-purpose flour

SPECIAL GUIDES

Substitutes, *continued*

If the recipe calls for:	Substitute:
1 cup flour (sifted, self-rising)	1 cup sifted all-purpose flour plus 1½ teaspoons baking powder and ⅛ teaspoon salt
1 clove garlic	⅛ teaspoon garlic powder
1 tablespoon ginger root, fresh	⅛ teaspoon ground ginger
1 cup half and half	1½ tablespoons butter plus enough whole milk to equal 1 cup
1 tablespoon herbs, fresh	1 teaspoon, dried
1 cup honey	1¼ cups sugar plus ¼ cup liquid
1 teaspoon Italian herb seasoning	½ teaspoon dried oregano plus ¼ teaspoon each, dried basil and thyme
1 tablespoon lemon juice	1 tablespoon white vinegar
1 cup milk, skimmed	⅓ cup nonfat dry milk powder plus water to equal 1 cup
1 cup milk, whole	½ cup evaporated milk plus ½ cup water
1 teaspoon mustard, prepared	1 teaspoon powdered mustard plus 1 teaspoon water
2½ teaspoons pumpkin pie spice	1½ teaspoons ground cinnamon plus ½ teaspoon each ground nutmeg and ginger plus a dash of cloves
1 tablespoon sherry, dry	1 tablespoon dry vermouth
Sweetened condensed milk	1 cup plus 1 tablespoon powdered milk plus ½ cup warm water plus ⅓ cup sugar (mix powdered milk and warm water), then dissolve sugar in that first mixture.
3 cups tomato juice	1½ cups tomato sauce plus 1½ cups water OR 1 (6 ounce) can tomato paste plus 3 cans water, a dash of both salt and sugar
1 teaspoon vinegar	2 teaspoons lemon juice
1 cup yogurt	1 cup buttermilk

Note: Substitutions are based on how ingredients interact in the recipe.

SPECIAL GUIDES

Healthy Ingredient Substitutions

Recipe calls for:	Use:
Whole or 2% milk	Skim milk, 1% milk or evaporated skimmed milk diluted equally with water
Whipping cream	Chilled evaporated skimmed milk, whipped
Cheddar, American, Swiss and Monterey Jack cheese	Cheeses with 5 grams of fat or less per ounce
Mozzarella cheese	Part-skim mozzarella cheese
Cream cheese	Light cream cheese products, or Neufchâtel cheese
Creamed cottage cheese	Nonfat or 1% fat cottage cheese or farmer's cheese
Ricotta cheese	Nonfat, lite or part-skim ricotta cheese
Sour cream	Nonfat or low-fat sour cream, or nonfat or low-fat yogurt
Whole egg	2 egg whites or ¼ cup egg substitute
Baking chocolate, 1-ounce square	3 tablespoons cocoa plus 1 tablespoon mono-unsaturated or poly-unsaturated vegetable oil or margarine
Fudge sauce	Chocolate syrup
White flour, 1 cup	½ cup whole wheat flour plus ½ cup white flour, or ⅔ cup white flour plus ⅓ cup oat bran
Sugar	Reduce amount by ⅓ to ½, substitute brown sugar or honey when flavor will not be affected
Salt	Reduce by ½ or eliminate - except in bread recipes

SPECIAL GUIDES

Healthy Ingredient Substitutions,
continued

Recipe calls for:	Use:
Margarine	Reduce amount using a margarine made from mono-unsaturated or poly-unsaturated oil or use reduced-calorie margarine
Vegetable oil	Reduce amount using a mono-unsaturated or poly-unsaturated oil
Mayonnaise	Fat-free reduced-calorie, or low-cholesterol mayonnaise
Gravy	Gravy made with bouillon granules or broth and thickened with flour or cornstarch
Condensed cream of mushroom soup	99% fat-free condensed cream of mushroom soup
Egg noodles	Noodles made without egg yolks
White rice	Brown or wild rice
Pecans, walnuts	Reduce by ⅓ to ½
Beef, pork, veal or lamb	Lean cuts of red meat trimmed of all visible fat, or substitute with chicken or turkey
Ground beef	Ground turkey or lean ground round
Bacon strips	Turkey bacon or Canadian bacon
Poultry	Skinned poultry
Self-basting turkey	Baste turkey with fat-free chicken broth
Tuna packed in oil	Tuna packed in spring water

SPECIAL GUIDES

Cooking Terms

BASTE — to moisten roasting meat or other food, while baking, with juices from the pan or with additional juice.

BLANCH — to pour boiling water over a food, then drain and rinse with cold water. Used to whiten or remove skins from almonds, or to prepare vegetables for freezing.

BRAISE — to cook meat or vegetables by simmering in a covered dish in a small amount of liquid, either in an oven or over direct heat.

CARAMELIZE — to heat sugar in a skillet until melted and brown, or to heat foods containing sugar until light brown and of caramel flavor.

FRICASSÉE — to stew meats, poultry, etc., in a stock or sauce.

GLAZE — to coat with a thin sugar syrup.

MARINATE — to soak in French dressing, vinegar, lemon juice, sour cream or other dressing; usually before cooking.

PARBOIL — to boil food until partially cooked.

RENDER — to free fat from connecting tissue by heating slowly until fat melts and can be drained off.

SAUTÉ — to cook in a small amount of fat, turning often.

SCALD — to heat liquid to a temperature just below the boiling point. To immerse food in boiling liquid for a short time.

SCALLOP — to bake food in an oven-proof dish in layers with sauce and crumbs.

SCORE — to make light cuts or gashes in surface of a food — usually meat.

SEAR — to brown the surface of the meat by the application of intense heat usually in a hot pan or oven.

SHRED — to cut into very thin slices or strips.

SIMMER — to cook in liquid just below boiling point.

SPECIAL GUIDES

Cooking Terms, *continued*

SLIVER — to cut or shred into lengths.

STEEP — to cover with boiling liquid, cover and let stand.

STOCK — liquid in which food has been cooked.

TRUSS — to tie a fowl or other meat so that it will hold its shape during cooking process.

TEXAS PINK RIBBON INNS

TEXAS PINK RIBBON BED AND BREAKFAST INNS

**The Highlander
Georgie McIrvin's
Pink Ribbon Charter Inn**
607 Highland Ave.
Houston, TX 77009
(800) 807-6110
(713) 861-6110

Bussey's Something Special B&B
202 Hereford/P.O. Box 1425
Glen Rose, TX 76043
(817) 897-4843

Casa De Leona B&B
P. O. Box 1829
Uvalde, TX 78802
(210) 278-8550

Country Lake B&B
Route 2, Box 94B
Royce City, TX 75189
(214) 636-2600

The Guilded Thistle
1805 Broadway
Galveston, TX 77550
(800) 654-9380
(409) 763-0194

Heathers Glen B&B
200 East Phillips
Conroe, TX 77301
(409) 441-6611

Indian Mountain Ranch
Rt. 1, Box 162A
Hico, TX 76457
(817) 796-4060

Ledbetter B&B
P.O. Box 212
Ledbetter, TX 78946
(409) 249-3066

TEXAS PINK RIBBON BED AND BREAKFAST INNS

The Little House
110 North Sanders
Nacogdoches, TX 75961
(409) 564-2735

The Lovett Inn
501 Lovett Blvd.
Houston, TX 77006
(713) 522-5224

Madame Dyers' B&B
1720 Post Office St.
Galveston, TX 77550
(409) 765-5692

Maison-Bayou: A Creole Plantation
300 Rue Bayou
Jefferson, TX 75657
(903) 665-7600

The Meerscheidt Haus
458 N. Monroe
LaGrange, TX 78945
(409) 968-9569

Page House B&B
1000 Leander House
Georgetown, TX 78628
(512) 863-8979

The Patrician Inn
1200 Southmore Blvd.
Houston, TX 77004-5826
(800) 553-5797
(713) 523-1114

The Pelican House
1302 First Street
Seabrook, TX 77586
(713) 474-5295

Rancho Cama B&B
2595 Flite Acres Rd.
Wimberly, TX 78676-9707
(512) 847-2596
(800) 594-4501

TEXAS PINK RIBBON BED AND BREAKFAST INNS

Robin's Nest B&B
4104 Greeley
Houston, TX 77006
(713) 528-5821

Roses and The River
7074 County Rd. 506
Brazoria, TX 77422
(409) 798-1070

Sara's Bed & Breakfast Inn
941 Heights Blvd.
Houston, TX 77008
(713) 868-1130

Schmidt Barn B&B
Rte. 2, Box 112-A3/231 West Main
Fredericksburg, TX 78624
(210) 997-5612

Sherwood Farm Retreat
Route 2, Box 219D
Omaha, TX 75571
(903) 884-3039

Sunset-Sunrise B&B
H.C. 52 Box 331
Hemphill, TX 75948
(409) 579-3265

Urquart House of Eleven Gables
301 East Walker
Jefferson, TX 75657
(903) 665-8442

The Whistler
906 Avenue M
Huntsville, TX 77340
(409) 295-2834

Ye Ole Maple Inn
1509 Van Zandt/P.O. Box 1141
Glen Rose, TX 76043
(817) 897-3456

Index

A

APPETIZERS AND DIPS
Almond Chicken Dip 16
Anchovy-Olive Dip 16
Angel of Death Cheese 13
Artichoke Dip 17
Avocado Dip 17
Black Bean Salsa 10
Broccoli Dip 19
Cheese and Sausage Biscuits 14
Cheese Ball 12
Cheese Dip 18
Cheese Roll 13
Chipped Beef and Olive
   Cheese Ball 12
Chipped Beef Dip 19
Cold Salmon Mold 15
Cousin Iola's Chili Dip 20
Curry Dip and Marinated
   Broccoli 18
Fruit Dip 22
Meat Popovers 15
Mexican Style Chips-N-Dip 20
Nopales con Queso (Cactus with
   Cheese) 8
Oyster Roll 14
Phil's Cheese Dip 19
Pizza Fondue 11
Quick and Easy Mexican
   Appetizer 10
Raw Vegetable Dip 18
Relish Dip 22
Sausage Balls 14
Shrimp Marinade 9
Shrimp Ring 8
Skip Dip 17
Spinach Dip 21
Stella's Spicy Pecans 16, 41
Stuffed Mushrooms 11
Sugar and Spice Pecans 220
Tortilla Roll-Ups 9

APPLES
Apple Butter Recipe 224
Apple Butter Squares 153
Apple Pudding 168
Applesauce-Cinnamon
   Christmas Ornaments 227
Dannon Apple Spice Cake 194
Diabetic Apple Cake 182
Glazed Apples 225
Glazed Apple Slices 164

My Favorite Apple Pie 212
Sparkling Pear-Apple Cider 219
Tzimmes 142
Waldorf Salad 40

APRICOTS
Apricot Salad 39
Sugarless Apricot Delights 169

ARTICHOKES
Artichoke Dip 17
Italian Artichoke Hearts 141
Quick Spinach and Artichoke
   Casserole 145
Spinach Artichoke Casserole 145
Sylvia's Casserole 144

AVOCADOS
Avocado Dip 17
Avocado-Cranberry Salad 40

B

BANANAS
Banana Carrot Bran Muffins 25
Banana Nut Bread 28
Banana Pancakes 226
Banana Split 156
Hummingbird Cake 195

BEANS
Bean and Cheese Casserole 134
Bean Casserole 79
Bean Gravy 133
Black Bean Cakes with Spicy
   Vegetable Sauce 133
Black Bean Pizza 87
Black Bean Salad 42
Black Bean Salsa 10
Black Beans and Pasta 119
Chili Con Carne 84
Jalapinto Rice Casserole 77
Laredo Ranch Beans 122
Mexican Style Chips-N-Dip 20
Patio Beans 137
Spicy Pinto Beans 139
Sylvia's Casserole 144
Taco Soup 57
Turkey Chili (Spicy) 84

BEEF
All-In-One Casserole 73
Baked Spaghetti 117
Baked Stuffed Cabbage 89
Bean Casserole 79
Beefy Mexican Lasagna 114
Belgian Pot Roast 92

243

INDEX

Best Yet Spaghetti 118
Biscuit-Topped Casserole 81
Broiled Flank Steak 94
Cabbage Soup 54
Chili Con Carne 84
Chipped Beef and Olive
   Cheese Ball 12
Chipped Beef Dip 19
Company Casserole 76
Cousin Iola's Chili Dip 20
Curly Noodle Dinner 88
E-Z Steak 93
Eggplant Parmesan 124
Fajitas 91
Hamburger Casserole 76
Hamburger Pie 85
Italian Beef Casserole 74
Lasagna 112
Meat Popovers 15
Mexican Casserole 72
Mexican Chef Salad 47
Million Dollar Meatballs 92
Mom's Macaroni Casserole 68
No-Work Meat Loaf 94
One-Pot Spaghetti 117
Phil's Cheese Dip 19
Pizza Fondue 11
Pizza Spaghetti Casserole 68
Quick and Easy Pastie Pie 86
Skip Dip 17
Spaghetti Olé 118
Steak Kabobs 93
Stroganoff Sandwiches 66
Stuffed Meat Loaf 94
Taco Soup 57
Tagglarene Casserole 82
Tigerina 73
Tijuana Torte 87
Tony Marsietti 116
BEVERAGES
   Amaretto Liqueur 218
   Fruity Punch Delight 219
   Holiday Punch 220
   Kahlúa 218
   Ola Mae's Wassail 219
   Sparkling Pear-Apple Cider 219
   Wine 218
BISCUITS
   Cheese and Sausage Biscuits 14
   Sour Dough Buttermilk Biscuits ... 34
BLUEBERRIES
   Blueberry, Cherry or Strawberry
      Dessert 170
   Blueberry Lemon Cake 174
BREADS
   Banana Carrot Bran Muffins 25
   Banana Nut Bread 28
   Beer Bread 29

Broccoli Cornbread 33
Brown Sugar Shortbread 31
Cinnamon-Raisin Scones-Sticks ... 26
Cornbread 31
Corny Cornbread 33
Dilly Bread 29
English Muffin Bread 30
Garlic Bread Sticks 30
Injun Fry Bread 34
Manuela's Greek Bread 30
Mexican Cornbread 32
Oatmeal Muffins 24
Orange Yogurt Muffins 24
Pineapple Muffins 24
Pumpkin Bread 25
Raisin Scones 26
Sour Dough Buttermilk Biscuits ... 34
Southern Cornbread 31
Whole Grain Wheat Bread 28
Zucchini Bread 26, 27
Zucchini Nut Bread 27
BROCCOLI
   Broccoli Casserole 129
   Broccoli Cheese Rice Casserole 78
   Broccoli Cornbread 33
   Broccoli Salad 41
   Broccoli with Rice 132
   Curry Dip and Marinated
      Broccoli 18
   Italian Beef Casserole 74

C

CABBAGE
   Baked Stuffed Cabbage 89
   Cabbage Soup 54
   Cheese and Cabbage Soup 54
   Napa Cabbage Salad 38
   Pineapple Coleslaw 42
   Red Cabbage 143
   Rolled Cabbage Leaves 88
   Sweet-Sour Cabbage 125
CAKES AND FROSTINGS
   1-2-3-4 Cake 188
   7-Up Pound Cake 191
   Angel Food Cake 187
   Better Than Sex Cake 189
   Birthday Cake 187
   Blueberry Lemon Cake 174
   Cajun Day Syrup Cake 175
   Carrot Cake 180
   Chocolate Angel Food Cake 194
   Chocolate Cake 189
   Chocolate Cherry Cake 180
   Chocolate Fudge Cake 176
   Chocolate Sheet Cake 181
   Coconut Pound Cake 186

INDEX

Cowboy Coffee Cake 186
Cream Cheese-Chocolate
   Cupcakes 151
Dannon Apple Spice Cake 194
Date Nut Cake 193
Delicious Chocolate Cake 183
Diabetic Apple Cake 182
Died-and-Went-to-Heaven
   Chocolate Cake 185
Dirt Cake 193
Earthquake Cake 183
Gooey Butter Cake 188
Hummingbird Cake 195
Light Amaretto Delight Cake 191
Microwave Mississippi
   Mud Cake 179
Milky Way Cake 182
Mississippi Mud 178
Mom's Pound Cake 184
Oatmeal Cake 177, 190
Orange Cake 184
Piña Colada Cake 178
Poppy Seed Cake 181
Pound Cake 176
Pumpkin Cake 174
Red Velvet Cake 192
Rum Cake 195
Seven Minute Icing 175
Sock-It-to-Me Cake 190
Turtle Cake 177
Zucchini Chocolate Nut Cake 192
CANDIES
Best Fudge You Ever Ate 173
Buttermilk Fudge 172
Coconut Bon-Bons 201
Dark Chocolate Fudge 171
Fudge 173
Heavenly Hash 172
Instant Candy Cookies 202
Melt-Aways 172
Peanut Butter Fudge 171
CANTALOUPES
Fruit Salad 39
Melon Salad 36
CARROTS
Banana Carrot Bran Muffins 25
Carrot Cake 180
Carrot Raisin Salad 43
Carrot Salad 43
Cheese Carrots 137
Copper Pennies 123
Roasted Root Vegetables 138
Sunshine Carrots 137
Sweet Potato and Carrot Crisp 130
Sweet-Sour Carrots 123
CASSEROLES
All-In-One Casserole 73
Almond Chicken Casserole 81

Arroz Central Cafe Rice Casserole . 79
Bean and Cheese Casserole 134
Bean Casserole 79
Biscuit-Topped Casserole 81
Breakfast Casserole 69
Broccoli Casserole 129
Broccoli Cheese Rice Casserole 78
Brunch Casserole 70
Can Can 84
Chicken and Rice Casserole 79
Chicken Casserole 80
Chicken Tetrazzini Casserole 80
Company Casserole 76
Corn Casserole 127, 134
Easy Egg Casserole 69
Eggplant and Zucchini
   Casserole 131
Eggplant Casserole 139
Fay's Shrimp Casserole 107
Green Chili Rice 78
Green Rice Casserole 75, 77
Hamburger Casserole 76
Hamburger Pie 85
Hash Brown Potato Casserole 147
Hominy Casserole 76
Italian Beef Casserole 74
Jalapinto Rice Casserole 77
Louisiana Crawfish Casserole 109
Make Ahead Breakfast Casserole .. 70
Mexican Casserole 72
Mom's Macaroni Casserole 68
Pizza Spaghetti Casserole 68
Pork Chops and Rice Casserole 74
Potato Casserole 124
Quick and Easy Pastie Pie 86
Quick Spinach and Artichoke
   Casserole 145
Sesame-Cheese Casserole Bread ... 71
Sloppy Joe Casserole 71
Spinach Artichoke Casserole 145
Squash and Okra Casserole 135
Squash Casserole 148
St. Paul's Rice Casserole 75
Sweet Potato Casserole with
   Praline Topping 146
Sylvia's Casserole 144
Tagglarene Casserole 82
Tigerina 73
Tuna-Noodle Casserole 82
Yellow Squash Casserole 143
CHEESE
Almost Fat Free Lasagna 115
Angel of Death Cheese 13
Baked Spaghetti 117
Bean and Cheese Casserole 134
Beefy Mexican Lasagna 114
Best Ever Macaroni and Cheese .. 112
Broccoli Cheese Rice Casserole 78

245

INDEX

Cheese and Cabbage Soup 54
Cheese and Sausage Biscuits 14
Cheese Ball 12
Cheese Carrots 137
Cheese Dip 18
Cheese Roll 13
Cheese-Stuffed Pasta Shells 115
Cheesy Chicken and Ham
    Bundles 103
Chipped Beef and Olive
    Cheese Ball 12
Cousin Iola's Chili Dip 20
Easy Baked Eggs with
    Cheese Sauce 86
Eggplant Parmesan 124
Lasagna 112, 113
Lazy-Day Lasagna 114
Macaroni and Cheese 116
Mexican Chicken Lasagna 113
Mexican Grits 136
Mexican Style Chips-N-Dip 20
Nopales con Queso (Cactus with
    Cheese) 8
Oyster Roll 14
Phil's Cheese Dip 19
Pizza Fondue 11
Pizza Spaghetti Casserole 68
Quiche Lorraine 85
Quick and Easy Mexican
    Appetizer 10
Sausage Balls 14
Sesame-Cheese Casserole Bread ... 71
Skip Dip 17
Southwestern Quiche 85
Spinach Dip 21
Tijuana Torte 87
Tortilla Roll-Ups 9

CHEESECAKES
Busy Day Cheese Cake 155
Miniature Cheesecakes 159
Pumpkin Swirl Cheesecake 156

CHERRIES
Cherry Crunch 155
Chocolate Cherry Cake 180
Miniature Cheesecakes 159

CHOCOLATE
'Almost' Fat-Free Brownies 202
Best Fudge You Ever Ate 173
Better Than Sex Cake 189
Blackbottom Cupcakes 159
Chocolate Angel Food Cake 194
Chocolate Cake 189
Chocolate Cherry Cake 180
Chocolate Dipped Chocolate
    Chip Cookies 209
Chocolate Fudge Cake 176
Chocolate Pie 214

Chocolate Sheet Cake 181
Cocoa Waffle Cookies 198
Coconut Bon-Bons 201
Cream Cheese-Chocolate
    Cupcakes 151
Dark Chocolate Fudge 171
Death by Chocolate 150
Delicious Chocolate Cake 183
Died-and-Went-to-Heaven
    Chocolate Cake 185
Dirt Cake 193
Earthquake Cake 183
Florence's Toffee-Chocolate
    Squares 198
"Forgotten Cookies" or
    Chocolate Chip Kisser 201
Fudge 173
Fudge Chews 152
Fudge No-Bake Cookies 196
Fudge Pie 170
German Chocolate Dream Bars .. 207
Heavenly Hash 172
Hello Dolly Bars 154
Instant Candy Cookies 202
Microwave Mississippi Mud
    Cake 179
Milky Way Cake 182
Mississippi Mud 178
Puppy Chow 165
Red Velvet Cake 192
Rum Balls 208
Snickers Frozen Bars 162
Turtle Cake 177
Zucchini Chocolate Nut Cake 192

COBBLERS
Cherry Crunch 155
Peachy Cobbler 151

COOKIES AND BARS
'Almost' Fat-Free Brownies 202
Apple Butter Squares 153
Chocolate Dipped Chocolate
    Chip Cookies 209
Cocoa Waffle Cookies 198
Coconut Bon-Bons 201
Coconut Macaroons 205
Cocoons 203
Florence's Toffee-Chocolate
    Squares 198
"Forgotten Cookies" or
    Chocolate Chip Kisser 201
Frosted Pineapple Squares 150
Fruit Cake Cookies 199
Fudge Chews 152
Fudge No-Bake Cookies 196
German Chocolate Dream Bars .. 207
Ginger Cookies 199
Gingerbread 154

246

INDEX

Grandma's Molasses Cookies 207
Hawaiian Kisses (Cookies) 205
Hello Dolly Bars 154
Instant Candy Cookies 202
Miz' Jeanette's Cocoons 203
Neiman Marcus Bars 157
Non Fat Oatmeal Cookies 197
Nut Coconut Bars 204
Oatmeal Cookies 200
Pecan Cookies 200
Pumpkin Squares 153
Rum Balls 208
Snickerdoodles 197
Starlight Sugar Crisps (Sour
 Cream Twists) 206
Texas Ranger Cookies 209
The Great Oatmeal Bar 196
Top-of-the-Range-Cookies 204
Walnut Balls 208

COOKING CHARTS AND GUIDES
Common Kitchen Pans 230
Contents of Cans 231
Cooking Terms 237, 238
Equivalent Amounts 232
Equivalent Measures 231
Healthy Ingredient
 Substitutions 235, 236
Liquid Volume 230
Mass Weight 230
Oven Temperature Chart 231
Substitutes 233, 234

CORN
Baked Corn 127
Corn Casserole 127, 134
Corny Cornbread 33
Maquechou 140
Mexican Cornbread 32
Scalloped Corn 122

CORNBREAD
Broccoli Cornbread 33
Cornbread 31
Corny Cornbread 33
Mexican Cornbread 32
Southern Cornbread 31

CRAB
Crab Sandwiches 64
Crawfish Gumbo 63
Quiche Lorraine 85

CRANBERRIES
Avocado-Cranberry Salad 40
Cranberry Crown Salad 37
Cranberry Crunch Pie 210
Cranberry Jelly Sauce 225
Cranberry Relish 224
Cranberry Salad 38

CRAWFISH
Crawfish Etouffée 109
Crawfish Gumbo 63

Louisiana Crawfish Casserole 109

CUCUMBERS
Cucumber Vegetable Side Dish ... 142
Yogurt-Cucumber Salad 46

D

DESSERTS
Apple Pudding 168
Banana Split 156
Blackbottom Cupcakes 159
Blueberry, Cherry or Strawberry
 Dessert 170
Brown Sugar Pudding 166
Busy Day Cheese Cake 155
Cherry Crunch 155
Cold Grand Marnier Soufflé 226
Cream Puffs 165
Date Pinwheel 161
Death by Chocolate 150
English Trifle 163
Français Parfait 155
Frosted Pineapple Squares 150
Fudge Pie 170
Ginger Snaps and Cream
 Cheese 152
Glazed Apple Slices 164
Melt-Aways 172
Miniature Cheesecakes 159
Orange Coconut Balls 160
Oranges, Provençal Style 168
Peachy Cobbler 151
Pistachio Salad 164
Poached Pear Gratin 162
Poached Pears 166
Pretzel Salad 167
Pumpkin Swirl Cheesecake 156
Puppy Chow 165
Rice Pudding 169
Snickers Frozen Bars 162
Soft Pretzels 220
Strawberries 'N Cream Chillout ... 163
Strawberry Dessert Roll 157
Strawberry Dips 163
Strawberry Shortcake 158
Sugar-free Ice Custard 161
Sugarless Apricot Delights 169
Tassies 167

DIPS AND SPREADS
Almond Chicken Dip 16
Anchovy-Olive Dip 16
Angel of Death Cheese 13
Apple Butter Recipe 224
Artichoke Dip 17
Avocado Dip 17
Black Bean Salsa 10
Broccoli Dip 19

INDEX

Cheese Ball 12
Cheese Dip 18
Cheese Roll 13
Chipped Beef and Olive
　Cheese Ball 12
Chipped Beef Dip 19
Cousin Iola's Chili Dip 20
Curry Dip and Marinated
　Broccoli 18
Fruit Dip 22
Mexican Style Chips-N-Dip 20
Oyster Roll 14
Phil's Cheese Dip 19
Pizza Fondue 11
Raw Vegetable Dip 18
Relish Dip 22
Skip Dip 17
Spinach Dip 21

DUCK
Ducks - Southern Style 105
Sweet-Sour Roast Duck 105
Wild Duck Gumbo 64

E

EGGPLANT
Eggplant and Zucchini
　Casserole 131
Eggplant Casserole 139
Eggplant Parmesan 124
Ratatouille with Olive Oil 134
Rice-Stuffed Eggplant 128

EGGS
Breakfast Casserole 69
Brunch Casserole 70
Easy Baked Eggs with
　Cheese Sauce 86
Easy Egg Casserole 69
Make Ahead Breakfast Casserole .. 70
Quiche Lorraine 85
Southwestern Quiche 85
Strawberry Omelet Supreme 160

EXTRAORDINARY EXTRAS
A "Home" Made Recipe 222
Amaretto Liqueur 218
Apple Butter Recipe 224
Applesauce-Cinnamon
　Christmas Ornaments 227
Banana Pancakes 226
Cold Grand Marnier Soufflé 226
Cranberry Jelly Sauce 225
Cranberry Relish 224
Dora's Mother's Waffles 222
Elephant Stew 227
French Soap 228
Fruity Punch Delight 219
Glazed Apples 225

Holiday Punch 220
Kahlúa 218
Lentil Sauce 227
Nancy's Sweet and Sour Pickles .. 221
Ola Mae's Wassail 219
Recipe for the Perfect
　Honeymoon 225
Soft Pretzels 220
Sparkling Pear-Apple Cider 219
Spiced Pear Preserves 223
Squash Pickles 223
Sugar and Spice Pecans 220
Wine 218
Yorkshire Pudding 221

F

FISH *(See also individual listings)*
Cold Salmon Mold 15
Fisherman's Supper 110
Glazed Red Snapper 111
Orange Roughy Fillets with
　Grapefruit Brûlée 110
Red Snapper Provençale 111

FRUIT *(See also individual listings)*
Blueberry, Cherry or Strawberry
　Dessert 170
English Trifle 163
Français Parfait 155
Fruit Cake Cookies 199
Fruit Dip 22
Fruit Salad 39
Glazed Fruit Salad 36
Low-Fat Chicken and Grape
　Salad 49
Melon Salad 36
Multi-Fruit Pie 212
Winter Fruit Salad 44

FUDGE
Best Fudge You Ever Ate 173
Buttermilk Fudge 172
Fudge 173
Fudge Chews 152
Fudge No-Bake Cookies 196
Fudge Pie 170
Peanut Butter Fudge 171

H

HAM
Cheesy Chicken and Ham
　Bundles 103
Jambalaya Rice Salad 50
Tortilla Roll-Ups 9

HOMINY
Hominy 126
Hominy Casserole 76

248

INDEX

I

INNS *(Texas Pink Ribbon Bed and Breakfast)*
Bussey's Something Special B&B 240
Casa De Leona B&B 240
Country Lake B&B 240
Georgie McIrwin's Highlander 240
Guilded Thistle, The 240
Heathers Glen B&B 240
Indian Mountain Ranch 240
Ledbetter B&B 240
Little House, The 240
Lovett Inn, The 241
Madame Dyers' B&B 241
Maison-Bayou: A Creole Plantation 241
Meerscheidt Haus, The 241
Page House B&B 241
Patrician Inn, The 241
Pelican House, The 241
Rancho Cama B&B 241
Robin's Nest B&B 241
Roses and The River 242
Sara's B&B 242
Schmidt Barn B&B 242
Sherwood Farm Retreat 242
Sunset-Sunrise B&B 242
Urquart House of Eleven Gables . 242
Whistler, The 242
Ye Ole Maple Inn 242

L

LAMB
Rolled Cabbage Leaves 88

M

MAIN DISHES
Arroz Con Pollo 89
Baked Stuffed Cabbage 89
Belgian Pot Roast 92
Black Bean Pizza 87
Boned Chicken Breasts with Parmesan 103
Broiled Flank Steak 94
Can Can 84
Chicken Cacciatore 99
Chicken Pot Pie 89, 90
Chili Con Carne 84
Curly Noodle Dinner 88
Dressing-Topped Chicken Pot Pie . 90
Easy Baked Eggs with Cheese Sauce 86

E-Z Steak 93
Fajitas 91
Hamburger Pie 85
Million Dollar Meatballs 92
No-Work Meat Loaf 94
Pork Chops With Oregano 92
Pork Roast with Miso 91
Quiche Lorraine 85
Quick and Easy Pastie Pie 86
Rolled Cabbage Leaves 88
Saltimbocca a la Romana 87
Sausage Ring 86
Southwestern Quiche 85
Steak Kabobs 93
Stuffed Meat Loaf 94
Sunday Pork Tenderloin 93
Tijuana Torte 87
Turkey Chili (Spicy) 84

MEXICAN AND TEX-MEX
Beefy Mexican Lasagna 114
Black Bean Salad 42
Black Bean Salsa 10
Chili Con Carne 84
Cousin Iola's Chili Dip 20
Fajitas 91
Mexican Casserole 72
Mexican Chef Salad 47
Mexican Chicken Lasagna 113
Mexican Chicken Soup 58
Mexican Cornbread 32
Mexican Grits 136
Mexican Style Chips-N-Dip 20
Nopales con Queso (Cactus with Cheese) 8
Pancho Villa Stew 58
Phil's Cheese Dip 19
Quick and Easy Mexican Appetizer 10
Southwestern Chicken and Vegetable Salad 51
Southwestern Quiche 85
Spaghetti Olé 118
Taco Soup 57
Tijuana Torte 87
Tortilla Roll-Ups 9
Turkey Chili (Spicy) 84

MISCELLANEOUS
A "Home" Made Recipe 222
Applesauce-Cinnamon Christmas Ornaments 227
Bed and Breakfast Inns, Texas Pink Ribbon 240, 241, 242
Elephant Stew 227
French Soap 228
Recipe for the Perfect Honeymoon 225

MUFFINS
Banana Carrot Bran Muffins 25

249

INDEX

Oatmeal Muffins 24
Orange Yogurt Muffins 24
Pineapple Muffins 24

O

OATMEAL
Fudge No-Bake Cookies 196
Instant Candy Cookies 202
Non Fat Oatmeal Cookies 197
Oatmeal Bar, The Great 196
Oatmeal Cake 177, 190
Oatmeal Cookies 200
Oatmeal Muffins 24
Texas Ranger Cookies 209
OKRA
Citrus Okra 145
Squash and Okra Casserole 135
ORANGES
Orange Cake 184
Orange Coconut Balls 160
Oranges, Provençal Style 168
Orange Yogurt Muffins 24

P

PANCAKES AND WAFFLES
Banana Pancakes 226
Dora's Mother's Waffles 222
PASTA
Almost Fat Free Lasagna 115
Baked Spaghetti 117
Beefy Mexican Lasagna 114
Best Ever Macaroni and Cheese .. 112
Best Yet Spaghetti 118
Black Beans and Pasta 119
Cheese-Stuffed Pasta Shells 115
Chicken Alfredo 95
Chicken Noodles 104
Chicken Tetrazzini 104
Chicken Tetrazzini Casserole 80
Ira's Special Pasta Sauce 120
Lasagna 112, 113
Lazy-Day Lasagna 114
Lentil Sauce 227
Light and Healthy Pasta Sauce ... 119
Macaroni and Cheese 116
Macaroni Salad 46
Mexican Chicken Lasagna 113
Mom's Macaroni Casserole 68
Multicolor Pasta 116
One-Pot Spaghetti 117
Pasta con Pomodora Crema 120
Pasta Salad 47
Pizza Spaghetti Casserole 68
Shrimp with Spanish Sauce
  over Pasta 107

Sloppy Joe Casserole 71
Spaghetti Olé 118
Tigerina 73
Tony Marsietti 116
Tuna-Noodle Casserole 82
PEANUT BUTTER
Frozen Peanut Butter Pie 214
Melt-Aways 172
Peanut Butter Fudge 171
PEARS
Poached Pear Gratin 162
Poached Pears 166
Sparkling Pear-Apple Cider 219
Spiced Pear Preserves 223
PECANS
Favorite Pecan Pie 211
Pecan Cookies 200
Pecan Crunch Pie 210
Stella's Spicy Pecans 16, 41
Tiny Pecan Tarts 211
PIES
Chocolate Pie 214
Cranberry Crunch Pie 210
Favorite Pecan Pie 211
Fresh Strawberry Pie 213
Frozen Peanut Butter Pie 214
Fudge Pie 170
Luscious Lemon Pie 215
Meringue Pie Crust 216
Multi-Fruit Pie 212
My Favorite Apple Pie 212
Never Fail Pie Crust 216
No Bake Pumpkin Pie 215
Pecan Crunch Pie 210
Pineapple Sour Cream Pie 213
Tiny Pecan Tarts 211
PINEAPPLE
Apricot Salad 39
Birthday Cake 187
Diana's Delight 45
Dump Salad 38
Frosted Pineapple Squares 150
Heavenly Salad 37
Hummingbird Cake 195
Piña Colada Cake 178
Pineapple Coleslaw 42
Pineapple Muffins 24
Pineapple Sour Cream Pie 213
Pistachio Salad 164
PIZZA
Black Bean Pizza 87
Pizza Fondue 11
Pizza Spaghetti Casserole 68
PORK
Baked Stuffed Cabbage 89
Creole Gumbo 62
Pancho Villa Stew 58
Pork Chops and Rice Casserole 74

INDEX

Pork Chops With Oregano 92
Pork Roast with Miso 91
Sunday Pork Tenderloin 93
POTATOES
Almost French Fries 135
Baked Potatoes 126
Great Grated Potatoes 132
Hash Brown Potato Casserole 147
O'Brien Potato Ring 138
Potato Casserole 124
Potato Salad for a Crowd 48
Potato Soup 55
Potato Wedges 140
Ro-Tel Potatoes 132
Tzimmes 142
POULTRY
Almond Chicken Casserole 81
Almond Chicken Dip 16
Arroz Con Pollo 89
Baked Chicken 101, 102
Bean Casserole 79
Best Yet Spaghetti 118
Boned Chicken Breasts with
 Parmesan 103
Can Can 84
Cheesy Chicken and Ham
 Bundles 103
Chicken Alfredo 95
Chicken and Rice Casserole 79
Chicken Cacciatore 99
Chicken Casserole 80
Chicken in Wine 98
Chicken Noodles 104
Chicken Paprikash 101
Chicken Pot Pie 89, 90
Chicken Salad in Orange Halves ... 49
Chicken Sherry 99
Chicken Teriyaki 100
Chicken Tetrazzini 104
Chicken Tetrazzini Casserole 80
Citrus Salsa Chicken 95
Country Cajun Chicken Fricassée . 97
Country Captain Chicken 97
Dressing-Topped Chicken Pot Pie . 90
Ducks - Southern Style 105
Fajitas 91
Grilled Chicken Sandwich 66
Herbed Chicken 100
Jambalaya Rice Salad 50
Lazy Ladies Salad 48
Low-Fat Chicken and
 Grape Salad 49
Maureen's Italian Chicken 96
Mexican Chicken Lasagna 113
Mexican Chicken Soup 58
Oven Fried Chicken 102
Pheasants à la Candlelight 106

Quick and Easy Chicken 106
Quick and Easy Pastie Pie 86
Rosemary Chicken 100
Southwestern Chicken and
 Vegetable Salad 51
Stir-Fried Chicken with Cashews
 and Green Onions 98
Sweet-Sour Roast Duck 105
Tandoori Chicken 96
Turkey and Sweet Potato Soup 56
Veggie Pita Pockets 65
PRESERVES
Apple Butter Recipe 224
Spiced Pear Preserves 223
PUMPKIN
No Bake Pumpkin Pie 215
Pumpkin Bread 25
Pumpkin Cake 174
Pumpkin Squares 153
Pumpkin Swirl Cheesecake 156

Q

QUICHES
Quiche Lorraine 85
Southwestern Quiche 85

R

RED SNAPPER
Glazed Red Snapper 111
Red Snapper Provençale 111
RELISHES
Black Bean Salsa 10
Cranberry Relish 224
Relish Dip 22
RICE
Almond Chicken Casserole 81
Arroz Central Cafe Rice
 Casserole 79
Arroz Con Pollo 89
Baked Stuffed Cabbage 89
Broccoli Cheese Rice Casserole 78
Broccoli with Rice 132
Chicken and Rice Casserole 79
Confetti—Wild Rice Toss 144
Garden Rice Salad with Lemon
 Herb Dressing 43
Green Chili Rice 78
Green Rice Casserole 75, 77
Jalapinto Rice Casserole 77
Jambalaya Rice Salad 50
Louisiana Crawfish Casserole 109
Pork Chops and Rice Casserole 74
Rice Pilaf 130
Rice Pudding 169

INDEX

Rice-Stuffed Eggplant 128
Rolled Cabbage Leaves 88
Spinach Rice Salad 45
St. Paul's Rice Casserole 75

S

SALAD DRESSINGS
French Dressing 52
Green Goddess Dressing 52
Honey Dressing 52
Zero Salad Dressing 52

SALADS
Apricot Salad 39
Avocado-Cranberry Salad 40
Black Bean Salad 42
Broccoli Salad 41
Carrot Raisin Salad 43
Carrot Salad 43
Chicken Salad in Orange Halves ... 49
Cranberry Crown Salad 37
Cranberry Salad 38
Diana's Delight 45
Dump Salad 38
Fruit Salad 39
Garden Rice Salad with Lemon
   Herb Dressing 43
Glazed Fruit Salad 36
Heavenly Salad 37
Jambalaya Rice Salad 50
Lazy Ladies Salad 48
Low-Fat Chicken and Grape
   Salad 49
Macaroni Salad 46
Melon Salad 36
Mexican Chef Salad 47
Napa Cabbage Salad 38
Oriental Salad 51
Pasta Salad 47
Pineapple Coleslaw 42
Pistachio Salad 164
Potato Salad for a Crowd 48
Seven Layer Salad 40
Sinner's Repent Big Time Salad 44
Southwestern Chicken and
   Vegetable Salad 51
Spinach Rice Salad 45
Stella's Spicy Pecans 16, 41
Sunshine Spinach Salad 45
Waldorf Salad 40
Winter Fruit Salad 44
Yogurt-Cucumber Salad 46

SANDWICHES
Cancun Tuna Sandwiches 66
Crab Sandwiches 64
Grilled Chicken Sandwich 66
Stroganoff Sandwiches 66

Vegetarian Pita Sandwiches 65
Veggie Pita Pockets 65

SAUCES
Bean Gravy 133
Cranberry Jelly Sauce 225
Fluffy Strawberry Sauce 160
Hard Sauce 136
Ira's Special Pasta Sauce 120
Lentil Sauce 227
Light and Healthy Pasta Sauce ... 119
Marinade 96
Shrimp Marinade 9

SAUSAGE
Breakfast Casserole 69
Cheese and Sausage Biscuits 14
Make Ahead Breakfast Casserole .. 70
Sausage Balls 14
Sausage Ring 86
St. Paul's Rice Casserole 75

SEAFOOD *(See also individual listings)*
Cajun Stir Fry Shrimp 108
Crawfish Etouffée 109
Fay's Shrimp Casserole 107
Fisherman's Supper 110
Glazed Red Snapper 111
Louisiana Crawfish Casserole 109
Orange Roughy Fillets with
   Grapefruit Brûlée 110
Oriental Salad 51
Red Snapper Provençale 111
Shrimp Creole 108
Shrimp Divine 108
Shrimp with Spanish Sauce over
   Pasta 107

SHRIMP
Cajun Stir Fry Shrimp 108
Creole Gumbo 62
Fajitas 91
Fay's Shrimp Casserole 107
Jambalaya Rice Salad 50
Shrimp Creole 108
Shrimp Divine 108
Shrimp Marinade 9
Shrimp Ring 8
Shrimp with Spanish Sauce
   over Pasta 107

SOUPS, STEWS AND GUMBOS
Cabbage Soup 54
Cheese and Cabbage Soup 54
Chili Con Carne 84
Cold Strawberry Soup 62
Crawfish Gumbo 63
Creole Gumbo 62
Farm Market Soup Stew 60
Fresh Spinach Soup 63
Gazpacho 59
Mexican Chicken Soup 58
Minestrone 61

INDEX

Old Fashioned Vegetable Soup 59
Pancho Villa Stew 58
Potato Soup 55
Sippy Consommé 62
Taco Soup 57
Turkey and Sweet Potato Soup 56
Turkey Chili (Spicy) 84
Wild Duck Gumbo 64

SPINACH
Fresh Spinach Soup 63
Green Rice Casserole 75
Lazy Ladies Salad 48
Quick Spinach and Artichoke
  Casserole 145
Spinach Artichoke Casserole 145
Spinach Dip 21
Spinach Rice Salad 45
Sunshine Spinach Salad 45

SQUASH
Spiced Acorn Squash 131
Squash and Okra Casserole 135
Squash Casserole 148
Squash Pickles 223
Yellow Squash Casserole 143

STRAWBERRIES
Cold Strawberry Soup 62
Fluffy Strawberry Sauce 160
Fresh Strawberry Pie 213
Pretzel Salad 167
Strawberries 'N Cream Chillout ... 163
Strawberry Dessert Roll 157
Strawberry Dips 163
Strawberry Omelet Supreme 160
Strawberry Shortcake 158

SWEET POTATOES
Baked Sweet Potatoes 129
Baked Yams Supreme 146
Cashew Yam Bake 125
Sweet Potato and Carrot Crisp 130
Sweet Potato Casserole with
  Praline Topping 146
Sweet Potato Soufflé 141
Turkey and Sweet Potato Soup 56

T

TOMATOES
All-In-One Casserole 73
Black Bean Salsa 10
Cabbage Soup 54
Creole Tomatoes 136
Fresh Tomato Tart 128
Gazpacho 59
Ira's Special Pasta Sauce 120
Light and Healthy Pasta Sauce ... 119
Pasta con Pomodora Crema 120
Ratatouille with Olive Oil 134

Relish Dip 22
Ro-Tel Potatoes 132
Taco Soup 57
Tijuana Torte 87

TUNA
Cancun Tuna Sandwiches 66
Tuna-Noodle Casserole 82

TURKEY
Almost Fat Free Lasagna 115
Bean Casserole 79
Biscuit-Topped Casserole 81
Curly Noodle Dinner 88
Eggplant Parmesan 124
Jalapinto Rice Casserole 77
Lasagna 113
Million Dollar Meatballs 92
Quick and Easy Pastie Pie 86
Sloppy Joe Casserole 71
Taco Soup 57
Tagglarene Casserole 82
Turkey and Sweet Potato Soup 56
Turkey Chili (Spicy) 84

V

VEAL
Saltimbocca a la Romana 87

VEGETABLES *(See also individual listings)*
Almost French Fries 135
Baked Corn 127
Baked Potatoes 126
Baked Sweet Potatoes 129
Baked Yams Supreme 146
Bean and Cheese Casserole 134
Bean Gravy 133
Black Bean Cakes with Spicy
  Vegetable Sauce 133
Broccoli Casserole 129
Broccoli with Rice 132
Cashew Yam Bake 125
Cheese Carrots 137
Citrus Okra 145
Confetti—Wild Rice Toss 144
Copper Pennies 123
Corn Casserole 127, 134
Creole Tomatoes 136
Cucumber Vegetable Side Dish ... 142
Eggplant and Zucchini
  Casserole 131
Eggplant Casserole 139
Eggplant Parmesan 124
Fresh Peas in Velvet Sauce 144
Fresh Tomato Tart 128
Great Grated Potatoes 132
Hash Brown Potato Casserole 147
Hominy 126

253

INDEX

Italian Artichoke Hearts 141
Laredo Ranch Beans 122
Maquechou (pronounced "Mock-
 shoo") 140
Marinated Vegetables 148
Mexican Grits 136
O'Brien Potato Ring 138
Patio Beans 137
Potato Casserole 124
Potato Wedges 140
Quick Spinach and Artichoke
 Casserole 145
Ratatouille with Olive Oil 134
Red Cabbage 143
Rice Pilaf 130
Rice-Stuffed Eggplant 128
Ro-Tel Potatoes 132
Roasted Onions 126
Roasted Root Vegetables 138
Scalloped Corn 122
Spiced Acorn Squash 131
Spicy Pinto Beans 139
Spicy Vegetable Couscous 147
Spinach Artichoke Casserole 145
Squash and Okra Casserole 135

Squash Casserole 148
Steak Kabobs 93
Sunshine Carrots 137
Sweet Potato and Carrot Crisp 130
Sweet Potato Casserole with
 Praline Topping 146
Sweet Potato Soufflé 141
Sweet-Sour Cabbage 125
Sweet-Sour Carrots 123
Sylvia's Casserole 144
Tzimmes 142
Vegetarian Pita Sandwiches 65
Veggie Pita Pockets 65
Yellow Squash Casserole 143

Z

ZUCCHINI
Eggplant and Zucchini
 Casserole 131
Zucchini Bread 26, 27
Zucchini Chocolate Nut Cake 192
Zucchini Nut Bread 27

The Rose
12700 No. Featherwood, Suite 260
Houston, TX 77034

Please send ____ copy(ies) of ***The Rose Cookbook*** @ $14.95 each _____
Postage and handling @   2.00 each _____
TOTAL _____

Name _____

Address _____

City _____ State _____ Zip _____

Please make checks payable to ***The Rose***.

- -

The Rose
12700 No. Featherwood, Suite 260
Houston, TX 77034

Please send ____ copy(ies) of ***The Rose Cookbook*** @ $14.95 each _____
Postage and handling @   2.00 each _____
TOTAL _____

Name _____

Address _____

City _____ State _____ Zip _____

Please make checks payable to ***The Rose***.

- -

The Rose
12700 No. Featherwood, Suite 260
Houston, TX 77034

Please send ____ copy(ies) of ***The Rose Cookbook*** @ $14.95 each _____
Postage and handling @   2.00 each _____
TOTAL _____

Name _____

Address _____

City _____ State _____ Zip _____

Please make checks payable to ***The Rose***.